# THE CANADIAN Criminal Justice SYSTEM

**Subhas Ramcharan**
University of Windsor

**Willem de Lint**
Victoria University of Wellington

**Thomas S. Fleming**
Seneca College

Prentice Hall

Toronto

*To our wives and children, who inspire us to excellence*

—*S. R.*

*To Vaughen, whose spirited optimism has been my torch, and to my mother, whose goodness continues to guide me*

—*W. de L.*

*To Patrick, Tom, Kate, Patricia, and Angel*

—*T. S. F.*

**Canadian Cataloguing in Publication Data**

Ramcharan, Subhas
    The Canadian criminal justice system

Includes bibliographical references and index.
ISBN 0-13-085594-4

1. Criminal justice, Administration of – Canada.   I. De Lint, Willem, 1959–    .
II. Fleming, Thomas, 1951–    .   III. Title.

HV9960.C2R35 2001      364.971      C00-931740-6

ISBN 0-13-085594-4

Vice President, Editorial Director: Michael Young
Editor-in-Chief: David Stover
Senior Editor: Sophia Fortier
Signing Representative: Michelle Fredericks
Developmental Editor: Lisa Phillips
Production Editor: David Peebles
Copy Editor: Marcia Miron
Production Coordinator: Peggy Brown
Page Layout: Phyllis Seto
Photo Research: Susan Wallace-Cox
Creative Director: Mary Opper
Interior and Cover Design: Lisa Lapointe
Cover Image: Paul Edmondson/Stone

1 2 3 4 5    05 04 03 02 01

Printed and bound in Canada.

Prentice
Hall

# Contents

# Preface

The challenge to produce a text on the Canadian criminal justice system can be daunting. On the one hand, we enthusiastically and conscientiously have drawn together the main themes that we believe need to be analysed and addressed in this introductory level book. On the other hand it is only the readers of the text who can truly judge whether it has met its goals of readability, up-to-date statistics and fair and objective analysis of the state of the criminal justice system. As well, we acknowledge that in a co-authored text ideological perspectives and interpretation of facts may differ. For us, this provides added strength to the analytical critique offered.

Any analysis of Canada's criminal justice system must offer the reader a clear and precise discussion of the historical development of the justice system, as well as the contemporary and evolving picture. Specifically our goal is to allow readers to obtain through the text a clear and precise interpretation of the structure of the criminal justice system as it may apply to their personal experiences. The twin dilemmas of individual and civil rights as espoused in our Canadian Charter of Rights and Freedoms on the one hand, and, on the other, society's demand for order, control, and predictability in behaviour are never far from the central theme of the text.

We believe that many distinctive features separate this text from its competitors. The historical and contemporary analysis of the criminal justice system, describing its evolution and future directions, is accomplished using an easily digested pedagogic style. Key terms, major references, key questions, and Weblinks are provided to assist the student in the learning process. As well, the introduction to the criminal law and criminal justice systems including the role of the police, judiciary and prisons is accomplished using analytical tools and examples from contemporary Canadian legal and iustice system cases. We hope that our presentation and sometimes provocative critique of theories of crime causation, the impact of crime on victims, the victim rights movement, and the issues of women and racial minorities in the criminal justice system will lead to forthright and productive debate among readers.

# Acknowledgments

This project from inception to conclusion took many years and involved many individuals. David Stover first encouraged the proposal for a Canadian criminal justice text and approved the project. Marta Tomins, Laura Pearson, Lisa Phillips, Marcy Miron, and David Peebles were all involved in various stages of development and editing of the text. Particular thanks to Lisa Phillips and David Peebles for seeing the project through the final stages of editing and production.

We must acknowledge the critical comments of the reviewers who allowed the authors the opportunity to strengthen the content of the text and improve its readability: Leanne Fitch of St. Thomas University, Ian Hepher of Lethbridge Community College, Uldis Kopstals of Seneca College, and Ken Smith of Confederation College. Anne Merner, Lena Razwan, Dina Labelle, and Andria Turner assisted in typing drafts of the manuscript over the years. We also express our appreciation to Murray Pomerance, Judith Limkilde, and Heather Dokeray. Finally, the authors collectively would like to acknowledge the contributions of the thousands of students in our courses in criminology who have acted as "guinea pigs" for our ideas, ideals, and critiques, which form the platform for this text on the Canadian criminal justice system.

# CHAPTER 1

# Criminal Justice: An Introduction

## Objectives

- To discuss the components of the criminal justice system: the police, the courts, and corrections.

- To outline the processing of criminal cases as they pass through the criminal justice system and the methods used to protect the legal and human rights of those charged.

- To introduce the sociological causes of crime.

- To identify the functions of criminal law and the role of the criminal justice system in administering the law.

## What Is Criminal Justice?

The criminal justice system is one of the most fascinating and at times controversial components of the legal institution in Canada. At any given time, national debates are being waged with fury and vitriol about some issue related to the system, be it the police, the judiciary, sentencing, incarceration, parole, capital punishment, or euthanasia. As Cunningham and Griffiths (1997) note, most Canadians believe that crime is increasing, and many believe that the criminal justice system is culpable in this breakdown of law and order. Whether or not it is based on fact, the perception that crime is on the increase has immense social and

political implications for the actions and behaviour of Canadians. For example, pollsters have found that politicians who advocate greater law and order, heavier and harsher sentences, and boot camps for young offenders have greater support from the electorate than do those who advocate social engineering as a method for reducing crime.

Examining the criminal justice system means taking into account public perceptions such as these, as well as considering the historical and social underpinnings of the society from which crime and crime control methods have evolved. Before we get into an analysis of the structural components of the criminal justice system, it is important to understand that the kind of system we have in Canada is a legacy of our political, philosophical, and legal history, developed and moulded over time to reflect our unique social, political, and cultural institutions. How we respond to crime and how we administer the process is clearly going to be markedly different from the methods used in the United States, which has a history, a political system, legal and philosophical values, and social institutions that contrast vividly with Canada's. Of importance, as well, is the impact of racial and cultural diversity on Canada's society, legal system, and criminal justice system. Contrary to majority opinion, not all Canadians believe that our justice system treats all racial groups equally. In fact, large segments of Canada's racial minority population were left out of the legal process when laws were being formulated and enacted. Native peoples, for example, may not agree with the process for prosecuting or sentencing offenders. They may have social or cultural value systems that view "deviant" behaviour in a different way from the majority society. As a multicultural society, Canada must adapt and become more sensitive to diversity if we are first to understand crime causation, and second to devise methods for effective crime control.

The Canadian **criminal justice system** has three components: the police, the courts, and corrections. According to Goff (1997), the direct cost of this system to provincial, territorial, and federal levels of government exceeded nine billion dollars in 1993. However, this figure did not include the hidden costs of crime, such as the loss of work and psychological and physiological trauma suffered by victims of crime. Travis (1990) states that viewing the process of criminal justice as a system allows us to understand the interdependency of the parts of the total process, as many factors influence the decisions in the criminal justice process. Yet, this interpretation of a cohesive, integrated justice system is a theoretical construct; in practice, there are many deviations from the model, as interagency competition, conflict, and other factors can hinder the interaction of the different parts of the justice system. Figure 1.1 illustrates the court procedure in a criminal case, from committal of the crime to arrest, court trial, and corrections outcome.

COURT PROCEDURE IN CRIMINAL CASES

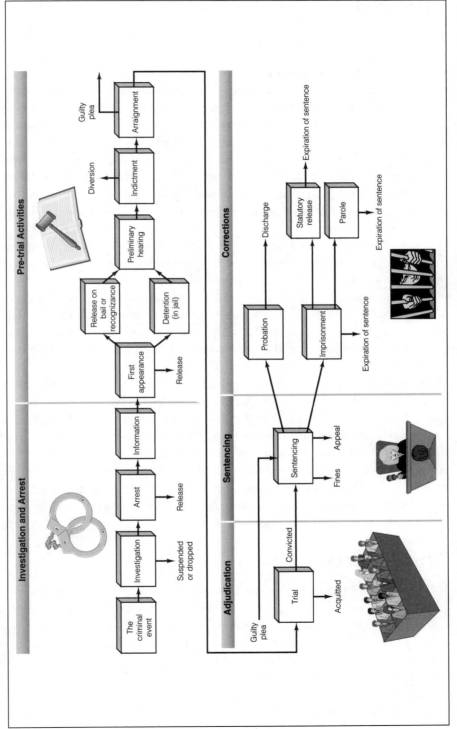

Source: F. Schmalleger, D. MacAlister, P. McKenna, & J. Winterdyk. 2000. *Canadian Criminal Justice Today.* Toronto: Prentice Hall.

# The Police

The modern justice system begins with the committing of a crime, report to the police, and subsequent investigation by the police. It is important to note that the police are the front-line soldiers in the criminal justice system. They not only conduct the criminal investigation, but they also decide whether to proceed with obtaining an arrest warrant from the Crown attorney, the official state prosecutor. Since an **arrest** involves suspension of the individual's rights and freedoms, it is a serious step in the justice process. Furthermore, since the police cannot arrest all offenders who commit criminal or noncriminal deviant acts, the discretionary powers of the police are immense. For this reason it is important that every effort be made to change the commonly held perception that the police selectively enforce the law against certain groups of people, for example, racial minorities or the poor.

Goff (1997) notes that policing in Canada is carried out at three levels: municipal, provincial, and federal. At the municipal level, there are over five hundred police forces in Canada, each of which provides all the policing needs of their communities. Three provincial police forces also operate in Ontario, Quebec, and Newfoundland. They enforce the **Criminal Code,** the federal statute comprising the criminal laws of Canada and requirements for criminal procedures and sentencing, and provincial laws in all jurisdictions that are not covered by a municipal policing force. The final policing body in Canada is the Royal Canadian Mounted Police (RCMP). The RCMP enforce all Criminal Code and provincial laws in the provinces that do not have a provincial police force. They also enforce all federal statutes in all provinces, including drug and tax offences, police airports, operate the Canadian Police College, operate forensic and DNA laboratories, and run the Canadian Police Information Centre. According to Cunningham and Griffiths (1997), policing is the largest component of the criminal justice system, costing the nation over six billion dollars annually. It is estimated that over sixty thousand police officers are employed in all branches of policing in Canada today.

# The Courts

If the police are the front-line soldiers in the war against crime, investigating criminal behaviour and laying charges, the courts are the core of the criminal justice system. For the majority of citizens, the court is the place where they can obtain justice. While the context of what is justice may differ depending on the particular interest group, undoubtedly the hallmark of the **court system** is that it is a place where all defendants should be treated fairly and equally.

The Canadian court system is a complex, tangled, and layered structure, which we will discuss in greater detail elsewhere. However, it can be broadly

classified into three levels: provincial courts, superior courts, and appeal courts. In some provinces the specific names may differ, but the role of each of these courts in the justice system is similar. The provincial courts handle the bulk of all criminal cases, including those prosecuted under the Young Offenders Act. At this level, courts may be organized according to specialties, such as criminal, family, or youth courts. According to Desroches (1995) the provincial court is one of rapid dispatch, with defendants rarely contesting the charges laid. He found in the cases he researched that 90 percent of those charged with robbery pleaded guilty in provincial court. While for most Canadians their only involvement with the court system is at this level, about 10 percent of those charged with indictable or serious criminal offences will be prosecuted in the superior court. Whereas at the provincial court level, the trial is before a judge alone, at the superior court level the case may be heard by either a judge or both a judge and jury. The appeals court hears appeals from both the superior and provincial courts, dealing mainly with issues related to procedural errors or sentencing processes.

At the top of the pyramid is the Supreme Court of Canada, which hears appeal cases from across Canada on any issue that it deems important. As well, it is entitled to interpret the **Canadian Charter of Rights and Freedoms (the Charter),** a document that formally states the rights and freedoms of all Canadians. Therefore, the Supreme Court of Canada acts similarly to the United States Supreme Court by not only interpreting the law, but also creating law.

## Corrections

**Corrections** refers to the system of treatment of convicted offenders. Anyone found guilty of a criminal offence is liable to be sentenced to a term in either a federal or provincial prison. Although Canada has a smaller percentage of its population incarcerated in prison compared with the United States, in recent years this percentage has been increasing markedly. According to Foran and Reed (1996) the total correctional population increased 34 percent between

1989 and 1995. There is considerable debate over the goals of sentencing in Canada. Is the purpose to punish, to rehabilitate, to humiliate, or to seek retribution? Analysis of decisions of judges or guidelines for sentencing provided by the Minister of Justice suggests that there is considerable latitude for discretionary sentencing by judges in the court system. However, this discretion can often lead to sentencing disparities, as an identical offence can result in many different sentencing options, depending on the province or the values of the judge.

Canada officially espouses the philosophy that its sentencing process is driven by the twin goals of rehabilitation and deterrence. The intent is to deter the offender from repeating the crime, as well as to identify the underlying causes that led to the criminal offence in the first place. Furthermore, in the last decade the courts have been taking into account the impact that the crime has on the victim. Cunningham and Griffiths (1997) note that victims of crime have demanded that the criminal justice system recognize the physical, emotional, and financial consequences of the crime. Advocates of victim impact statements suggest that those who carry out crimes, rather than victims, were getting the most attention from the authorities. Today, victim impact statements have an important role in the sentencing process.

The corrections system is still under heavy societal criticism. A 75 percent recidivism rate suggests that prisons have failed to rehabilitate convicts. High-profile parolees who reoffend often mar the record of a generally successful parole system, and there are many critics who believe that prison life has become too soft and cushy, with the authorities condoning a deviant prison subculture. However, as Goff (1997) notes, the correctional system is a major cog in the criminal justice system, one that attempts to juggle contradictory goals, including deterring crime, rehabilitating offenders, and punishing those who have committed serious offences against the state.

# The Canadian Justice System

As we have stated, each component of the criminal justice system—the police, the courts, and corrections—plays a unique and complementary role in ensuring that the system works. The process begins with a police investigation, resulting either from a complaint or a discovery of a crime in progress. After gathering evidence, the police arrest the offenders, or a justice of the peace issues a summons for the offender to appear in court.

An arrest is a serious matter, as it involves potential loss of freedom and brings the criminal sanctions of the state down on the accused. At the stage of questioning and prior to arrest, the individual's protections under the Charter are outlined, including the right to legal counsel and the right not to answer the questions of the police. In the course of the arrest, the accused is fingerprinted, photographed, weighed, measured, booked, and placed in a detention cell. At this stage, the process moves from the police to the courts, with the law stating that within 24 hours of arrest the accused must be brought before a justice of the peace or a magistrate. The purpose is for the court to determine the question of bail for the defendant. Since the Bail Reform Act of 1970, most defendants are released on their own recognizance. However, in the case of more serious criminal charges, the accused will have to post a cash or property bond, and in the rare case that the court officer believes the defendant may fail to appear for trial, bail is denied. In this situation the accused is taken to a pretrial detention centre, usually the local city jail, to await court appearance. Our justice system also allows defendants who are indigent to apply for legal aid; if granted, a lawyer drawn from a list of available defence lawyers is assigned to the accused.

The formal court process begins with the preliminary hearing, where a judge hears the police evidence, presented by an assistant Crown attorney, and the defence attorney attempts to debunk and deny the validity of this evidence. The judge at this stage seeks to determine only that there are reasonable grounds to believe that the defendant committed the crime. Having determined that there is a "bona fide" case against the accused, the judge sends the case to trial. Should the judge believe that insufficient evidence is presented, the case will be dismissed and the defendant freed.

It should be mentioned that the majority of criminal cases never come to trial, and in our criminal courts, the majority of those convicted are found guilty of a lesser offence than they were originally charged with committing. Because trials are expensive and long drawn out, the common outcome is either a plea bargain or a dismissal. In those cases that involve a criminal court trial before a judge or before a judge and jury, the process is formal and regulated. The rules of evidence, of cross-examination by the Crown and defence, and of the role of the judge in applying the law are clearly defined. If the jury is unable to obtain a unanimous verdict, a mistrial is declared, and a retrial could be ordered by the Crown attorney. The Crown could also decide not to retry the accused, and at that point the accused will be released.

When the offender is convicted of a Criminal Code violation, the judge has the role of imposing punishment, including probation, community service, a monetary fine, imprisonment, or a combination of fine and imprisonment. For serious offences, such as first or second degree murder, the judge must impose a minimum mandatory sentence that the offender must serve before becoming eligible for parole. In many instances before sentencing, the judge will request a presentence report from a parole officer and will inquire about the offender's socioeconomic position, previous criminal record, and family and community status. Because for most offences the Criminal Code does not impose strict min-

imum sentences, judges have wide discretion in the sentencing process. A major problem with this latitude is that judges in different jurisdictions could impose vastly different sentences for similar offences. Critics of this discretionary sentencing policy believe that specific mandatory maximum and minimum sentences will lead to fairer and more equitable sentencing across Canada. The final stage in the court process is the right of the accused to appeal the sentence and the conviction imposed by the judge. In serious cases of a criminal or constitutional manner, the Supreme Court of Canada could agree to hear the case, although less than one hundred cases a year reach this court.

Those sentenced to a term in a correctional facility find themselves in either a provincial or a federal institution. The determining factor is length of sentence, with those offenders sentenced to longer than two years ending up in a federal institution. Canada places its prisoners in maximum, medium, or minimum security institutions, depending on the risk and the treatment needs of the offender. Newer prisons are moving away from the fortress, razor wire, and "stone wall" structures of the past century, but in all except the minimum security institutions, rehabilitative programs are all but nonexistent. The challenge is to improve the life chances of the offender, so that on release to day parole, full parole, or to a halfway house, the opportunity to participate in the normative structure of the society will have been enhanced and recidivism opportunities reduced.

The goal of the Canadian justice system is not to reduce crime at any cost, but to obtain fair justice for all accused and to protect the legal and human rights of those charged with criminal offences by following established rules; this system is known as **due process.** The bottom line is that the innocent should never be found guilty, and if these injustices ever occur, it must be determined where the system broke down and the problem must be fixed. All along the process, from arrest to the courts and finally corrections, limits to the power of criminal justice officials are in place, with the goal of preventing the miscarriage of justice. All offenders are treated as innocent until proven guilty, every effort is made to provide legal representation for the accused, and the police and the prosecution are continually monitored by watchdog agencies. The premise is that the abuse of power by law administration officials is always a possibility—these officials will bend the rules to obtain convictions if given the opportunity. In fact, recent high-profile cases in Canada have shown that innocent people have been convicted of murder and other crimes and that police and court officials have presented evidence that they knew was false to juries. In the last few years, the first degree murder convictions of Donald Marshall, Guy Paul Morin, and David Milgaard were all overturned by the Supreme Court of Canada, and after public inquiries, further legal measures to control law administration officials were introduced. Given these high-profile cases of the maladministration of justice, the evidence seems to support the view that police and court officials could bend the rules if given the opportunity in order to obtain convictions. That the accused could be innocent seems hardly to matter in this obsession with proving guilt. In this model of justice, any tampering with the criminal procedures as set by the legal statutes is a violation of the rights of the offender and is grounds for the acquittal of the accused.

# Criminal Justice and Criminology

To a large extent, the study and analysis of criminal justice grew from the need for better training and a professional ethic for practitioners in the field, be they the police, court workers, or correctional officials. According to Schmalleger (1997), early criminal justice education was practice oriented and a technical form of education with on-the-job training. **Criminology,** on the other hand, is an academic discipline with roots in sociology and psychology. However, the discipline of criminology is central to the analysis of criminal justice. As well, both disciplines deal with the same content, with criminal justice covering the practical, applied content and criminology examining the theoretical underpinnings provided by criminology.

It is important that as a society we understand the sociological and psychological causes of crime. If, for example, crime is rooted in the way our society is organized, then crime reduction through the criminal justice system will be successful only if it addresses the structural roots of criminality. As Hagan (1989) notes, only if we understand crime causation, prevention, and the rehabilitation and punishment of offenders can we devise methods for the fair and just administration of the criminal justice system. Barkhan (1997) further notes that crime victimization and criminal justice cannot be fully understood without appreciating their structural context. They originate in communities, in the relationships and interactions among people and the social inequalities of race, ethnicity, or social class. It is through criminological insights and understanding of human behaviour that we can improve the applied discipline of criminal justice. For example, research on crime victimization or punishment provides insight for officials in the criminal justice system into the nature and purpose of crime in various contexts.

That the study of the criminal justice system has grown in similar leaps and bounds as the discipline of criminology in Canada is not surprising. The turbulence of the past three decades has brought increasing concern with social issues, especially the administration of justice. At the same time, the dramatic increase in crime rates in the United States and, to a lesser extent, in Canada has heightened interest in crime causation and prevention. The increased importance of crime prevention led to emphasis on law and order and to the professionalization of practitioners in the justice system. As well, academic programs in criminal justice were created in postsecondary institutions, often side by side with criminology programs or sometimes integrated within these programs.

With Canada increasingly caught up in a critical examination of the criminal justice system and of the protection of individual and legal rights, the direction that justice studies will take remains open. It is today an important applied discipline grounded in developing increased understanding of the branches of the justice system: the police, the courts, and corrections. With an enshrined "due process" model of justice, combined with the Charter of Rights and Freedoms, the pressure is always to reduce inequities and corruption in the system.

Criminal justice and criminology also question why some behaviours are defined as crimes, while others are not. Regoli and Hewitt (1996) note that crimes are both legal and social constructs. Social thinking and interaction play an important role in determining which acts are defined as criminal. This is a fascinating premise, for it explains why, for example, as social and legal views about the role and status of women to control their own bodies shifted in Canada, Parliament legalized abortion and the Supreme Court upheld its legality. Furthermore, it explains why blue-collar crime continues to receive the most attention from the justice system, whereas white-collar crime is not treated as serious malfeasance. Gallup polls in Canada show that the public continues to view blue-collar crime as societally dangerous and threatening to social order, but it sees white-collar crime as a mild deviation.

Regardless of how we view criminal violations of the law, criminologists invariably agree that in complex, multicultural societies such as Canada's, law has become an increasingly necessary tool in regulating behaviour. Regoli and Hewitt (1996) note three commonly identified functions of criminal law: to define socially unacceptable behaviour, to control behaviour and maintain social order, and to design punishment for unacceptable behaviour. It is important to understand that the role of the criminal justice system is to administer the criminal law that the society has codified in the criminal statutes. For example, when people take part in socially unacceptable behaviour and break the law, the role of the police is to investigate the incident and, based on the evidence, lay a charge. The role of the court is to prosecute the accused using established legal techniques, and the role of the corrections system is to carry out the court's sentencing process. Although the law may not reflect fairness and equity for all groups in society, it is not the role of the criminal justice system to be biased in interpreting the criminal law. This link between the administration of justice and the criminal law becomes particularly complicated in cases where the criminal law may reflect the biases of a dominant group. Powerful groups legislate laws that protect their interests, such as property laws, while women, the poor, and racial minorities have seldom seen legislation that protects their interests enshrined in the law.

# Conclusion

The tremendous growth in the importance of criminal justice and criminology studies in Canada in the past two decades reflects the importance that crime causation, prevention, and administration play in the lives of Canadians. In 1988 the Canadian General Social Survey polled ten thousand Canadians about their attitudes toward crime and criminal justice and the degree of their victimization by criminals. Although the crime rate in Canada is four times lower than in the United States (Barkhan, 1997), 25 percent of those surveyed were concerned about crime, and over 75 percent felt that punishment by the courts for crimes was too lenient. Women and the elderly also felt more unsafe in their neighbourhoods and on the streets. Given these attitudes, it is likely that interest in the administration of justice will continue to be important to the Canadian public. While not an impossibility, creating a justice system based on following due process and protecting the legal rights of individuals, while enforcing the criminal laws fairly and efficiently, is a great challenge. In the following chapters, we hope to provide a comprehensive analysis of the operation of the criminal justice system and its components. As well, we will critically analyze and provide constructive solutions to the dysfunctional parts of the criminal justice system.

# Summary

In this chapter, we have discussed the historical and social underpinnings of the society from which crime and crime control methods have evolved. Examining the various branches of the criminal justice system—the police, the courts, and corrections—allows us to analyze both the methodology and the practice of criminal justice. While the twin goals of crime control and due process are the linchpins of the system, they often can be in conflict. The crime control approach emphasizes law enforcement and punishment, while the due process model stresses the rights of individuals to fair treatment before the law and holds the law enforcement agencies accountable for upholding justice. Within this mix is thrown the Canadian Charter of Rights and Freedoms, which further enshrines individual rights and limits the operation of the Canadian criminal justice system. The challenge for the justice system is to balance the collective needs of the society for effective law enforcement with the need to be fair and equitable and to recognize individual rights.

# Key Terms

arrest (p. 4)

Canadian Charter of Rights and Freedoms (p. 5)

corrections (p. 5)

court system (p. 4)

Criminal Code (p. 4)

criminal justice system (p. 2)

criminology (p. 9)

due process (p. 8)

# Discussion Questions

1. What are the main goals of the Canadian criminal justice system?

2. Discuss the concept of social order in the context of the purpose of criminal law in society.

3. Discuss some of the factors that influence why certain behaviours are defined as criminal and others are not.

4. Outline some changes you would institute in the various parts of the criminal justice system to improve the efficiency of its operations.

5. Does the Charter of Rights and Freedoms affect the promotion of social order and social control in society?

# Weblinks

**www.library.utoronto.ca/libraries_crim/crimhome.htm** The University of Toronto's Centre of Criminology is an excellent starting point with a list of links to various online criminal justice resources. The information covers a wide range of subject areas, including public and private policing, violence, deviance and social control, young offenders, criminology, and criminal law.

**www.canadalegal.com/gosite.asp?s=1352** Duhaime's Canadian Criminal Law Centre site offers plain language articles on criminal justice issues ranging from abortion law to traffic tickets.

**www.acjnet.org/** This site is a gate to Canadian justice and legal information and services. The Access to Justice Network (ACJNet) opens doors to legislation, people and organizations, publications, databases, and discussion forums on justice and legal issues. These resources are organized under subject headings such as: aboriginal people, crime prevention, plain language, women, and youth.

**insight.mcmaster.ca/org/efc/pages/law/cc/cc.html** This McMaster University site provides the text of the entire Criminal Code of Canada.

**www.icclr.law.ubc.ca** The International Centre for Criminal Law Reform and Criminal Justice Policy is a Vancouver-based, independent, non-profit institute, officially affiliated with the United Nations. The organization is dedicated to national and international efforts to reduce crime and improve justice. Their site contains publications, occasional papers and reports, event and conference listings, an on-line forum facility, and links to partner institutes around the world.

# CHAPTER 2

# Crime Statistics

## Objectives

- To provide a statistical analysis of crime in Canadian society, including who commits crime, the prevalence of crime, and the incidence of crime.

- To analyze self-report and victimization data to enhance our understanding of crime, risk factors for crime and victimization, and locations of crime.

- To analyze over- and underreporting of crime owing to bias in the justice system in the forms of racism, sexism, and classism.

- To provide a comprehensive analysis of crime patterns in Canada by region, type of crime, age, sex, race, social ecology, and demographics.

## The Crime Picture

Most Canadians believe that crime is a major social issue. Polls show that Canadians frequently view the "crime problem" as among the top priorities for government intervention. But what is the extent and nature of crime in Canadian society? Who commits crime, what sort of crimes are most frequently committed, and under what conditions do these crimes occur?

This chapter will provide an overview of the **demographics** (the pattern or distribution in a population) of crime in Canadian society. We will begin by explaining some key terms and concepts that aid in the interpretation of crime rates. Next, we will discuss the sources of knowledge about crime statistics and

patterns. Finally, we will discuss some possible reasons for the demographics, reasons that are tied to theories about crime.

A *preconception* is an understanding or a view formed prior to thoroughly reviewing the evidence. Before reading this chapter, you might want to jot down some of your own preconceptions about crime in Canada. Is the crime rate going up or down? Is violent crime on the increase? How does Canada rank compared with other countries in measures of crime?

You might also want to ask yourself what the *sources* are of your preconceptions of the Canadian crime picture. If you are like most people, your sources will be television news and talk shows, major newspaper and magazine stories, and news and information posted on the Internet. These are mass media sources because they are a form of communication aimed at very large markets. However, the mass media tend to transmit a distorted image of crime. Violent street crimes are widely covered, while nonviolent corporate and white-collar crimes are underreported. Canadian mass media sources also tend to view the crime situation through American lenses, giving the illusion that Canadian society suffers the same degree of social problems that exist south of the border. Furthermore, although the Internet contains much accurate and valuable information, it also contains unreliable and inaccurate material.

Your impression of the crime picture might also be informed by your own experiences. Your view of the bigger picture often—and quite naturally—comes from your own experience. Have you been a victim of crime? Was the victimization brutal? Your "gut feeling" about the extent of crime out there can be shaped and distorted by your individual situation and experience.

Your situation may be unusual in a number of ways that we will discuss, using demographic measures like age, sex, class, ethnicity, and ecology. Even if your situation represents many demographic norms, it still doesn't provide the best place from which to draw inferences on what is happening in the whole of Canadian society. To get a relatively accurate measure of the extent and nature of crime in Canada, we need to look at the number of incidents within *populations,* rather than at the number of incidents an *individual* has experienced. To get a feeling for the difference, speak to some of your classmates and compare notes on your experiences of victimization. The more people you compare notes with, the more you will see be able to see how individual experiences are deviations from the average.

You might also compare experiences with criminal acts. Have you ever shoplifted? How often? Ask some of your classmates to describe their criminal history. You may have some compunction about disclosing your past criminal behaviour, however insignificant it was. Your classmates might also have reservations about sharing their criminal history, however trifling, with you. Nevertheless, these exercises are unsophisticated versions of two of the tools social scientists use to get a picture of crime: victimization and self-report surveys. These, plus official and unofficial statistics, form the basis of a rendering of the crime picture that is *sociologically sound*—or valid and reliable according to social science standards.

Although they may be sociologically sound, we shall also see that each of these techniques is far from perfect. Your own survey of your classmates' criminal histories and experiences of victimization will likely leave you with the suspicion that much of the true picture has not been fully revealed. Similarly, social scientists using the most advanced methods will also admit that problems persist with the reporting and counting that they use to arrive at their findings. However, it is important to stress that the crime picture drawn in this way is still more reliable and accurate than one drawn from an ad hoc sampling of mass media stories and individual experience. While the picture of crime in Canadian society presented in this chapter is far from flawless, it is derived from the best methods and tools at our disposal.

## The Purpose of Crime Statistics

Why do we record, or try to record, the amount of crime in society? Why is the study of crime often a war of words (and numbers) between those who believe crime is increasing and society is becoming destabilized, and those who believe crime is on the decrease and society has a handle on its social problems? In part, crime is political, and crime statistics frequently serve political masters. In Canada, crime has not yet reached the level of politicization exhibited in American politics, but it almost always sits among the top five or ten planks of a party platform. Crime sells votes.

But there are other reasons why crime measurement is important. One reason is that many theories explaining crime depend on some kind of mapping of the frequency and distribution of crime. Without reasonably solid information on the incidence and prevalence of crime, it is difficult to begin the work of explaining crime. Theories of crime causation are important if governments wish to create policies aimed at reducing—or redistributing—criminality in society.

Let us take the example of drunk driving. Before they will see drunk driving as a problem requiring action, governments will want to study the evidence of the prevalence and frequency of this behaviour. The argument that more money, changed laws, or redistributed governmental resources, such as more police officers, are required hinges on some evidence that this is a social problem that governmental policy can do something about. To understand the dimensions of the problem, such as increasing frequency, prevalence, and cost, the government needs a picture of the problem based on a collection of records of incidence. If Mothers Against Drunk Driving can tell the government that accidents owing to impairment have increased nationally from, say, 5000 in 1996 to 10 000 in 1997, then the federal government may agree that the issue is worthy of further governmental intervention.

So crime recording is a picture of a population or of society as a whole from the angle of criminality. How much criminality there is, what kinds of criminality are common, and where the criminality takes place are questions that provide a basis from which policy can attack the social problem of crime. The facts and figures of crime can mobilize political action and social policy.

Underlying crime statistics are the insecurities and anxieties that crime elicits. The reason politicians can win votes and government can organize resources in the area of crime policy is that protection from criminal depredation is at the heart of why we have government in the first place. Thomas Hobbes argued that we have a strong central authority in order that we may be secure from such depredations by others, and we sacrifice some of our freedoms to this central authority (today, it can be more local) in order to maximize our security. Where there is a great deal of crime, or in Emile Durkheim's term, *anomie* (or normlessness) in a society, there is evidence of a breakdown of the norms by which a population of people is constituted as a society. Therefore, crime statistics represent a barometer of the extent to which there are "bad people" among us and provide a way of checking on our contract with government: Is our social contract being upheld? Does it need to be reviewed?

# Methods for Mapping Crime

## Terms and Concepts

When you hear criminal justice officials and social scientists speaking about the crime picture, you likely encounter unfamiliar terms and concepts. Before venturing out into the hazardous terrain occupied by numbers and graphs, we will review some of these terms in order to gain a basic understanding of the terms used in crime statistics.

### Prevalence of Crime

The **prevalence of crime** is the number of people participating in crime at a given time. Prevalence is measured by dividing the number of offenders by the size of the population.

If, for instance, there are 50 people in your class and 5 of these students are offenders, then you can determine the prevalence of crime in your class by dividing the population of offenders (5) by the population of your class (50). This gives you a ratio of 1/10.

## Incidence of Crime

The **incidence of crime** is the frequency with which offenders commit crime, or the average number of offences per offender. Incidence is measured by dividing the number of offences by the number of offenders.

Let us say that the 5 hypothetical offenders in your class committed the following number of offences: 1 committed 1 offence, 3 committed 2 offences, and 1 committed 17 offences. You would calculate the incidence by adding up the offences and dividing that number (20) by the number of offenders (5). This would leave you with an incidence rate of 4 offences per offender, or 4/1.

## Crime Rate

The **crime rate** is the number of offences that occur per population. A population, or a cohort, is simply a group of people with a common demographic. The group can be as large as all of the people in Canada or as small as all of the people in your class. A crime rate is calculated by totalling all the offences occurring in a given population and dividing that number by the population. The population is the *denominator*—the figure underneath the line. The frequency is the *numerator*—the figure above the line. A crime rate uses a given denominator of 100 000. It is usually measured as a frequency of offences per 100 000 people.

Let us take the hypothetical example of your class again. You have 5 offenders who have committed a total of 20 offences in a population of 50 students. You can calculate the crime rate by simply dividing the number of offences by the total population: 20/50 = 2/5. Or, you can calculate it by multiplying prevalence (1/10) by incidence (4/1). This would give you the following 1/10 x 4/1 = 4/10.

Now, remember that crime statistics are usually presented as a figure per population of 100 000. The easiest way to calculate this statistic is to divide the number of offences by the meaningful population in which those offences occurred to get a percentage and then multiply the percentage (a figure out of 10), by 100 000. In this case, that would give us a rate of 40 000/100 000—presented in short form by just citing the numerator, or 40 000. This is an astronomical rate indeed! Most crime rates are lower than this.

One of the reasons the rate is so high is that we failed to properly account for *time*. In our example, we did not specify a time period in coming up with our rate of 40 000. But a time period is important. When we look at crime, we are always concerned with a rate of crime in a specified period of time. The crime rate is almost always calculated *per year*, but it can also be given per month in month-to-month comparisons.

Let's apply this principle to our hypothetical class. Say those 20 offences were spread out evenly over 15 years. This would give us a rate per year of 1.33; 1.33 divided by the total population of 50 equals a rate of 2066. This figure is more realistic, but it is still higher than what you might reasonably expect to find were you to rely on official statistics.

It is important to remember that a crime rate always refers to the incidence and frequency of offences per a given population. At its most general, the rate consists of *all* offences committed and *all* of the population in a territorial jurisdiction, such as Canada. However, crime rates are also given for specific offences, such as burglary, murder, and auto theft. For example, if there were 70 homicides in Metro Toronto in 1995, and Metro Toronto at the time had a population of 2 million, we would compute a murder rate of 70/2 000 000 = 3.5.

As an illustration of differences in crime rates for various offences, Table 2.1 compares total robberies and breaking and entering in Canada for 1996. Adding the total number of offences in both categories gives us a crime rate of 9489 (2 785 953/ 29 963 600). Remember, the crime rate for the whole country is calculated using the census population in the denominator. For 1996, according to Statistics Canada, the population was 29 963 600. By the year 2000, the population is projected to be slightly over 32 000 000.

## TABLE 2.1

### ROBBERIES AND BREAKING AND ENTERING, 1996

| OFFENCE | TOTAL NUMBER | CRIME RATE |
|---|---|---|
| Robbery | 31 242 | 104 |
| Breaking and Entering | 396 085 | 1322 |

## Problems with Crime Rates

There are problems in calculating crime rates that should induce you to read them with some skepticism. First, what really belongs in the denominator? Some analysts have suggested that to calculate car thefts or property thefts in general, what we really ought to put in the denominator is the property available to be stolen. With car thefts, for example, does it not make sense to consider the number of cars available to steal? Certainly, we would learn more precisely the extent of auto theft as a problem if we could compare places according to the proportion of cars stolen.

Second, which numbers should be used for the numerator? Above, we used Statistics Canada figures for total Criminal Code offences. StatsCan figures depend on the police becoming aware of an offence and recording it. As we shall shortly see, for the police to record the offence, a number of things had to have happened—a citizen had to call the police, and the police had to correctly identify and record the event as an offence.

Third, what is the true relationship between official records and the extent of real crime? We refer to this problem in the term "the dark figure," which we will discuss next.

## BOX 2.1

### CALCULATING CRIME RATE: SPEND-IT-HERE, ONTARIO

Let us take the example of a tourist city, Spend-It-Here, Ontario. Crime reports include all break and enters reported to the police in a given year. Let's say that this figure was recorded as 1500. Therefore, 1500 would go above the line in calculating the crime rate for car theft. If Spend-It-Here has a population of 200 000, that would give us the following:

$$\frac{1500}{200\ 000} = 750$$

The trouble is that Spend-It-Here's population on any given day can also include many nonresidents who are not enumerated, which makes the denominator smaller than it should be. If, for instance, there are an extra 15 000 visitors on a Saturday night, and if this is when most car thefts occur, then the denominator of the population of the city ought to be 215 000, giving us a lesser rate of 698.

This is perhaps more extreme in a city like Atlantic City, New Jersey, or Washington, D.C. In Washington, a great deal of nonresidents commute from surrounding states to work every day, making the daily population count much higher than the enumerated residential population. Washington has a very high murder rate, but this rate does not include nonresidents among the denominator, thus deflating it and inflating the crime rate.

## The Dark Figure of Crime

From time to time in your study of criminology you will come across the term *the dark figure of crime,* or simply *the dark figure.* What does this term mean? Simply put, the **dark figure of crime** refers to the amount of actual crime in society, which official crime statistics do not show because not all crimes are reported to or recorded by the police. When you hear the radio announcing that the crime rate is up, the report is based on police statistics or on official crime statistics of reported and recorded crime. However, since the first victimization survey in the mid-1960s, criminologists have confirmed what most people in the criminal justice system and in society have long suspected: many people who commit crimes are not caught and brought to justice, and many crimes remain unreported and unrecorded because many victims choose not to pursue the case. The dark figure is this unreported and unrecorded crime; it is a figure that is unknown.

We are beginning to know more about this dark figure, however. We know, for instance, that unreported crimes for some offences are much higher than others. Victimization surveys reveal that the proportion of unreported to reported cases of sexual assault is very high. On the other hand, cases of unreported or unrecorded homicides are very low. The underreporting of homicide is on the low end of the scale because victims are often missed if they disappear. For these and other reasons, the reporting of homicides is not shadowed by a sizeable dark figure. The exceptions are cases where someone is murdered but the death is officially reported as resulting from natural causes or accident.

The dark figure is important for a number of reasons. The deterrent effect of punishment cannot take place if the offender is not prosecuted. As well, the picture of crime trends is skewed if "real" criminality is very different from "official" criminality. Insurance programs, compensation programs, and even policy objectives are also best served by the most reliable data about crime.

Before we leave our discussion of the dark figure, one caveat is in order. According to our criminal law, a crime is a violation of the Criminal Code that is attended by the requisite mens rea and actus reus, as determined by a court of law (we will discuss these elements of criminal offences in Chapter 3). The legal profession would argue that criminologists who claim that there is a dark figure of crime and criminality are using the terms *crime* and *criminality* too liberally, given that only the courts can determine legal criminality, and some of those who make up the dark figure would be found legally not guilty. The problem is exacerbated because "actual" criminality represented in the dark figure depends on information that is most often documented without the benefit of cross-examination. This information may be based on compounded, unchallengeable interpretations of a given event as a legal offence.

## Crime Recording

Our understanding of the picture of crime depends on two sources: official statistics and unofficial statistics. As we have learned, **official statistics** detail *recorded* criminal activities. This recording is done by the police, the courts, and provincial and federal corrections agencies. **Unofficial statistics,** on the other hand, are *estimates* of criminal activity based on self-report and victimization surveys.

We have already noted that crime statistics are a necessary starting point for policy and for some theorizing on criminality. However, we will see that official statistics do come with problems, as the numbers that they provide can be skewed by systematic biases and errors. In our discussion of crime reporting we will begin by addressing the various kinds of official statistics on crime we have in Canada and some specific problems with them. Next, we will look at self-report and victimization reports as a way of augmenting the crime picture with unofficial statistics. Finally, we will look at sources of bias and error in statistics.

## Official Statistics

Official statistics begin with individual cases of offences recorded by the police. These cases need to be gathered as a collection of more manageable data. In Canada, the Uniform Crime Reporting Survey (UCR) allows us to do this. The UCR contains simply rules, definitions, and categories by which data on incidents are scored according to nationally approved criteria.

The UCR was inaugurated in 1962 as a shared project of Statistics Canada and the Canadian Association of Chiefs of Police. The UCR includes almost all Criminal Code offences, as well as federal and provincial statutes. The Canadian Centre for Justice Statistics (CCJS) assumed responsibility for the program in 1981. The CCJS offers an annual compilation of the UCR. You can see the latest available data by going to the Statistics Canada Web site (www.statcan.ca/english/Pgdb/State/justic.htm) and looking at the table "Crime by Type of Offence."

Before analyzing what these data tell us, we need to consider their limitations. First, not all incidents are reported to the police. Victimization surveys have found that such reporting depends on whether there is a complainant or victim, whether the victim perceives the seriousness of the crime, and whether the victim feels the police can be of help or views the crime as a private matter that can be resolved. Some victims may also fear retaliation, and sexual assault victims are particularly hesitant about having their lives further disrupted by "secondary" victimization through the justice process itself. Some victims also experience a sense of shame, and many do not wish to subject themselves to further violation. The official scrutiny that attends the fact-finding of a criminal event is itself painful, and many victims believe that the criminal justice system will fail to remedy their loss or offer them justice.

Second, violations include summary conviction offences such as traffic violations and thus mislead us into equating a rise in such offences with a rise in the crime rate. In the United States, the FBI resolves this problem somewhat by listing eight serious offences as Part 1 offences, which together constitute a crime index. The index is intended to match what most people identify as "true crime." These crimes include murder and manslaughter, forcible rape, robbery, aggravated assault, burglary/breaking and entering, larceny/theft, motor vehicle theft, and arson.

Third, often a number of separate offences are committed in an incident, but only the most serious is scored. As Silverman (1980) has argued, the result is that the total crime count is underestimated because those other crimes are lost in the analysis. Another result is the misleading impression that a larger percentage of crimes are serious crimes (Linden, 1996).

Fourth, the numbers are only as good as their faithfulness to the events they represent. If the police begin to clamp down on prostitution through more "proactive policing," or if they decide to look the other way for possession of small amounts of cannabis even though there are no changes to legislation, then the numbers they feed into the UCR will show increases and decreases that reflect changes in police practices, rather than changes in crime patterns. Also, if the police decide to enforce "zero tolerance" policies with regard to violence in schools or "affirmative arrest" practices in cases of spousal assault—where the police officer is not to use discretion, but is to arrest if any sign of physical assault is present on the body of the complainant—then crime rates will rise as a result of these changes in policies. If there is a rise in the number of police officers available to the public, again, crime rates may go up. In a study by McDonald (1969), one of the best predictors of increasing crime rates was found to be growth in the size of police forces.

In addition to the discretion and enforcement practices of the police, there are differences in other subsystems of the criminal justice process that can produce variations in the crime rate. For example, Sprott and Doob (1998) have found huge variations in incarceration rates between provinces, which are partly the result of vast differences in provincial policies and the administration of justice.

Fifth, in addition to changes in crime control policies, changes in legislation can affect crime rates. If the Criminal Code creates new offence categories or broadens existing ones, crime rates will reflect these legislative changes in the form of increases. Recent changes to drug legislation are a prime example.

## Unofficial Statistics

### Self-Report Data

In addition to official statistics, criminologists use unofficial statistics to obtain a picture of crime. A **self-report survey,** as the word implies, is one that asks people to report on their own delinquency or criminal past. In our earlier example, your classmates' reports of their past criminal behaviour were rudimentary self-reports. Self-report surveys, then, are merely questionnaires asking for some demographic data in addition to information about the respondents' criminal history.

The first self-report study of crime was conducted by Austin Potterfield in the early 1940s. Of the college students he surveyed, 90 percent admitted to a felony crime. Wallerstien and Wyle (1947) and Nye and Short (1957) did further studies to corroborate Potterfield's initial findings that criminality was widespread across the adolescent population. The dark figure of crime suddenly began to appear, and it loomed large—it seemed that many crimes were neither reported nor recorded.

Self-report studies were important not only as criticism of official data. These studies also held the potential to reveal the work of the criminal justice system. They were key evidence of the claim that there existed law enforcement biases that gave a skewed or distorted rendering of criminality. Indeed, self-report studies have been important in painting a picture of the relationship between class and crime, as well as in demystifying the assumption that delinquency is an almost exclusively lower-class phenomenon.

In the United States in 1976, a large self-report study, the National Youth Survey, discovered that more than 90 percent of juveniles admitted to at least one act for which they could have served a custody sentence, had they been caught. It also found that the actual rate of delinquency was 4 to 10 times higher than was officially reported in the UCR.

As with official statistics, there are persistent problems with self-report studies. For example, it has been found that lower-class males and black males are more likely to underreport their delinquency (Hindelang, Hirschi, & Weis, 1981). In addition, the method depends on one person's interpretation of events (the perpetrator), which may not accord with how others interpret the events. People can more easily admit to things through confession in a confidential questionnaire, and this sort of confession may exaggerate criminality. There have been strong criticisms of the reliability and validity of self-report surveys because respondents depend on their memory of events, and they may misunderstand questions or simply lie (Huizinga & Elliott, 1986).

## Victimization Data

**Victimization surveys** are another source of unofficial information to augment the crime picture and to cast light into the dark figure. Victimization surveys are questionnaires that ask people to provide information about their experience as the object of criminal activity, rather than as the perpetrator. Respondents are asked to tell if and how often they have been robbed, raped, had things stolen from among their possessions, and so forth. They are asked if they knew the offender; whether they reported the event to the police, and why or why not; and what the circumstances of the crime were. In addition, they are asked detailed questions about their own life circumstances.

Victimization surveys capture many petty crimes and crimes that may occur in the household, such as burglary, domestic assault, and incest, which often are not reported to the police. According to the 1982 Canadian Urban Victimization Survey, personal theft, vandalism, simple assault, and sexual assault were more likely to go unreported than to be reported. However, victimization surveys fail to report many frauds, as the victim is often unaware of the crime.

In Canada, there have been three victimization surveys that have taken a national sampling. The first of these was the Canadian Urban Victimization Survey, conducted in 1982. It consisted of a random sample of the population aged 16 and over in seven cities. Over 60 000 telephone interviews were conducted. Residents were asked questions covering a wide range of victimization experiences over the previous year. In 1988 and 1993, the General Social Survey (GSS) was conducted through telephone surveys of a smaller sample of Canadians (10 000). It asked respondents for more detailed information on a more limited set of crimes (CCJS, 1994). Finally, a small national sample was taken as part of an international study of crime victimization (van Dijk & Mayhew, 1997; van Dijk, Mayhew, & Kilias, 1991).

All of these studies showed that about 40 percent of crimes go unreported to the police. The survey findings confirmed U.S. reports that revealed a very low reporting of sexual assault (just 10 percent). The GSS also found an annual rate of spousal assault of between 3 and 4 percent. However, if a relationship lasts 10 years, then at 4 times 10, we see 40 percent of women reporting assault by their partners during the life of the relationship. They also found that some petty crimes were very likely to be reported (68 percent of break-and-enter offences) (CCJS, 1994).

The relationship between official statistics and victimization rates as reported in victimization surveys is shown in Table 2.2. The table compares the major crime categories in the Uniform Crime Reports index in the United States with responses of victimization from the National Crime Victimization Survey, which began operation in 1972 in the United States. Can you think of why so many motor vehicle thefts are reported?

Victimization surveys have revealed much about the characteristics of criminal incidents, such as the time, the location, the offender–victim relationship, and the victim's decisions before and after the victimization, such as whether to call the police and the reasons why or why not. Victimization surveys have also helped to change our understanding of crime as a distributed phenomenon, or one that is spread out across time and space in certain predictable ways. By looking at crime from the point of view of the victim, victimization surveys highlight risk factors, focusing attention on the behaviours, locations, relationships, and activities that could increase a person's chances of victimization. In general, much of the dark figure of crime has been revealed through victimization surveys.

There are two noteworthy shortcomings of victimization surveys. One problem is that they depend, for the most part, on the victim's uncorroborated statements. In most cases, these statements are not or cannot be verified. The respondent may be mistaken as to the nature of the event, the time of the event, and the circumstances surrounding the event. People who decide to respond to

## TABLE 2.2

---

COMPARISON OF CRIMES REPORTS

| OFFENCE | UNIFORM CRIME REPORTS | NATIONAL CRIMINAL VICTIMIZATION SURVEY |
|---|---|---|
| **VIOLENT CRIME** | | |
| Homicide | 23 305 | – |
| Forcible rape | 102 096 | 316 000 |
| Robbery | 618 817 | 1 299 000 |
| Aggravated assault | 1 119 950 | 2 478 000 |
| **PROPERTY CRIME** | | |
| Burglary | 2 712 156 | 5 482 000 |
| Larceny | 7 876 254 | 23 765 000 |
| Motor vehicle theft | 1 539 097 | 1 764 000 |

Source: UCR figures adapted from FBI data by Schmalleger, 1997, p. 40.

the survey may be somewhat more keen to talk about their victimization than those who decide not to respond. Some of these methodological problems are addressed and partially resolved in good surveys, but problems remain. A second broad area of concern is how victimization relates to crime. Crime, it must be stressed, is a determination of the court, and many instances of victimization will not constitute legal crimes. The relationship of victimization to crime is not as clear cut as might be assumed (see Quinney, 1972).

## Longitudinal Research

Another noteworthy research technique is known as longitudinal or cohort research. This method involves observing a sample of people or a cohort of people who share a like characteristic over time. The longitudinal method is much like the British documentary series *28 Up* and *35 Up*, which follow a small sample of people by interviewing them every seven years to see how their lives are coming along. Every so often, the sample in a longitudinal survey is investigated on a number of criteria in order to gauge the incidence of crime or victimization.

One of the first of these studies was done by Wolfgang, Figlio, and Sellin in a 1972 study, *Delinquency in a Birth Cohort*. These authors followed 9945 boys in Philadelphia from their birth in 1945 until they were 18 years old. The authors used official police records to identify delinquents and found that over a third of the boys had some police contact. They also found that some of these boys were what they called *chronic offenders* (boys who offended fives times or more up until the age of 18); these boys made up 6.3 percent of the total of the group.

When Wolfgang replicated the study in a 1958 birth cohort, he found that the rate of chronic delinquency had increased to 7.5 percent.

The advantage of this kind of study is that it allows researchers to trace patterns in criminal careers or biographies. Such tracing is possible because both official data and some biographical data can be cross-tabulated. The more biographical data, the more that can be discovered above the limited dimensions, such as age and sex, that official statistics make available. In addition, the longitudinal study, if the sample is properly selected, can be a highly reliable indicator of the rates of criminal activity in particular populations.

## New Methods

In the United States, the National Incident-Based Reporting System (NIBRS) records crime by detailing the date, time, location, offender characteristics (age, sex, ethnicity, race), victim characteristics (age, sex, ethnicity, circumstances), and offence characteristics. This method is very promising as it incorporates much of the data that other systems omit, leaving victimization and self-report data to fill in the blanks.

# Systemic Biases and Sources of Error

Thus far, we have discussed specific problems in the reporting and recording of crime and the development of crime statistics. There are also some more structural and systemic causes of error in the development of crime figures. Three sources of errors are systemic racism, sexism, and classism. As well, the goals and interests of efficiency in justice institutions may affect crime statistics.

## Racism

Earlier, we mentioned that the police have a great deal of discretion in determining who is selected for criminal prosecution. Such discretion is more pronounced when police are more proactive (in cases where there is no complainant or victim), but it is also relatively greater in minor offences, such as littering, jaywalking, disorderly conduct, and minor traffic violations. The decision of the police and the courts of whether to prosecute may be influenced by professionalism and by weighing the perceived harm to the community or society against the principle of upholding the privacy and liberty of the individual. But it has often been found that professionalism and liberal principles are not the driving forces of prosecutorial decision making. Instead, as inquiries into the wrongful convictions of David Milgaard and Donald Marshall have found, sometimes even in serious cases the police look for the best available target to clear cases, and they look for them within marginalized groups and minorities—in these cases, Aboriginal Canadians.

David Milgaard (right) at a press conference in 1998.

## Sexism

It has also been contended that sexism may play a role in the over- or underreporting of crime. In the past, the juvenile justice system was preoccupied with status offences, or offences stemming from the moral regulation of girls and young women. Girls were more likely than boys in the early and mid 20th century to be apprehended and brought to court for status offences (Chesney-Lind, 1977). More recently, feminists have contended that girls and women are more harshly treated when their behaviour suggests that they are not following traditional roles (Carlen, Christina, Hicks, O'Dwyer, & Tchaikowsky, 1985). A competing view is the *chivalry hypothesis*—the theory that officials in the criminal justice system, from police officers to judges, are more lenient with female criminals, whom they consider "damsels in distress." Today, however, self-report and victimization rates fail to support the chivalry hypothesis. Women appear to be processed by the law in a way that is appropriate to their offending.

## Classism

The crime picture is also distorted through classism. Not everyone's interests are equally reflected in decision making about which kind of conflicts warrant criminalization. Partly, this problem is related to who occupies a position of power in determining right and wrong conduct. People with wealth and status in society can much more easily identify with the interests of others like them. If they occupy the ranks of judges, lawyers, and politicians, then their interests will affect who is processed and how. But they will also influence how social problems are categorized as crime or regulatory offences or as legitimate risks that are not prohibited.

For example, even though many people in high-pollution areas, such as southern Ontario, are put at risk by environmental degradation and the presence of nitrogen oxides, benzene, ground-level ozone, and other pollutants, and many early deaths are attributable to environmental contamination, we still prefer to view repeat health and safety violators as good citizens who should be given a chance to correct their actions. In many jurisdictions, industry and governmental regulators set flexible goals that permit recurrent violations of existing environmental and occupational health and safety codes. Infractions against labour codes are similarly subject to regulatory law, as governments operate to encourage compliance rather than to punish deviation. To get an idea of the differences in the policing of corporate deviance and "street crime," try to picture a drug dealer and a police officer sitting down to work out goals or targets for the quantity and quality of infractions (drug deals) that the dealer will be allowed to make. Jeffrey Reiman (1990) argues that there are two laws in our society: one for the rich and one for the poor.

The difference cannot be justified by referring to the greater economic importance of corporate polluters and white-collar offenders, because the cost to society of corporate and white-collar crime is estimated to be far greater than the cost of street crime. Rather, the distinction between the two is better understood as a difference of political power. Political power serves the interests of those in society who have a bigger slice of the economic pie. Under this argument, the criminal law is seen as the poor person's law—it is applicable more often and with greater consequences to those in society who have less. This view of the class basis of criminal selection, argued by criminologists such as Richard Quinney, Robert Elias, and Jeffrey Reiman, is important to our picture of the distribution of wrongdoing in society, as it alerts us to the possibility that there is another dark figure of transgressions against society that are not revealed by official crime statistics, self-reports, and victimization surveys (see, for example, Muncie, McLaughlin, & Langen, 1997).

A further problem of classism is that the distribution of resources in society works against the rights of the marginalized. Legal aid programs are intended to the right the imbalance for accused of few means, but for the most part they fail to do so because the quality and availability of legal aid rarely comes close to what is available to those with vast resources for their legal defence. Again, the distribution of wealth in society skews the crime picture to present a much greater distribution of crime in the lower classes.

## Institutional Practices in the Police, the Courts, and Corrections Systems

Each subsystem of the criminal justice system—the police, the courts, and corrections—has goals and the means to achieve these goals. These subsystems attempt to maximize their efficiency while operating with some level of accountability and attending to the rule of law. Sometimes, however, the effort to make each of these systems more efficient competes with considerations of due process. Herbert Packer (1964) saw crime control and due process as two competing objectives. But even where law is flexible so that it operates efficiently to control crime, the professionals who work within these subsystems often take shortcuts to achieve their objectives.

Plea bargaining is an example of such a shortcut, because it trades some amount of due process for enhanced efficiency, often rewarding accused persons who agree to such deals with shorter sentences than they would have received had they insisted on a full trial. Plea bargaining is therefore an institutional practice, or a routinized, officially sanctioned procedure used across the whole criminal justice system. Institutional practices like plea bargaining affect the crime picture because they allow for more guilty verdicts than would be possible without it.

Another example relates more to how institutions, as Mary Douglas puts it, *think*. Police forces can be understood in terms of their objectives, one of which is to find a suspect who can be processed criminally for a crime. As the Guy Paul Morin inquiry showed, this objective can lead police to seek not so much the person who actually committed the crime, because proving guilt goes beyond the epistemology of police work, but rather a person who can be prosecuted or arrested. Once an arrestable person is found, as discovered in the Morin inquiry, the police may ignore evidence of the suspect's innocence, to the point of failing to disclose such key evidence to prosecutors. Therefore, the distribution of resources in society influences who is more and who is less arrestable.

# Crime Patterns in Canada

Is Canada a safe country in which to live? Are cities more crime prone than towns? Are women more likely to be victims of crime than men? These are just some of the questions that a comprehensive crime map can provide answers to.

A crime map is simply a graphical presentation of the official crime statistics published by Statistics Canada. In this section, we will look at how crime is distributed. We will see how it is distributed by region, season, time of day, ecology, age, gender, class, ethnicity, and citizenship. We will also see how the crime rate has changed over time in Canada and how Canada's crime rate compares with those of other nations.

## Historical Trends

Probably the most frequently asked question about crime is, "Are crime rates going up?" We look at crime rates as a barometer of social cohesion and quality of life. As Canadians, many of us regard the historically high violent crime rates in the United States as evidence of a lack of social cohesion and of a poorer quality of life.

Figure 2.1 shows us what has happened to the crime rates in Canada between 1962 and 1996, the latest year for which figures are available. We cannot go further back with much reliability because the UCR began compiling data only in 1962. The crime rate increased consistently between 1962 and 1991, and over five consecutive years, between 1991 and 1996, the rates decreased. In fact, the decrease was 3.2 percent between 1991 and 1992, 5.3 percent between 1992 and 1993, 4.3 percent between 1993 and 1994, 1.6 percent between 1994 and 1995, and 1.6 percent between 1995 and 1996. The decreases in the crime rate include violent crime. After fifteen straight years of an increase, between 1977 and 1992, violent crime decreased in the four years between 1992 and 1996.

FIGURE 2.1

CRIME RATES PER 100 000 CANADIANS, 1962–1996

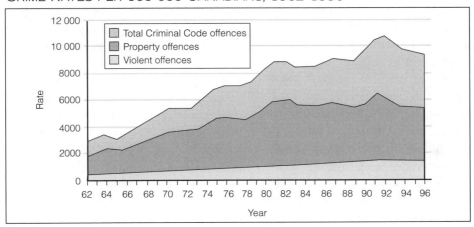

Source: CCJS. 1997. "Canadian Crime Statistics, 1996." *Juristat*, 17(8).

It is impossible to say whether the reduction in crime rates will be long-term or whether these recent figures are simply a break before the final assault on the mountain. The main cause of the break may be due to demographics, as there were relatively fewer young people in the population during the years with lower crime rates. As we will see later, young people are more likely to be involved in criminal activity. In fact, prevalence of offending peaks in the teenage years and then decreases during the third decade of life. In Canada, the number of young people aged 15 to 24 between 1991 and 1996 dropped to 4 million from 4.5 million in the late 1980s. It is expected that the number of young people will climb to this level again by 2006 (Foot, 1996).

## Comparative Trends

How does Canada's crime picture compare with those of other countries? Is our society more dangerous to live in, or less so? Are we relatively safe from depredation?

Before we look at cross-cultural or comparative data on crime rates, a note of caution should be sounded. We have already pointed out many problems with official reporting methods. When we attempt to compare rates between different countries, these problems become even more pronounced owing to differences in law enforcement practices, police data-gathering techniques, and definitions of categories. International victimization surveys might provide more reliability in comparing crime rates.

However, there are rather sizable differences in crime rates between countries that are not simply the result of differences in recording and enforcement. For instance, the rates of murder vary significantly, as is shown in Figure 2.2. The highest murder rate in 1990 was recorded by Swaziland, at 87.76 percent. The lowest rate, 0.47 percent, was found in the Czech Republic. The difference between these two rates is enormous, with the rate of murder 187 times as high in Swaziland as in the Czech Republic. Although a chart like this presents a window on crime and offers a gross representation of anomie, we need to remember that crime rates also vary within countries and shift over time. We also must remember that political turmoil, which may be temporary, will have a great impact on crime, although not always on official crime rates, since these depend on the definitions of events by political authorities whose interests may compete with international standards of human rights.

Nevertheless, if we contrast murder rates in the United States, Canada, England and Wales, and Norway, we are comparing relatively stable democracies, and yet we still see rather strong differences, with the United States having a rate more than 9 times greater than Norway's. Reasons for the differences are many and varied, but some of the most pressing are those related to urbanization, community cohesiveness, economic disparity, and the presence of individ-

FIGURE 2.2

--------------------------------------------------------------------------------

## MURDER RATES BY COUNTRY

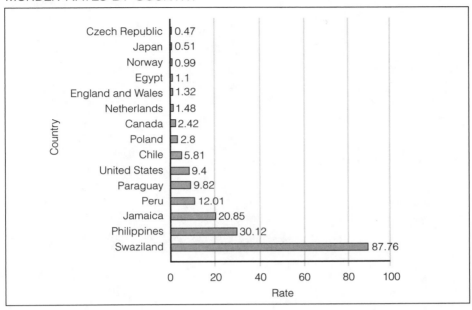

ualist and libertarian versus socialist or communal social policies and infrastructures (see Hartnagel & Lee, 1990).

For property crimes, the differences between countries are more complicated. These crime rates may also be influenced by the growing internationalization of organized crime affecting major categories such as auto theft.

## Crime by Region

Let us look at Table 2.3 and Figure 2.3. Table 2.3 presents all offences in Canada and breaks them down by province. Figure 2.3 converts the data into an area graph showing the distribution of offences by region. Notice the incline in crime rates in the western and northwestern regions of Canada. With the exception of Quebec, the further west across the country, the higher the rates of violent crime and of the total offences. The trend is not as pronounced with property crime. Notice also the very high rates in the territories. Crime rates in the North tend to be much higher than the Canadian average.

Now have a look at Figure 2.4. The rates are difficult to generalize, but the property crimes were lowest in Quebec City and highest in Vancouver. Vancouver also recorded the highest violent crime rate. In general, as we head north and west, crime rates increase.

TABLE 2.3

## CRIME BY REGION, 1996

| | CANADA | NFLD. | P.E.I. | N.S. | N.B. | QUE. | ONT. | MAN. | SASK. | ALTA. | B.C. | Y.T. N.W.T. |
|---|---|---|---|---|---|---|---|---|---|---|---|---|
| **All Offences** | 2 720 619 | 35 230 | 10 845 | 81 748 | 53 842 | 527 810 | 922 654 | 126 626 | 123 710 | 256 761 | 559 183 | 22 210 |
| **Criminal Code** | 2 624 148 | 33 828 | 10 247 | 78 739 | 50 950 | 510 375 | 893 824 | 121 167 | 118 961 | 248 296 | 536 547 | 21 214 |
| *Violent crimes* | 291 437 | 5 531 | 1 118 | 10 548 | 6 903 | 48 391 | 101 413 | 16 897 | 13 563 | 27 938 | 54 784 | 4 351 |
| Murder | 572 | 7 | 0 | 15 | 8 | 143 | 174 | 37 | 27 | 46 | 112 | 3 |
| Attempted murder | 848 | 6 | 1 | 12 | 9 | 311 | 249 | 32 | 58 | 42 | 121 | 7 |
| Manslaughter | 60 | 0 | 1 | 3 | 1 | 10 | 12 | 8 | 4 | 7 | 13 | 1 |
| Robbery | 31 242 | 52 | 17 | 433 | 202 | 9 799 | 9 413 | 1 838 | 803 | 2 328 | 6 305 | 52 |
| *Other violent crimes* | 258 715 | 5 466 | 1 099 | 10 085 | 6 683 | 38 128 | 91 565 | 14 982 | 12 671 | 25 515 | 48 233 | 4 288 |
| *Property crimes* | 1 555 800 | 15 425 | 4 813 | 37 880 | 25 174 | 331 742 | 527 119 | 63 779 | 64 323 | 141 120 | 336 869 | 7 556 |
| Breaking and entering | 396 085 | 4 223 | 1 091 | 9 502 | 6 882 | 106 286 | 120 469 | 16 532 | 18 433 | 31 326 | 78 622 | 2 719 |
| Theft of motor vehicles | 178 580 | 553 | 209 | 2 409 | 1 492 | 48 071 | 58 419 | 10 231 | 6 494 | 14 321 | 35 747 | 634 |
| Theft | 849 529 | 8 790 | 2 828 | 21 600 | 13 423 | 155 905 | 299 249 | 32 148 | 31 629 | 78 855 | 201 372 | 3 730 |

*continued*

| | | | | | | | | | | | | |
|---|---|---|---|---|---|---|---|---|---|---|---|---|
| Possession of stolen goods | 30 599 | 196 | 61 | 430 | 565 | 3 026 | 12 868 | 797 | 2 245 | 4 077 | 6 217 | 117 |
| Fraud | 101 007 | 1 663 | 624 | 3 939 | 2 812 | 18 454 | 36 114 | 4 071 | 5 522 | 12 541 | 14 911 | 356 |
| *Other crimes* | 776 911 | 12 872 | 4 316 | 30 311 | 18 873 | 130 242 | 265 292 | 40 491 | 41 075 | 79 238 | 144 894 | 9 307 |
| Prostitution | 5 912 | 4 | 1 | 116 | 12 | 1 239 | 2 568 | 180 | 222 | 817 | 750 | 3 |
| Gaming and betting | 710 | 6 | 2 | 37 | 6 | 137 | 214 | 13 | 10 | 243 | 37 | 5 |
| Offensive weapons | 16 132 | 167 | 44 | 496 | 341 | 1 279 | 6 567 | 1 127 | 776 | 2 063 | 3 048 | 224 |
| *Other Criminal Code offences* | 754 157 | 12 695 | 4 269 | 29 662 | 18 514 | 127 587 | 255 943 | 39 171 | 40 067 | 76 115 | 141 059 | 9 075 |
| Federal statutes | 96 471 | 1 402 | 598 | 3 009 | 2 892 | 17 435 | 28 830 | 5 459 | 4 749 | 8 465 | 22 636 | 996 |
| Provincial statutes | 0 | 0 | 0 | 0 | 0 | 0 | 0 | 0 | 0 | 0 | 0 | 0 |

Source: Statistics Canada, CANSIM, Matrix 2200 and Catalogue no. 85-205-XIB.

FIGURE 2.3

CRIME RATES BY REGION, 1996

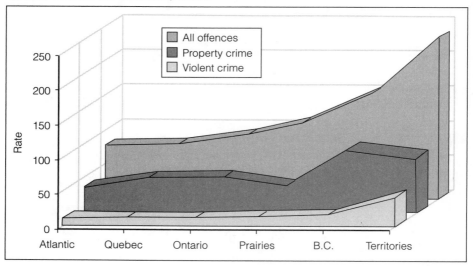

FIGURE 2.4

PROPERTY AND VIOLENT CRIME IN MAJOR METROPOLITAN AREAS, 1996

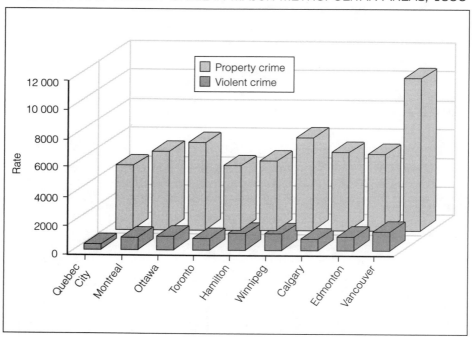

Many reasons have been offered to account for the higher crime rates in western Canada. Take a moment to consider what some of these reasons may be. Why would rates be lower in the Maritime provinces and higher in British Columbia and the Territories?

Some have argued that we should look at age and sex, but the evidence is scanty that there are more young males in the West and the North (Hartnagel, 1978). Another possibility is economic differences. Although we see high unemployment rates in the Territories and Newfoundland, economic disparity may be greater in the West and North. But economics alone is probably an insufficient reason.

One reason for the difference may be cultural. Communities are relatively unsettled, as people move frequently, and informal norms and controls are less established in the West than in the East. Kennedy, Silverman, and Forde (1991) have attributed higher homicide rates to greater levels of economic inequality and social disorganization. Ross (1995) suggests that violence in Canada is dependent on varying social attitudes and patterns of public policy, whereas environmental criminologists suggest that certain geographic factors play a role in creating opportunities for certain types of crime (see, generally, Brantingham, Mu, & Verma, 1995). Vancouver, for example, being a seaport, provides drug smugglers with a destination for unloading great quantities of drugs, particularly heroin. As a result, there are much higher rates of heroin trafficking and drug addiction in Vancouver, which, in turn, lead to increases in property crime and violence.

## Crime by Age

A good snapshot of crime in Canada must highlight the effect of age. In Canada in 1996, 84 percent of those charged with a violent crime were adults and 16 percent were youths, while for property offences, adults made up 71 percent and youths 29 percent of the cases. When the distribution of crime is examined according to age, the relationship between crime and age is quite striking.

In Figure 2.5, notice how property crime rises rapidly in the teen years but stabilizes throughout the 20s and 30s. Remember, the chart shows only the percent distribution by age, and does not compare the actual numbers between property and violent crime. In general, violent crimes decline more slowly, and property crimes tend to be more exclusively a young person's phenomenon. The highest incidence for many property crimes occurs between the ages of 13 and 15. But as you can see, both violent and property crime are at their highest percentage at age 15.

FIGURE 2.5

------------------------------------------------------------------------

PERSONS ACCUSED OF PROPERTY AND VIOLENT CRIME BY AGE, 1996

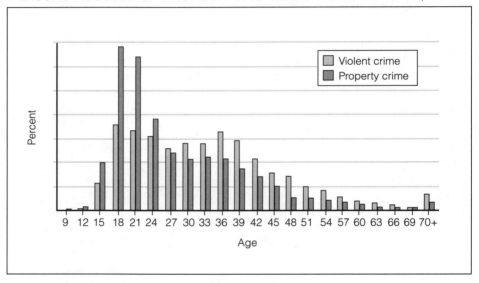

There are many reasons given to account for the distribution of crime in youths. Adolescent youths are involved in testing the boundaries of the societies in which they live. Family controls are loosened at the same time that there is an increased desire to express individuality and competence in adult roles, whether in socially constructive ways or not. Peer group influences become paramount, and often peer group selection demands risk taking and demonstrations of fearlessness. Peer bonds are secured in the solidarity of shared risks.

Again, there are economic and sociobiological as well as cultural explanations for the distribution of crime in youths. Young people are acutely sensitized to the need to dress fashionably in order to be accepted by their peer groups, but there is a wide variation in their ability to afford the latest fashions. Adolescence is also a time when much energy goes into attracting the attention of the opposite sex.

The tools to do so may be difficult to attain legitimately. So biological imperatives and economic necessity come together in criminal activity. The violence, too, is a testing and perhaps a forming of identity, whereby the adolescent becomes aware of the vast social world outside of the family, in which he or she is only one among many. Violence, in this respect, is an attack on this social world in order to assert individualism or empowerment. But as people get older, the vast majority recognize that violence as a means of assertion is counterproductive.

## Crime by Sex

Males accounted for almost 84 percent of all Criminal Code violations in 1996. The pie charts in Figures 2.6 and 2.7 show the distribution of all Criminal Code offences and violent crimes by sex. The number of adult males charged with violent offences was 99 192, compared with the 14 263 for females. Males accounted for 85 percent and females 15 percent of adult violent offences. With respect to juvenile violent offences, 16 620 male juveniles and 5191 female juveniles were charged, meaning that female juveniles accounted for more than 25 percent of juvenile violent crime.

As Doob and Marinos (1995) note, "zero tolerance" programs in schools have likely been a factor in more juveniles being charged with minor crimes and have resulted in some higher figures for juvenile females. However, it will be necessary to watch the figures closely in the next few years. While there is a narrow-

FIGURE 2.6

TOTAL CRIMINAL CODE OFFENCES BY SEX, 1996

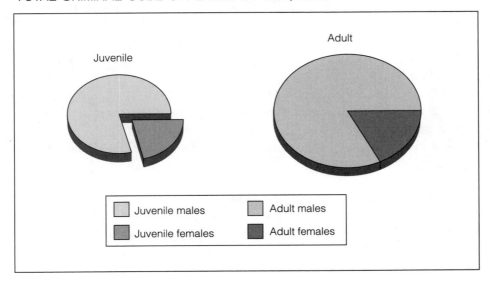

Juvenile

Adult

| Juvenile males | Adult males |
| Juvenile females | Adult females |

FIGURE 2.7

VIOLENT OFFENCES BY SEX, 1996

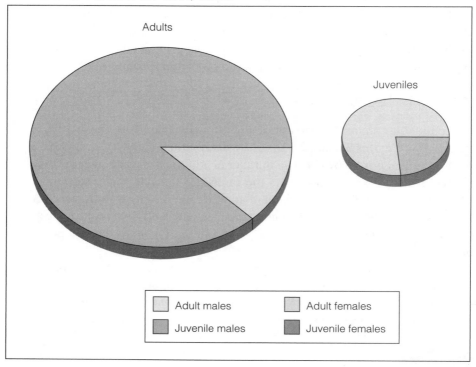

ing of the gap between males and females for minor offences (mostly property crimes), the gap remains substantial for violent offences.

Victimization and self-report surveys confirm that violent offences are most frequently committed by males. The Canadian Urban Victimization Survey estimated that about 90 percent of robberies and assaults in 1981 were committed by males (Johnson, 1986). Research by Hagan (1985) found that males exceeded females in self reported delinquency in the United States in 1970 by a margin of a little more than two to one.

Looked at historically, the relationship between female and male offending shows a pattern that invites the hypothesis that involvement in the breadwinner role will increase the chances of involvement in criminal offending. For example, between 1912 and 1920, there was a sharp rise in the rate of convictions of females for indictable offences from 20 to over 100. The male rate during this period rose gradually from approximately 450 to 500. A similar spike occurred during World War II. The 1970s saw the next upsurge in female criminality. Each of these periods is associated with new role demands or changing roles of women. During wartime, women worked in factories and were more active working in the public sphere while many of the men were away at war. During the 1970s, there was a major recession and the women's movement was popularized, leading to a fundamental shift away from the model of the male as the single family breadwinner. Indeed, Adler (1975) at this time put forth the liberation and opportunity hypothesis that as women began to perform roles previously reserved for men, they would also begin to take on the more aggressive, competitive, and risk-taking characteristics associated with the working world and with masculinity. Others, such as Johnson (1986), have argued that women are still committing crimes—credit card fraud and shoplifting—that are associated with their traditional role as consumers and homemakers.

It should be noted that there are other explanations offered for the differences between male and female criminality that are related not to culture and economics, but rather to biology.

## Crime by Race

According to Ontario's report on systemic racism in the criminal justice system, *racialization* involves classifying people into racial groups by referring to signs of origin (Gittens et al., 1995). Such signs include skin colour and place of birth. Judgments based on these signs are then made about the character, talents, and belongingness of people in a country. Social constructions of race have been used to rationalize economic exploitation and unequal treatment by social institutions, such as those enforcing criminal justice.

In Canada, Chinese, Japanese, black, and Aboriginal peoples have been subject to discrimination. During World War II, Canadians of Japanese descent were forced into internment camps, and Aboriginal people laboured under a system of what today would be known as ethnic cleansing, by which their traditions and cultural heritage were subjected to assimilation and genocide by the colonizing Europeans.

Today, the overrepresentation of Aboriginal and black people in the Canadian justice system continues to be a key dimension of the crime picture, as is reflected in official figures (see Figure 2.8). Especially in Manitoba, Saskatchewan, and Alberta, but also in the other provinces, these groups are charged and imprisoned at much higher rates than are whites. In the Prairie provinces, Aboriginal people account for nearly half of provincial prison admissions, even though they represent less than 15 percent of the population of those provinces.

In Ontario, the *Report on Systemic Racism in the Criminal Justice System* found that rather than improving in the period covered by their research, the situation in Ontario showed signs of getting even worse. It found a dramatic increase in admissions to prison of black adults between 1986/87 and 1992/93. Black adults were admitted to prison at over 5 times the rate of white adults, pro-

ADULT PRISON ADMISSION RATES IN ONTARIO, 1992–1993, BY RACE AND SEX

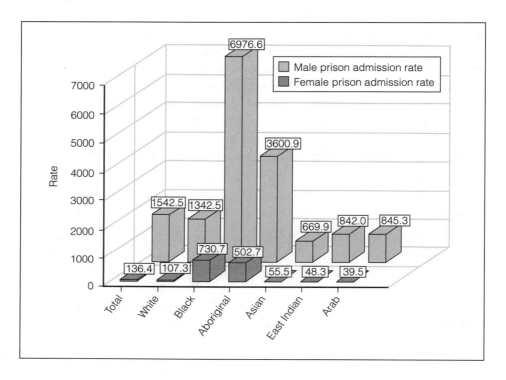

portionate to the representation in Ontario's population. As well, the admission rate for black women was almost 7 times that of white women. The report attributed some of these differences to the greater rate of imprisonment of blacks before trial; by 1992/93, the pretrial admission rate for drug trafficking/importing charges was 27 times higher than the rate for whites. Even for simple possession, the rate for blacks was 15 times that of whites. For the typically more discretionary charge of obstructing justice, the pretrial admission rate for blacks was 13 times higher than for whites. As the commission noted, it was obvious that black accused were jailed only because they were black, and white accused were not held before trial because they were white (Gittens et al., 1995).

Some criminologists have argued that criminal justice agents actively discriminate against Aboriginal and black people. This argument has been tested by Hagan (1974). In a study of correctional institutions in Alberta, Hagan found that Aboriginal people were being incarcerated for fine default, and their incarceration for this offence accounted for two-thirds of the sentences for Aboriginal people. These fines originally stemmed for minor offences related to alcohol abuse.

It must be pointed out that some of the disparity between the groups represented in Figure 2.8 can be accounted for by various quasi-judicial criteria, such as the economic and social standing of the accused. Whether or not accused persons have secure employment and secure social ties will have an impact on whether they are remanded in custody to await trial, and these factors have spin-off effects throughout their involvement with the justice system.

Apart from quasi-judicial criteria, which have a greater effect on some minorities, there is the actual rate of crime. The higher crime rates among black and Aboriginal Canadians, in particular, result, at least in part, because these groups commit more crimes than those groups that are underrepresented. While some of the difference can be accounted for by selective enforcement, by the quasi-judicial criteria, by the composition of law enforcement professions, and by other biases in the criminal justice system, not all of the difference can be accounted for in this way.

The relatively higher economic depravation does account for some of the wide disparity in incarceration. The social segmentation of some groups inhibits their economic integration (LaPrairie, 1983) LaPrairie views overrepresentation of Aboriginal people as a result of economic and social disadvantages, including the relative lack of education and employment. The economic argument also can be applied to blacks in Canadian society. In Nova Scotia after World War II, for instance, blacks were subjected to blatant economic, political, and social discrimination to such a degree that their whole community was forced to move from an economically valuable area of Halifax. Discrimination has forged an economic legacy of blocked opportunities both in education and in employment, which have contributed to overrepresentation in offending, offence categories, and imprisonment.

But it is particularly the relationship between cultural supports and economic opportunity that must be addressed. James (1989) argues that Aboriginal values are placed under stress in a "complex urban society." One key dimension of this stress relates to property values. Aboriginal traditions emphasize the reciprocity of possessions, rather than permanent ownership, and in some such transactions, this translates into theft under the law. When majority Canadian and Aboriginal values conflict in court, Aboriginal people tend to be the overwhelming losers, adding to the escalating spiral of deprivation.

## Social Ecology and Crime

In addition to age, race, sex, and comparative and regional measures, crime can be seen as distributed according to time and place. There are places and times that have higher rates of criminal activity than others. Victimization surveys have done much in recent years to present a map or a social ecology of crime. By *social ecology,* we mean the study of environmental features or factors as criminogenic or crime-inviting phenomena.

For example, the National Crime Victimization Survey in the United States found in cases of rapes and sexual assaults that two-thirds were committed by someone acquainted with, known to, or related to the victim, two-thirds occurred in the evening or at night, about six in ten occurred in the victim's or someone else's home, more than one-third occurred as the victim engaged in activities in the home, and another third occurred during leisure activities away from the home.

In general, risk of victimization is increased among the following: people in western Canada, people in urban areas, young people, people with active lives, and people who are single, separated, or divorced.

One of the clear findings of victimization surveys, such as the Canadian Urban Victimization Survey, as shown in Figure 2.9, is that the more frequently people are involved in activities outside the home, the more likely they are to be the object of victimization. However, it should also be kept in mind that in the case of sexual assaults and assaults on women, many of these crimes occur within the home and often are committed by persons known to the victim. In addition, ex-boyfriends or ex- or estranged husbands tend to be the offenders.

FIGURE 2.9

INCIDENT RATES BY AVERAGE ACTIVITIES OUTSIDE THE HOME

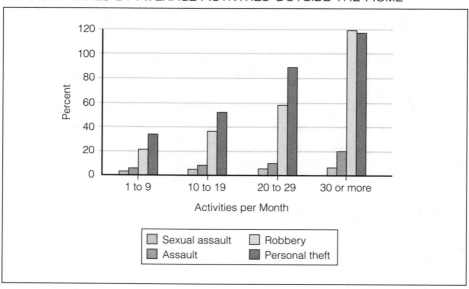

The Canadian Criminal Justice System

# Conclusion

Is the crime rate going up in Canada? Will it continue on the upward slope that we have seen since the mid-20th century? Or will it follow the more recent downward trend that we have seen between 1991/92 and 1996? It would be fair to predict that we will see another rise in crime rates very soon. One reason for the expected rise is that there will be a change in demographics, so that more youths will be of prime crime age. The greater the proportion of such youths, the greater the likelihood of higher crime rates. Another reason is structural, or related to how society is organized according to the distribution of power. Canadian society is becoming increasingly polarized into "haves" and "have-nots." Economic disparity is identified as a condition in which there tends to be more marginalization and less adherence to norms, both by the rich and by the poor (Braithwaite, 1997; Tittle, 1995). Simply put, when there is an increase in the number of those who have very little and who have little chance of improving their lot, there will be more criminalization of such people, both through the enactment of more laws to punish them and through the self-selection of criminal activity by these groups. In Canada, we have already seen cities pass bylaws intended to criminalize homeless persons, creating new categories of offenders. We have also seen policies of zero tolerance enacted in the schools and in the policing of minor offences, which will bring more individuals into the criminal justice system. Finally, our approach to social problems appears to be in a period of malaise—we are politically unwilling or unable to think beyond using the weapons of law enforcement and penalization. Rather, these blunt instruments have become the preferred solution in the absence of the resources of the welfare state.

# Summary

In this chapter we have painted a picture of Canadian crime and the methods we use to create this picture. We began by reviewing official crime statistics in such sources as the Uniform Crime Reporting Survey, and we described the shortcomings of these sources. We then looked at some unofficial sources for uncovering the dark figure of crime, including victimization surveys and self-reports. Finally, we looked at recent trends in crime, and we identified some factors that influence the crime rate, including sex, age, and population demographics.

# Key Terms

crime rate (p. 18)

dark figure of crime (p. 20)

demographics (p.14)

incidence of crime (p. 18)

official statistics (p. 21)

prevalence of crime (p. 17)

self-report survey (p. 23)

unofficial statistics (p. 21)

victimization survey (p. 24)

## Discussion Questions

1.  What is one reason that may account for the change in the crime rate in the last eight or nine years?

2.  Describe two factors that could account for the rise and decline of crime rates.

3.  Why are homicide rates seen as fairly good general indicators of overall crime rates?

4.  What are some problems with official statistics?

5.  What is meant by systemic bias?

## Weblinks

**www.statcan.ca/english/Pgdb/State/justic.htm** Statistics Canada's site provides statistics on the topic of justice and crime, categorized by crimes, victims, suspects and criminals, and police and the courts.

**qsilver.queensu.ca/rcjnet/** Queen's University's Network for Research on Crime and Justice (RCJ-Net) brings together research on the topic of crime and justice. The site provides links to the RCJ journal and to current and future research topics.

**www.hc-sc.gc.ca/hppb/familyviolence/bilingual.htm** The National Clearinghouse on Family Violence, a Health Canada site, is a resource centre for information about violence within the family. The Clearinghouse provides research findings and information on prevention, protection, and treatment.

**www.ncjrs.org/stathome.htm** The US Department of Justice's Bureau of Justice Statistics page is an excellent resource for US statistics on topics such as crime, victims, law enforcement, prosecution, courts, and corrections. There is also a link to the world factbook of criminal justice systems.

**www.fbi.gov/ucr/ucrquest.htm** This helpful FBI page provides clear and comprehensive answers to the most commonly asked questions regarding the Uniform Crime Reporting Survey (UCR), as well as links to UCR reports and to the FBI home page.

CHAPTER 3

# Criminal Law

## Objectives

- To outline the use of criminal law to maintain social order and control.

- To offer two main explanations of the purposes of criminal law: the value consensus model and the conflict model.

- To outline the operations of the Criminal Code and its distinctions among types of criminal offences and defences.

- To discuss the goals of the Canadian Charter of Rights and Freedoms.

## What Is Criminal Law?

In their classic definition, Sutherland and Cressey (1970) describe **criminal law** as a body of specific rules regarding human conduct that have been promulgated by political authority and that apply uniformly to all members of society. As well, criminal laws are enforced by punishment administered by the state. Criminal law, therefore, is codified and explicitly defines acts that violate the law—in other words, **crime**—delineating penalties and sanctions as authorized by the laws of the land and its legislators. The main categories of law that affect Canadians include criminal law, case law, and civil law. Although we are most concerned in this chapter with the role and function of the criminal law in the administration of criminal justice in Canada, we will also discuss other forms of law and their purposes.

The fundamental premise underlying modern criminal law is that criminal acts injure not just individuals, but all of society. Social order and control are invariably challenged when criminal acts are committed; hence, to maintain social order, rules governing social behaviour have been enacted to protect members of the society. As Cunningham and Griffiths (1997) note, all legal systems in Canada are governed by the principle of the rule of law, and we are all required to obey the law and to be punished if we break it. We also look to the legal system to respond to crimes committed against us. Furthermore, a law must apply equally to everyone, and a penalty must be defined for proscriptions of the law. Most importantly, commission of crime offends not only members of society, but society itself; therefore, in criminal cases, the government as the injured party begins the process of prosecuting the offender. The premise is that since crime is harmful to society, it is the government's responsibility to seek redress and to obtain justice.

## The Purpose of Criminal Law

Criminologists see two main explanations for the original purpose of criminal law. Under the *value consensus model,* society is characterized by a set of core values for which there is consensus among all members. In this perspective, criminal behaviour results from the offender's failure to be socialized into accepting the values of the society. According to this school of thought, society maintains its important social values by punishing deviation from them. Although there is widespread agreement that many offences, such as murder, assault, or incest, violate societal values, in a modern, heterogeneous society such as Canada's, there may be considerably less consensus concerning victimless and nonviolent criminal acts. Cunningham and Griffiths (1997) also refer to the fact that laws under Canada's Criminal Code are always subject to modification and change by legislators. For example, in the past it was a criminal offence to practise homosexuality, but today that law has been repealed. Also, "moral entrepreneurs" can entrench their moral values by instituting laws against gambling, prostitution, soft drugs, abortions, and so on, regardless of public opinion.

In contrast to the consensus model, the *conflict model* suggests that some groups have a greater role and power in having laws passed that protect their interests. According to this view, Canada is made up of various interest groups, and legal codes are enacted to represent the interests of the powerful over the interests of the powerless. Because of the unequal distribution of power among segments of society, the rich and powerful enact laws, such as those related to property, to protect their position of influence and power. Chambliss (1975) describes, for example, how England's vagrancy laws in the 18th century created legal norms that favoured business interests and penalized the poor and the homeless. Undoubtedly, there is some truth to the argument that powerful business interests lobby governments to ensure that environmental laws or security and business practices laws remain weak and ineffective, while an inordinate amount of time, effort, and expense is spent prosecuting perpetrators of property crimes.

# The Forms of Law

Regardless of why certain behaviours are labelled criminal, violations that are prosecuted result in punishment. The rationale is that society condemns the offensive behaviour, and the criminal knowingly intended to do harm in committing the offence. Criminal law operates under a set of procedures enshrined in the criminal justice system and is composed of both statutory and case law. **Statutory law** includes all those laws passed by legislation and known as the Criminal Code. Parliament continually adds to and revises this body of law, as well as sentencing procedures. **Case law** is often referred to as laws based on precedence. This type of law is established on the basis of the accumulated wealth of knowledge of trial and appellate jurists over the years, in both criminal and civil cases. In Canada, case law has had a great influence on the trial process in criminal law cases. While the decisions of the Supreme Court of Canada are invariably used as guidelines for all arguments in lower courts, all branches of the trial phase use arguments based on case law in attempting to influence the judicial decision. Often, the judge also relies heavily on case precedents in handing down the decision. The purpose of case law is to ensure that there is consistency and predictability in the interpretation of the law and that both the defence and the prosecution can be adequately prepared in their submissions.

According to Schmalleger (2000), **civil law** provides a formal means for regulating noncriminal relationships between persons, business and other organizations, and agencies of government. This body of law contains the rules and regulations for the enforcement of contracts, divorce, child support and custody, property matters, negligence, libel, consumer and commercial practices legislation, and many other laws pertaining to contractual obligations.

The key difference between criminal law and civil law is that civil lawsuits seek compensation for alleged wrongs, rather than punishment. Violations of civil law are not crimes; instead, they are contract violations. In this instance the individual, not the state, files the lawsuit that brings the matter before the justice system. Civil legal claims may arise in connection with criminal actions, and victims may choose to pursue a civil suit after a criminal trial has been completed, regardless of whether the defendant was found guilty. For example, parents of the victims of multiple murderer Clifford Olsen successfully sued to have proceeds from the sale of his memoirs divested from his estate. Similarly, in the United States the family of Nicole Simpson successfully sued O.J. Simpson for millions of dollars, even though he had been acquitted of her murder in a criminal trial. Because of the difference in degree of proof between a civil and a criminal matter, a not guilty verdict in a criminal case does not preclude the awarding of damages to the victim in a civil suit.

In conclusion, although criminologists often have different perspectives as to the functions of law in Canada, they almost unanimously support the premise that in our complex, heterogeneous society criminal law functions to define socially unacceptable behaviour, to control behaviour and maintain social order, and to regulate the punishment of deviant behaviour. However, public perception of what is inappropriate behaviour changes over time, and the law often lags behind public opinion in terms of adapting to societal change. To remedy this problem, the Law Reform Commission of Canada has been established by Parliament to revise all criminal laws and to remove obsolete laws from the statute books. This process of legal change, while excruciatingly slow, at least allows for public input into definitions of criminal behaviour and sanctions. In terms of regulating the punishment of proscribed behaviour, the criminal law serves multiple purposes. It prevents vigilante groups from imposing their own punishment, and it prevents arbitrary or excessive punishment. It bases punishment on the severity of the offence, and, most importantly, because we have a national criminal code, ensures that punishment for similar crimes committed is uniform across Canada.

# Categories of Criminal Offences

While violations of criminal law can vary in severity, Tappan (1960) notes that a crime is always an intentional commission or omission of an act, in violation of the criminal law. *Commission* includes such acts as assaults, thefts, and illegal drug use or possession. *Omission* includes such acts as neglect of a child and failure to obey a police officer. The Criminal Code does not define all crimes as equally harmful, nor does it require similar punishment for all crimes. Our Criminal Code distinguishes between indictable summary conviction, and treasonous offences. Indictable offences **(felonies)** are the most serious crimes and thus carry the severest punishment. Examples of felony charges under the Criminal Code include first or second degree murder, manslaughter, armed robberies, drug possession, aggravated assault, sexual assault, burglary, and arson. Invariably, a guilty conviction and a record of previous convictions for Criminal Code violations would lead to a period of imprisonment for offenders. For those convicted of first and second degree murder, a mandatory period of incarceration is provided under the Criminal Code. For lesser felonious offences, punishment could include imprisonment and fines. A concern among many Canadians is the wide variation in sentencing allowed under the Criminal Code for many felonies, which leads to disparities between provincial jurisdictions.

Summary conviction offences (**misdemeanours**) are minor crimes, such as petty theft, disorderly conduct, or possession of marijuana. Punishment is usually a fine for a first offence and probation or a short prison sentence for repeat offenders. In recent years, the Canadian judiciary has been sentencing those found guilty of misdemeanours to community service in an attempt to divert them from the criminal justice system. Juvenile offenders, in particular, have been major beneficiaries of this program. Under normal circumstances an officer needs to witness the misdemeanour being committed or to seek an arrest warrant to apprehend the offending person. However, the police need only believe that there are "reasonable grounds" to proceed with an arrest for a felonious offence.

Under special circumstances, the criminal law allows for the arrest of persons presumed to have committed the offences of treason or espionage. **Treason** is defined as helping a foreign government overthrow or make war against the Canadian government. **Espionage** involves gathering information related to national defence by spying and is aimed at damaging the government or people. Both of these violations are extremely rare in Canada in peacetime, although the growth of industrial espionage has become a growing concern in an age when trade secrets can have serious national repercussions.

# Elements of Criminal Offences

Many of us may have heard the term *corpus delicti* and wondered what it meant. Goff (1997) notes that under our criminal law, certain essential facts and features must exist in every criminal act, hence the meaning of **corpus delicti** as literally "the body of the crime." In order to obtain a conviction it is essential that the Crown prove these elements in a court of law. The most important facts or foundation of the crime include **actus reus,** meaning the guilty act, and **mens rea,** meaning intent, or, as Regoli and Hewitt (1996) state, the coinciding of the guilty act with the guilty mind.

Actus reus refers to the physical carrying out of the crime in violation of the law. It includes the actual committal of the crime, but it could also include making threats or attempting to intimidate witnesses to a crime. In either case, the person carrying out the act is solely responsible for his or her actions.

The Criminal Code also states that a criminal violation has taken place if we act in a criminally negligent way that leads to bodily harm against someone. As well, a person can violate the Criminal Code by conspiring to commit a crime, even though an actual crime did not occur in the strict meaning of actus reus. So even though it may be an incomplete crime, or a criminal conspiracy or perjury, it is a violation of the criminal law and thus the offender is subject to arrest, conviction, and punishment.

Mens rea means the guilty mind, or having a criminal intent. In Canadian criminal law a defendant has not violated the Criminal Code unless it can be proved that criminal intent was present at the time the crime occurred. As Regoli and Hewitt (1996) state, the mere fact that a person engages in deviant behaviour that violates the law is not enough to prove criminal liability. The crux is being able to prove that the defendant *intended* to commit the criminal offence.

Criminal responsibility or intent involves committing a criminal act purposely, knowingly, recklessly, and negligently. Canadian common law, as well, distinguishes between general and specific intent. *General intent* means that there was a prior intent to violate the Criminal Code. For example, in committing a burglary, a defendant may have intended only to rob the victim; however, if the burglar confronted and killed the victim, the prosecutor does not have to prove that the burglar intended to kill the victim, but only that he or she had a general intent to violate the criminal law. *Specific intent* involves the committal of a crime with due deliberation and planning, for example, assault with intent to rape. Verdun-Jones (1997) notes that in these cases the prosecution must prove not only that the defendant had an intention to commit a crime, but also that the defendant plotted for the purpose of committing the crime.

As we noted earlier, for an act to be considered criminal, both the act that is proscribed by the Criminal Code (actus reus) and the intent to commit the crime

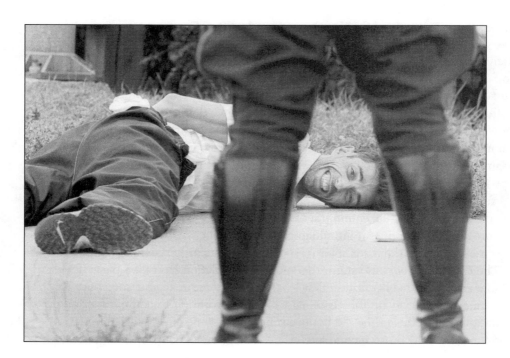

(mens rea) must occur concurrently. As Regoli and Hewitt (1996) state, it is integral to the committal of a crime that the offender have the guilty mind and also commit the act. In the vast majority of cases, it is relatively simple to prove the connection between intent and committal of the criminal act; therefore, simultaneous occurrence is not a major legal argument for the defence.

Goff (1997) also notes that an integral part of our legal system is the fact that behaviour must be societally harmful if it is to be prosecutable as criminal. Although there is considerable debate over the prosecution of so-called victimless crime, such as prostitution or gambling, the Criminal Code sees these offences as not morality related but criminally related. As violations of the criminal law, they are perceived as societally harmful. Of course, changing societal attitudes can lead to changes in the criminal law, and just as abortions in particular circumstances have been legalized, gambling and prostitution could eventually be perceived as societally harmless. Also, whereas death and physical injury are obvious evidence of criminally harmful conduct, less obviously damaging behaviour can be criminally harmful, as well. For example, lying under oath, crimes against property, embezzlement, or behaviour that violates the rights of specific groups, such as women or ethnic minorities, also contravene the Criminal Code. These behaviours are societally harmful; thus, in addition to being liable for whatever personal harm may have been inflicted against the victims, the offenders can be prosecuted under criminal law.

# Criminal Defences

One of the core principles of Canadian criminal law is the fact that under certain special circumstances, violations of the Criminal Code may be found to be justifiable and thus are not legally prosecutable and are excusable. These justifications are then the major defence in the argument to refute the criminal charge.

Regoli and Hewitt (1996) note that *justifications* are based on the defendant's accepting responsibility for the offence while attempting to prove that there were mitigating circumstances for the act. *Excuses* are made the basis of the defence when the defendant admits to contravening the Criminal Code but attempts to prove that criminal responsibility was absent at the time the offence was committed. In both of these circumstances, the onus is on the defendant to prove that his or her actions were justifiable or excusable. For example, a defendant who has committed a crime in front of witnesses may plead criminal insanity as an excuse for the crime. Police officers charged with assaulting or shooting alleged offenders almost invariably deny criminal responsibility for their actions as well, claiming that their actions were necessary to bring the situation under control.

We will now briefly outline some possible lines of defence for criminal charges.

## Self-Defence

Besides law enforcement officers, many other defendants deny criminal responsibility for their actions by raising the argument of **self-defence** as a justifiable action. Recently in Nova Scotia, a convenience store owner was charged with manslaughter for killing an intruder who attempted to rob his store. The defence was justifiable homicide, and the question for the court was what degree of force was necessary to protect the shop owner's property. Canadian legal precedent suggests that deadly force may be used only if there is imminent threat of serious injury or death. In this case, the robber was armed with a butcher knife and demanded money. The question was, Should a person confronted with a butcher knife respond with a gun? The court ruled against the claim of self-defence but it did accept a plea bargain for a lesser sentence.

The conjunction of attitudinal change and the greater number of wife abuse cases brought to court in Canada recently has resulted in the reduction of convictions for women who murdered abusive partners or stalkers. The law now allows women to plead self-defence in using deadly force if it can be proved that she was the victim of "battered woman syndrome," the result of physical and psychological abuse over a period of time. Ten years ago in Canada this argument was not an acceptable defence, but today Canadian courts are increasingly accepting the societal definition of wife abuse as grounds for justifiable homicide.

It is clear, therefore, that Canadian criminal law does not provide for the use of deadly force to protect property. However, the argument of self-defence has been successfully used in cases where actual bodily harm or death would have been imminent had force not been used. In response to attitudinal change, the courts are increasingly allowing this defence for rape or attempted sexual assault, stalking, and wife abuse. In cases of citizens resisting arrest by police officers, as can seen by looking at the decisions of the judiciary in the last decade, the courts invariably give the benefit of the doubt to the police officers, rather than to the victims of the police.

## Criminal Insanity

The defence of **criminal insanity** has attracted considerable public attention and debate in Canadian jurisprudence. Verdun-Jones (1997) notes that since our criminal law is based on the premise that a person should be convicted only if she or he knowingly and deliberately breaks the law, it may be inappropriate to apply the criminal law to someone who is incapable of making real choices because of mental illness. However, he believes that because the insanity defence is rigidly interpreted, it is often an unsuccessful defence. Even if the accused can prove that at the time of committing the offence he or she could not comprehend the illegality or moral reprehensibility of the act, acquittal is not automatic. Furthermore, acquittal often leads to the accused being detained in a mental health institution until deemed rehabilitated.

While it is not surprising that our contemporary insanity defence mechanism, including treatment of the offender deemed not guilty by reason of mental disorder, is based in 19th-century English jurisprudence, it is objectionable that the defence is still so narrowly interpreted. The lower courts continue to not only take the narrowest definition of criminal insanity as set out in law, but they also often state that an acquittal is possible only if the accused was incapable of knowing that she or he was committing a murder or that such an act was a crime under the criminal law. Of late, however, the Supreme Court of Canada has been taking a more liberal interpretation of the mental capacity of the accused to know that the act was wrong. As Verdun-Jones (1997) notes, this court is addressing the question of whether the accused should be exempted from criminal responsibility because the mental illness deprived him or her of the capacity to rationally perceive right and wrong. Also, Criminal Code amendments in 1992 modernized and streamlined the disposition process of those found not guilty by reason of mental illness. The accused can be discharged absolutely, with conditions, or can be detained in custody in a mental hospital or clinic. Provisions are also made for periodic review of detainees. The goal of the review tribunals is to monitor the treatment of the patient and to ensure that rehabilitated patients are reinstated into the community, rather than being given indeterminate sentences, as in the past. At the same time, fearing negative public opinion, Criminal Code amendments allow the courts to extend periods of detention in mental hospitals in order to protect society.

## Mistake of Fact and Mistake of Law

Other defences that are commonly raised to a criminal charge are **mistake of fact** and **mistake of law.** Verdun-Jones (1997) notes the courts may accept as a legal defence the statement that the defendant committed the actus reus of the offence but was mistaken as to the facts. In this case, the defendant had no reason to believe that he or she was committing a crime and therefore lacked the mens rea, or the guilty mind, which the Crown must prove to obtain a conviction. However, in using the mistake of fact defence, the defence counsel must prove not only that there was an honest mistake, but also that the mistake of fact would have been made by a reasonable person. This defence of honest mistake is commonly called upon by defendants in sexual assault cases who plead that the victim gave consent. The Supreme Court of Canada has been careful to weigh this issue so that the burden of proof lies overwhelmingly with the defendant.

The Criminal Code of Canada, however, is quite specific that ignorance of the law is no defence. As well, the courts have shown that while mistakes of fact may be a valid excuse for committing a criminal offence, mistakes related to the law are no excuse in criminal matters. Nevertheless, in some circumstances the courts have leaned toward a lenient interpretation of this section of the Criminal Code, in particular ruling that a mistake as to the legal interpretation of the civil law, rather than criminal law, could be used as a defence against a criminal charge. Verdun-Jones (1997) also notes that the increase in regulatory laws and statutes has created a situation whereby Canadians can be contravening laws that they have never heard of because the laws were never published widely. In these cases, the courts may be willing to recognize that regulatory laws may leave the door open for misinterpretation, and hence the benefit of the doubt could be given to the defendant. In one instance, the Supreme Court of Canada noted that "the complexity of contemporary regulations makes the assumption that a responsible citizen will have a comprehensive knowledge of the law unreasonable." In other words, a reasonable person could not be expected to understand the complexity of this regulation. The concept of *officially induced error* has also been accepted by the courts in limited circumstances, as has the defence called *colour of right,* in which an accused person can be acquitted if it is proved that the defendant acted under an honest mistake of law in believing that he or she had a legal right to the property in question.

## Intoxication

Verdun-Jones (1997) notes that until 1996, the Criminal Code did not define the defence of **intoxication.** This form of defence was based on common law and shaped by judicial decisions, first in England and later by Canadian courts. The main purpose of this defence through the 19th and 20th centuries was to use intoxication as a partial defence to serious criminal charges. If accepted, the defence would serve to mitigate the severity of the charge and allow for its reduction, for example, from second degree murder to manslaughter.

In 1996, Parliament passed legislation amending the Criminal Code to state that intoxication, however extreme, will not be accepted as a defence to a charge of any general intent offence that includes assault or bodily interference. This amendment came about because the Canadian public was unhappy with a Supreme Court decision in 1994 that acquitted a defendant charged with sexual assault on the grounds of intense alcoholic intoxication. The criticism was related to the concern that defendants could avoid taking responsibility for criminal behaviour by pleading intoxication. The debate over whether this amendment to the Criminal Code, section 33(1), contravenes the Canadian Charter of Rights and Freedoms continues. Parliament, acting on behalf of the Canadian public, believes that people who commit a criminal act while in a state of self-induced intoxication should be held responsible for their actions. The Supreme Court of Canada believes that it is a violation of sections 7 and 11(d) of the Charter of Rights to convict a person who lacks the ability to comprehend her or his actions as criminal because of intoxication. However, as of this time, the dictates of Parliament and its Criminal Code amendments prevail.

## Necessity and Duress

The two other forms of defence in a criminal charge that we will discuss are **necessity** and **duress.** In the case of necessity, the defendant does not dispute the facts of law and that he or she broke the law. However, the contention is that the defendant should not be convicted because breaking the law was the only option and therefore was necessary. While in minor cases the courts have accepted this defence, in more serious criminal cases they have been more reluctant to do so. For example, in the *Latimer* case (1998), the Court of Appeal in Saskatchewan denied the defence of necessity, which had been accepted by the trial judge. In this case, Latimer claimed that the murder of his daughter was necessary to end her immense pain and suffering caused by severe mental and physical illnesses. Essentially, the appeal court's view was that "the criminal law cannot recognize any principle which would entitle a person to violate the law because in his view the law conflicted with some higher social value." This view has been upheld by the Supreme Court of Canada, which states that the defence of necessity can never be accepted as a means of avoiding a peril that is lawfully authorized by the law.

It has been claimed that no modern criminal code can be just unless it allows for some recognition for an accused who committed a crime under duress. Section 17 of our Criminal Code does just that, when it states that "a person who commits an offence under compulsion by threats of immediate death or bodily harm, is excused for committing the offence if the person believes that the threats will be carried out." However, it does not allow this defence for any serious Criminal Code offences, including murder, sexual assault, kidnapping, or aggravated assault. Also, a member of a gang that may be inciting the compulsion cannot use this defence. The courts have once again been conservative in their interpretation of the defence of duress. They are quite clear that only if the threats involved immediate death or grievous bodily harm could duress be a successful defence. As well, the Supreme Court of Canada has stated that an accused cannot rely on this defence if there was an opportunity to safely extricate him- or herself from the situation of duress.

It should be noted that proposed amendments to the Criminal Code would treat the defences of necessity and duress under similar legal principles. Under this proposal, a person would be not guilty of an offence other than murder to the extent that the person acted under duress of circumstance or duress of threats. Although these proposals have never been enacted, the recent trend in court decisions has been the premise that it is wrong to convict a person who acts in a manner that can be characterized as defensive and aimed at avoiding death or serious bodily harm.

# The Canadian Charter of Rights and Freedoms

The Canadian Charter of Rights and Freedoms, entrenched in the Constitution Act of 1982, was one of the most significant additions to the Canadian legal system. Boyd (1998) believes that it signalled an important shift in power from the legislature to the judicial branches of government. The role of the judiciary has become one of interpreting whether federal or provincial legislation contravenes the core values of the Charter and the nation. One of the major requirements of the Charter is to allow the judiciary the right to define as unconstitutional legislation that contravenes the protected rights of citizens. However, as we will see, it is not an easy task to define many of these protected rights in ways that allow for consensus in an increasingly heterogeneous society. Whereas prior to the proclamation of the Charter, Canada was governed by the doctrine of parlia-

The signing of the Constitution Act of 1982.

mentary supremacy, the Charter is today the overarching document, with the courts entitled to test all laws against the values it enshrines. Since 1982, when the Act incorporating the Charter was signed, the Supreme Court of Canada has found that many pieces of legislation and some sections of the Criminal Code contravene the Charter rights of individuals or groups and thus has invalidated these particular legislative acts.

The Charter guarantees the rights and freedoms of Canadians, subject to certain limitations. As shown in Figure 3.1, the Charter is composed of several sections guaranteeing fundamental freedoms, legal rights, equality rights, enforcement rights, voting rights, mobility rights, language rights, and Aboriginal rights (see the appendix for the complete charter). It also provides opportunities for those whose rights are infringed to obtain remedies and redress from the courts. Section 1 of the Charter spells out limitations and makes it clear that no right is absolute. Federal and provincial governments can pass legislation limiting the rights in certain exceptional cases, subject to the grounds of being reasonable and prescribed by law. The Supreme Court of Canada in 1986 addressed this issue and set ground rules for the overriding of constitutionally protected rights and freedoms, stating that it must not be arbitrary, unfair, or based on irrational considerations. The means should be reasonable and impair as little as possible the infringement of the right, and there must be a proportionality between the effects of the measures and the objective to be achieved.

Section 2 of the Charter sets out the fundamental freedoms that are guaranteed to Canadians. These include freedom of religion, thought, belief, and expression, including freedom of the press and communication. As well, this section guarantees freedom of assembly and association. Boyd (1998) notes that the Supreme Court of Canada has not backed down in ruling on cases that involve  these freedoms. In a 1992 case, the accused challenged the constitutionality of obscenity provisions within the Criminal Code. Specifically, the accused was charged with selling materials that depicted explicit sex and violence. The Supreme Court held that while the obscenity section of the Criminal Code contravened the section of the Charter guaranteeing freedom of expression, there was a reasonable ground under the limitations section of the Charter to allow for this contravention. Ruling that materials portraying explicit sex with violence were harmful to society and women and were contrary to public opinion and the equality rights of women, the Court allowed the conviction. On the other hand, the Court ruled that the federal government's prohibition of tobacco advertising  contravened Section 2 of the Charter, related to freedom of expression. The Court stated that this legislation could not be justified, as tobacco was a legal product and the federal government could not prove a cause-and-effect relationship between a ban on advertising and a reduction in smoking.

-------------------------------------------------------------------------------

## KEY SECTIONS OF THE CHARTER OF RIGHTS AND FREEDOMS

**The Charter of Rights and Freedoms: Legal Rights and the Canadian Criminal Justice System**

**Legal Rights**

7. Everyone has the right to life, liberty and security of the person and the right not to be deprived thereof except in accordance with the principles of fundamental justice.

8. Everyone has the right to be secure against unreasonable search and seizure.

9. Everyone has the right not to be arbitrarily detained or imprisoned.

10. Everyone has the right on arrest or detention

    (a) to be informed promptly of the reasons therefor;

    (b) to retain and instruct counsel without delay and to be informed of that right; and

    (c) to have the validity of the detention determined by way of habeas corpus and to be released if the detention is not lawful.

11. Any person charged with an offence has the right

    (a) to be informed without unreasonable delay of the specific offence;

    (b) to be tried within a reasonable time;

    (c) not to be compelled to be a witness in proceedings against that person in respect of the offence;

    (d) to be presumed innocent until proven guilty according to law in a fair and public hearing by an independent and impartial tribunal;

    (e) not to be denied reasonable bail without just cause;

    (f) except in the case of an offence under military law tried before a military tribunal, to the benefit of trial by jury where the maximum punishment for the offence is imprisonment for five years or a more severe punishment;

    (g) not to be found guilty on account of any act or omission unless, at the time of the act or omission, it is constituted an offence under Canadian or international law or was criminal according to the general principles of law recognized by the community of nations;

    (h) if finally acquitted of the offence, not to be tried for it again and, if finally found guilty and punished for the offence, not to be tried or punished for it again; and

    (i) if found guilty of the offence and if the punishment for the offence has been varied between the time of the commission and the time of sentencing, to the benefit of the lesser punishment.

12. Everyone has the right not to be subjected to any cruel and unusual treatment or punishment.

13. A witness who testifies in any proceedings has the right not to have any incriminating evidence so given used to incriminate that witness in any other proceedings, except in a prosecution for perjury or for the giving of contradictory evidence.

14. A party or witness in any proceedings who does not understand or speak the language in which the proceedings are conducted or who is deaf has the right to the assistance of an interpreter.

**Equality Rights**

15. (1) Every individual is equal before and under the law and has the right to the equal protection and equal benefit of the law without discrimination and, in particular, without discrimination based on race, national or ethnic origin, colour, religion, sex, age or mental or physical disability.

    (2) Subsection (1) does not preclude any law, program or activity that has as its object the amelioration of conditions of disadvantaged individuals or groups including those that are disadvantaged because of race, national or ethnic origin, colour, religion, sex, age or mental or physical disability.

**Enforcement**

24. (1) Anyone whose rights or freedoms, as guaranteed by this Charter, have been infringed or denied may apply to a court of competent jurisdiction to obtain such remedy as the court considers appropriate and just in the circumstances.

(2) Where, in proceedings under subsection (1), a court concludes that evidence was obtained in a manner that infringed or denied any rights or freedoms guaranteed by this Charter, the evidence shall be excluded if it is established that, having regard to all the circumstances, the admission of it in the proceedings would bring the administration of justice into disrepute.

Source: C. Goff. 1997. *Criminal Justice in Canada.* Toronto: ITP Nelson.

---

Sections 7 through 14 focus exclusively in the legal rights of accused persons when they become part of the criminal justice system. As Goff (1997) notes, the Charter spells out the legal rights of those accused of crimes and the powers of the police, the courts, and the corrections system. Although they contain a complex series of provisions, the sections related to the administration of the criminal justice system clearly have a wide-ranging impact on the entire legal system. Whether they apply to the rights of the accused, the powers of the police to investigate or arrest, or the powers of the courts to prosecute and sentence, the Charter has redefined such fundamental issues as due process, the guarantee of a fair trial, and freedom from harsh or unjustified punishment.

Some of the highlights of the Charter protection of the legal rights of the accused include the right to life, liberty, and security and the right to fundamental justice. The Charter also spells out the right to be protected from unreasonable search and seizure, and from arbitrary detainment or imprisonment. Furthermore, on arrest or detention everyone has the right to be informed of the reason, to retain and instruct counsel, to have the validity of the detention subject to *habeas corpus* (a writ requiring investigation of unlawful detention), and to be released if the detention is illegal. The Supreme Court of Canada has ruled that evidence obtained by the police without the suspect being informed of the right to legal counsel is inadmissible. In fact, the Supreme Court has ruled that the police must not only give the accused the opportunity to contact legal counsel, but must not question an accused person until a reasonable time had elapsed after legal counsel had been contacted. In this way, the Court tries to ensure that anyone detained by police has the right to representation by legal counsel.

Section 11 delineates the rights of those charged with a criminal offence and their process through the criminal justice system. For example, it specifies the rights of presumed innocence, a speedy trial, granting of bail, and specific sentences for offences, as well as the right not to be retried for an offence if acquitted. One of the areas that the courts have been grappling with involves the right to be tried within a reasonable time. In one instance, the Supreme Court found that five years from arrest to trial was a reasonable time, yet in another it found that sixteen months was an unreasonable delay. The test is whether the accused was responsible for any delay, and if not, whether the Crown was acting responsibly in delaying justice. Hundreds of charges across the country have been dismissed, stayed, or withdrawn as a result of the 1990 Supreme Court decision that an eight-month delay was the outside limit of the test of reasonableness. The Court has proclaimed that the government has a constitutional obligation to commit resources so that unreasonable delay will not occur for the defendant. As well, the Supreme Court has ruled as unconstitutional those parts of the Narcotic Control Act that violate the presumption of innocence of the accused. Its ruling states that no defendant should have to prove to the court that any narcotics possessed were not for the purpose of trafficking. Instead, that was for the police and the Crown to prove.

Section 12 is also designed to protect the rights of the accused, by prohibiting cruel and unusual punishment. In 1987, the Supreme Court struck down the section of the Narcotics Control Act that set out a minimum sentence of seven years upon conviction for importing any amount of a narcotic, such as heroin, cocaine, or marijuana. The Court held that in certain circumstances, for example, importing a couple of grams of marijuana, a minimum sentence of seven years was "grossly disproportionate" and could be conceived as cruel and unusual punishment. However, the same Court had no problem in affirming that twenty-five years of imprisonment without parole were justified for first degree murder, particularly because this conviction involves premeditation. Sections 13 and 14 deal with the rights of witnesses during a criminal trial and the right against self-incrimination. As well, witnesses who do not speak the language of the court proceedings or who have physical disabilities have the right to a court interpreter.

The equality rights protection of sections 15, 25, and 28 enforce the equality of all Aboriginal peoples, as well as gender equality, and reinforce the multiculturalism of Canada. Section 15, in particular, reinforces the nondiscriminatory nature of the law and prohibits discrimination based on race, ethnic origin, colour, religion, sex, age, or mental or physical disability. Furthermore, this section allows the Court and the government the right to allow a program that has as its object amelioration of conditions for these disadvantaged peoples, including those disadvantaged by reason of race, colour, gender, age, or mental or physical disability. While the equality sections of the Charter seem all encompassing, the interpretations by the courts are not as liberal, with wide variations occurring in cases of race and gender equality. However, rulings in 1999 by the Supreme Court seem to be focusing on the overrepresentation of Aboriginal men and women in Canadian prisons. Lower courts have been advised to rethink the alternatives to incarceration and to use them whenever possible.

Finally, we would like to discuss section 24 of the Charter, which is the enforcement mechanism, empowering the court to exclude evidence that may have been improperly obtained. This section also provides remedies for infringement of Charter rights. Boyd (1998) notes that law enforcement agencies have been extremely critical of this section, claiming that by excluding evidence deemed to be tainted, the courts are releasing guilty people on a technicality. However, civil libertarians support this exclusionary rule as a necessary deterrent to the overzealousness and misconduct of the police. The Supreme Court has used as its test the concept of what would "bring the administration of justice into disrepute." For example, in one glaring case, the police arrested an individual for outstanding traffic tickets, subjected him to a rectal examination, found heroin on him, and then charged him with heroin possession. The Court found this chain of events reprehensible, excluded the evidence of the heroin, and stated that the administration of justice would be brought into disrepute if Canadian courts accepted evidence gathered in this manner. Since there were no reasonable or probable grounds for believing that the accused had committed a criminal offence, this was not a case of a good faith error, but rather an intentional violation of the Charter.

Boyd (1998) notes that the Supreme Court has been charting a careful course with respect to the exclusion of evidence obtained, the methods used by the police to obtain the evidence, and the overall impact on justice if the evidence is excluded. Given the fact that the Charter is less than two decades in existence, and that it has changed the historical supremacy of Parliament to make and interpret law, it is to be expected that there will be intense debate over its impact on the administration of justice. One of the major criticisms of the Charter is that because it is part of the Constitution, it gives judges the power to make law, a power that should be the prerogative of elected officials accountable to the electorate. The police are also highly critical of the emphasis on legal rights, which they claim hinders their ability to investigate, arrest, and prosecute criminals.

The bottom line for the Canadian people in judging the effectiveness of the Charter will be whether the decisions of the courts have created a more fair, just, and equitable Canada. Undoubtedly, spelling out our fundamental freedoms, our legal rights, and our equality rights cannot be construed as anything but positive protection in our democracy. Given the heterogeneous nature of our society, it will be impossible to obtain consensus as to what constitutes mainstream political, economic, or social values. However, Hogg (1992) states that the Charter protects the basic values of the nation as supported by the majority of Canadians. While we may disagree with the specific details of interpretation, we all agree on equality and freedom. While we may debate the fine points of meaning, we all agree that legal rights and equality before the law are fundamental rights. Finally, we have no alternative but to trust the courts to be the forum for delineating and ruling on what constitutes fairness and justice for all Canadian people.

# Conclusion

This chapter has analyzed the goals and purposes of Canadian criminal law in the context of the criminal justice system. It is within the justice system that the law is administered and enforced. While law serves many purposes, one of its main roles is to reflect the values of society, and just as Canadian society continually evolves and changes, so must the criminal law. What is defined as a violation of the law and harmful to the social order must always reflect the experiences and opinions of society. Similarly, criminal law must distinguish between serious felonies and misdemeanours that can be best administered by nonjudicial tribunals. The presumption of innocence on the part of the defendant is the linchpin of our criminal justice system, and the guilt of the defendant must be established in a court of law, such that it is proved beyond any reasonable doubt that a crime was committed. Canada's legal system allows for a series of defences. The purpose of the defence is to show that the defendant should not be held accountable for his or her actions, even though they may have violated the Criminal Code. New and innovative defences are continually being tested in our courts, but insanity and self-defence remain the two most important defences. Finally, we have addressed one of the most important additions to our legal system, the Canadian Charter of Rights and Freedoms, which was incorporated into the Constitution in 1982. That this document has had profound influence in our society and in our courts is without dispute. Although it is not without its critics, the Charter is the document that guarantees our legal rights and that places in the hands of the courts the role of final arbiter of our values, as well as of our belief in what constitutes a just and fair society.

## Summary

The basic premise of Canadian criminal law is that social order and social control are challenged by the commitment of criminal acts, and that these acts injure not just individuals but society itself. In terms of purposes of criminal law, criminologists see two opposing models. The value consensus model sees society as characterized by a core set of values held by all members. When these values are deviated from, society seeks ways to punish offenders through the Criminal Code. The conflict model, on the other hand, sees society as composed of various interest groups, with the criminal laws mainly protecting the power and property of those who are rich and influential and who enact the laws.

Guilt for any criminal law infraction must be proved by the prosecution in a court of law, and the accused is presumed innocent until proven guilty. There are many defences that an accused can claim to rationalize her or his behaviour, including the defence of insanity. One of the most significant additions to our legal system is the Canadian Charter of Rights and Freedoms, which outlines the protected rights of citizens, including the legal rights of accused persons when they become part of the criminal justice system. As well, the Charter defines the rights of the accused to legal counsel and guarantees of a fair trial, release on bail, and protection from harsh or unjustified punishment. While law serves many purposes, one of its main roles is to reflect the values of the society, and from this perspective what is a violation of the criminal law must always reflect the experiences and changes in the society.

## Key Terms

actus reus (p. 51)

case law (p. 49)

civil law (p. 49)

corpus delicti (p. 51)

crime (p. 47)

criminal insanity defence (p. 54)

criminal law (p. 47)

duress (p. 57)

espionage (p. 51)

felony (p. 50)

intoxication defence (p. 56)

mens rea (p. 51)

misdemeanour (p. 51)

mistake of fact (p. 55)

mistake of law (p. 55)

necessity (p. 57)

self-defence (p. 54)

statutory law (p. 49)

treason (p. 51)

## Discussion Questions

1. Discuss the goals and purposes of criminal law.
2. Discuss the differences between the defences of necessity and duress.
3. Discuss the defence of mental illness and its relevance to criminal law.

4.  The emphasis in the criminal law is on property offences. Discuss reasons for the lesser emphasis on white-collar and environmental crime in Canada.

5.  Discuss the importance of Charter provisions in protecting the legal rights of the accused.

## Weblinks

**www.canadalegal.com/gosite.asp?s=4286** This site is run by Professor David Paciocco, an expert on the law of evidence. He explains in detail the role of defence counsel. He begins by asking. "How can you defend those criminals?" and goes on to explain how!

**home.istar.ca/~ccja/angl/index.shtml** The Canadian Criminal Justice Association is dedicated to the improvement of criminal justice in Canada. The Web site offers their Justice Report, position papers on special issues such as crime prevention and young offenders, excerpts from the Canadian Journal of Criminology , and links to other sites of interest.

**canada.justice.gc.ca/Loireg/charte/const_en.html** The Web site of the Canadian Charter of Rights and Freedoms, with the full text made more accessible through links to specific areas.

**www.extension.ualberta.ca/legalfaqs/** The Legal Studies Program at the University of Alberta offers a Canadian Legal FAQs site, with questions and answers provided by topic and by provincial or federal jurisdiction.

**www.lexum.umontreal.ca/csc-scs/en/index.shtml** The Faculty of Law at the University of Montreal has searchable online collection of case law including the Supreme Court of Canada decisions on the Canadian Charter of Rights and Freedoms.

# CHAPTER 4

# Theories of Crime Causation

## Objectives

- To discuss theories explaining why people break the law.
- To outline classical and neoclassical theories of crime.
- To analyze modern theories of crime causation, including deterrence theory, rational choice theory, and routine activities theory.
- To put crime causation into sociological perspective by analyzing the relationship of the individual to society and to various informal and formal institutions, such as the family or peer networks.

## What Causes Crime?

Why do people transgress the norms of society? Why do some people continually break the law? These are questions penologists and criminologists have been wrestling with for more than two centuries.

You may be surprised to learn that the answer depends somewhat on how you perceive the world and the individual's place in it. In an important way, the answer depends on whether you believe that people are rational actors who have autonomy to choose their actions, or that people are in basic ways shaped by their social, economic, and cultural environments.

It may also depend on how you view society. Is the social world in which you live one that has much consensus about what is right and proper? Or is it full of profound divisions regarding these issues, with the law serving and representing only a powerful fraction of the whole?

Finally, your answer as to why some people commit crime may presuppose that it is individuals we need to worry most about when it comes to disruptions to society. Another consideration when we analyze causes of crime is how assumptions about policy or about the application of law lead us to focus on the individual as an object of intervention. But we know that there are larger social forces that are *criminogenic*, or crime causing. For this reason, many sociologists and criminologists look to the operation of the market or the state, or at relative economic deprivation, as the agent of criminality and therefore the object toward which policy needs to be directed.

In this chapter, you will be exposed to some examples of how people have explained crime. We will start with the classical school and the positivist school, and then take up some of the more recent thinking about this question. As we proceed, keep in mind that each theory or school of theories is distinguished from others in terms of the three questions below. In particular, we will address how each theoretical school addresses the following:

1. Free will versus determinism. (What is the assumption about the individual's freedom to choose?)

2. A consensus versus conflict view of society. (Is there equal representation of each status group in the law?)

3. The object of intervention. (What is the preferred site at which policy will be introduced?)

## Why Theorize?

When we assess a theory, we ask ourselves whether it is logical or makes sense as a coherent explanation. We also ask whether it satisfies us as an *explanation* for the phenomena we observe. Does it help us to predict when and if a phenomenon will occur? Do known facts behave in ways that conform with the theory's predictions? In other words, theories must be *internally logical, explanatory of the phenomenon,* and *empirically verifiable*. Theories must make sense, provide an explanation, and be testable and provable.

If you tell me that your bad hair day is related to school violence, you have provided an explanation, and we can test the relationship, provided we agree on what you mean by a "bad hair day." However, the relationship between your grooming behaviour and the phenomenon of school violence is not logical.

In the meantime, it is important for us to distinguish between sociological or scientific inquiry into causes of behaviour and legal or policy questions of responsibility and accountability.

In Figure 4.1, we see the continuum between causal agents of crime and responsibility agents, as well as the flow from informal to formal causal agents. The *causal agent*, whether school, family, social structure, peer group, or individual action, is understood in terms of some pathology in its operation or function. The social structure, the peer group, or the family is pathological or breeds dysfunctional actions. This is not to say that the individual cannot be seen as crime prone by nature; the individual's natural inclination to commit criminal acts is also investigated.

Positive science and the distribution of social forces are both relevant to crime etiology (the study of causation). Virtually every criminologist will acknowledge that various factors contribute to the criminal act. Thus, rather than pinpointing one cause, criminologists try to discover the sum of forces that together produce a criminal act or actor.

FIGURE 4.1

----

CRIME CAUSATION VERSUS LEGAL LIABILITY

| | | |
|---|---|---|
| *discipline* | **Causal agent** <br> social scientific principles <br> knowledge | *scientific methodology* |
| | function—pathology | |
| institution | school     peer group     family | individual |
| *society* | —— formal organization —— *informal organization*—— *self* | |
| constitution | incorporation <br> intent—liability | legal subject |
| *jurisdiction* | legal standing/societal values <br> obligations/protections/rights <br> **Responsible agent** | *legal discovery* |

global market
transnational organization
multinational corporation

--------------------------\\ society

multilateral agreements
trade agreements
global regulatory bodies

The *legally responsible agent,* on the other hand, refers to the culpability of the individual or society, depending on one's theoretical orientation. Sanctions are mechanisms to correct and to maintain the values and the goals of a group, society as a whole, or international trading systems. A large measure of responsibility is attributed by default in rules of participation. The Criminal Code and the law are based on the assumption that actions are intended, unless the court hears legally compelling evidence to the contrary. Such evidence is heard not according to principles of scientific discovery of causation, but rather according to principles of legal discovery, in which legal precedents and recognized social and political values play a large role. You will notice, if you give it some thought, that dysfunction is in this way the *limit* of legal correction and sanction: some people may be excused from criminal liability because they do not have the functional capacity to form a criminal intent. In legal jargon, a person can be held criminally liable on the basis of actus reus—the person's conduct or physical carrying out of a criminal act as distinguished from criminal intent.

If you look down the right side of Figure 4.1, you will see that it is the most simplified route to the sanctioning of individual criminal responsibility. Here we find the cause of criminality in the nature of the individual, which we deem the consequence of free choice. This concept of free will provides us with a nonproblematic relationship between an inquiry into ultimate cause and an inquiry into legal responsibility. Individuals choose to cause their own actions, for which it follows they can be held responsible.

If you look down the left side, however, you will note that the dysfunction or pathology is attributed to a societal object; an institution may function in such a way that it rewards behaviour that violates societal norms and competes with other societal values. International financial institutions, such as the World Bank and the International Monetary Fund, provide loans to Third World countries under "adjustment policies." These policies require austerity measures, which means removing much of the social safety net. Elliott Currie (1998) argues that these policies spur or create the criminogenic conditions under which a great number of people slide into poverty and desperation.

However, how we analyze causes and responsibility is also a function of how disciplines and jurisdictions are divided up. Some criminologists do not allow that scientific methodology will necessarily determine causal agents of criminality because much of the "data" is determined by societal values. These criminologists eschew a scientific methodology in favour of such alternatives as historical analysis. Many critical criminologists, therefore, are seen as being nontraditional within the discipline.

The legal agency is also divided—in this instance, by jurisdiction. Legal attribution of responsibility depends on an assignment of jurisdiction, whether according to standards of liability (civil, administrative, or criminal) or according to a division of geographic authority (local, provincial, national, or international).

For instance, O.J. Simpson was acquitted according to the legal standard of criminal law (his guilt was not proven beyond a reasonable doubt), but he was convicted in a civil court trial (on the balance of probabilities). To avoid attribution of responsibility and to ensure limited liability, many companies place warning labels on their products.

How we conceive of the parameters of legitimate jurisdiction and the boundaries of a discipline is a matter of politics, ideology, and power. Criminological theory and the attribution of responsibility for wrongs, losses, or harm depend on important questions of citizenship, representation, societal standing, and access to information. Although the practice of criminology or criminal justice administration may be presented as a straightforward discovery of knowledge or application of the law, it is important to remember that theories apply assumptions and that decisions have political context.

# Classical and Neoclassical Theories of Crime

## Before the Enlightenment

Before the classical period of crime theory, which is really the first period in which a rational, logic-informed approach was advocated for the social problem of criminality, there existed a mix throughout Europe of private vengeances between kinship groups, known as *blood feuds,* and of state-controlled sanctions, in which the Church played an important role.

For the most part, people were expected to take care of their own affairs. Formal policing did not exist before the 18th century in most jurisdictions. If wronged, a person could challenge the perceived wrongdoer to a duel. If robbed, the victim could hire a *thief-taker,* who would recover goods for a fee. There were also various voluntary organizations, such as *felons associations* or *regulators,* which members paid, in the form of duty or money, to protect them from depredation or to recover goods or catch and bring offenders to justice.

In Britain, and later in America, Australia, Canada, and other colonies, the justice system was essentially private. The offended party had to bring the offender to justice, either through the payment of money or through a form of collective membership.

In Europe, the justice system was much more strongly influenced by centralization and by the Catholic Church. On the Continent, from the 12th century through the 18th century, the Church allied itself with incipient states and helped them to rule through fear. Secular authorities had to demonstrate their allegiance to the Church by showing a willingness to purge their kingdoms of alleged non-

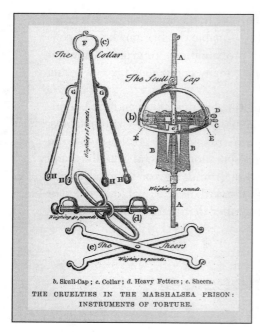

b. Skull-Cap ; c. Collar ; d. Heavy Fetters ; e. Sheers.

THE CRUELTIES IN THE MARSHALSEA PRISON:
INSTRUMENTS OF TORTURE.

believers and heretics through periodic show trials and executions.

Much of what stood for what we would today call *criminal justice* was dedicated not to the discovery of crime, but rather to the expunging of evil from the community. During the period of the Inquisition, the Catholic Church saw crime as possession by evil and elicited confession through brutal tortures, both before and during public executions. Punishment was dedicated to the task of confirming the solidarity and sanctity of the whole, often represented by a deity or a figurehead. In the 1700s, witch trials were still common. In Massachusetts Bay, the Puritan colony believed that the crime waves it experienced were caused by satanic forces. In places such as Salem, Massachusetts, famous witch trials were conducted. Guilt was determined by many novel devices in a trial by ordeal, which was designed to reveal a sign of God's will. Brutal execution practices included burying alive, burning at the stake, quartering, beheading, stoning, and breaking on the wheel. Death was the major method of punishment. Nonlethal forms were also unsavoury, including branding, pilloring, and whipping.

In addition to the brutality, the perceived arbitrariness of punishment, the unpredictability of its administration, and the class bias in its distribution became unpalatable both to an increasing segment of the merchant class and to many of the long-established elites. Enlightenment thinkers captured much of this sentiment, leading to a rethinking of sin as crime and of atonement as punishment. The key distinction between classical theory and the view of crime and punishment that preceded it was that classical theory offered a *naturalistic* rather than a supernatural explanation for criminal behaviour. Both Enlightenment and classical thinkers would argue that crime was not a possession of the person by evil, external forces. Rather, crime was a product of the rational individual's free will.

## The Enlightenment and the Birth of the Classical School

The Enlightenment was a reform movement that was spread throughout Europe by philosophers who rejected the belief that Church doctrine was a sufficient and rational account of how people existed in relation to institutions, society, and other people. In his 1748 treatise, *l'Esprit des Lois* ("the spirit of the laws"), Montesquieu repudiated torture and espoused a rational basis for the administration of criminal law. In 1762 Jean-Jacques Rousseau wrote the *Social Contract*, in which he argued that people could be made bad not by God, necessarily, but rather by social institutions; therefore, he believed a concerted effort should be made to reform these institutions.

The classical school applied the philosophy of this large body of work to the area of criminal law and punishment. Two main proponents of **classical criminology** were Cesare Beccaria of Italy and Jeremy Bentham of England. Both believed that the criminal law should mainly operate to deter crime, and that this function could best be achieved through principles of rationality, transparency, proportionality, and humaneness.

Bentham is important mainly for his *happiness principle*, which brought the notion of hedonism into the business of governance. Recognizing the pursuit of happiness as a legitimate part of humanity, Bentham sought to work *with* the idea of happiness rather than against it. He came up with his famous dictum: the greatest happiness for the greatest number. Because crime reduced the sum total of happiness, it needed to be deterred. It could be deterred, in turn, through a *pleasure/pain calculus,* in which the individual seeks to maximize his or her own happiness and to minimize pain. The weighing of pleasure and pain Bentham called the **hedonistic calculus;** the pain from crime always had to be greater than the pleasure derived from it.

Cesare Beccaria is most famous for his little volume *On Crimes and Punishments*, first published anonymously in 1764. Like other texts challenging doctrine or policy, it was denounced by the Catholic Church. Following Enlightenment thinkers and Social Contract thinkers, such as John Locke and Thomas Hobbes, Beccaria argued that punishment was a necessary instrument of deterrence, or crime prevention. He said that it was "always better to prevent crimes than to punish them" (Beccaria, 1764/1963, p. 93). He insisted, however, that only laws, and not magistrates, ought to be able to decree punishments for crimes. Only the legislator represents the will of the people, so it is the rightful maker of laws. So vigorous was his opposition to the arbitrary power of magistrates that he also argued against the right of judges to interpret law. Beccaria believed, furthermore, that legal punishment ought to be reserved for acts that were harmful to society; in this way, he hoped to restrict the scope of punishment to secular considerations.

## Principles of Classical Thought

The philosophy of the classical school can be summed up in the principles of rationality, deterrence, proportionality, transparency, and humaneness.

## Rationality

If people are free to choose crime rather than driven to it by external forces, then they can be reached through their cognition. When crime is considered an evil caused by external sources, it makes no difference what sort of reason you use on suspected or potential evildoers. But when crime is considered a freely chosen act, reason makes a vast difference. Rationality, important to Enlightenment thinkers, was also important to the development of sound policy in criminal justice. But for the utilitarians, rationality was considered in the context of hedonism. They believed that it was hedonism, or the desire for satisfaction or pleasure, that attracted rational people to crime. The classical thinkers, therefore, thought that free-willed humans were both rational and inclined to hedonism.

## Deterrence

The thought underlying deterrence is that prevention is better than punishment. Punishment during the Middle Ages consisted of outrageous tortures for often petty crimes. A theft could easily result in a sentence of death. Such punishments were not very different from sacrifices to appease the vengeance of a god. Moreover, if religious belief and Church doctrine held that people were either good or bad and acted accordingly, then deterrence would be of little value— people were more or less determined by their grace, as the Calvinists also believed.

But if people are rational actors seeking to maximize pleasure, deterrence makes much more sense. One of the assumptions of the classical school is that a *just measure of pain* will deter people from attempting to gain pleasure by harming others. The positive side of hedonism is an attraction to pleasure, the negative side, the avoidance of pain. Bentham argued that punishment deterred repeated criminality because people would respond to a subjective pleasure/pain calculus. Beccaria divided deterrence into the three principles of *celerity, certainty,* and *severity.* The pain of punishment must come swiftly, must be certain to come, and must be adequately severe to have value.

## Proportionality

Simply put, punishment must be proportionate to the criminal act. In this sense, proportionality is the opposite of arbitrary punishment. Proportionality has been a long-lasting concept in corrections and penology, and current penology still rests on this principle. Beccaria stated that punishment should be deployed only to deter people from actions that were harmful to society, and that punishment should be proportionate to that harm.

## Transparency

Beccaria also said that no crime ought to be without a law. Laws ought to be known to people before they act, not after the fact. Laws must exist before punishments can be applied, and these laws must be made by legislators.

## Humaneness

In *The Spectacle of Suffering* (1984), Pieter Spierenburg argued that one of the reasons for the great changes to crime and punishment in the 18th century was the closer social proximity of the classes. The upper classes began to worry that if the state expressed too much public violence through punishment, the public's appetite for violence would be keen and thus would put the elites in greater danger. In his view, the call for more humane punishments was merely an expression of self-interest. According to Beccaria, it was justice or just punishment that was served by humaneness. The end of proportionality was thus the end of humaneness. Punishment needed to reflect the social harm, rather than the power and majesty of the sovereign, as Douglass Hay (1975) expressed it.

# The Legacy of the Classical School

Much of the focus of the classical school was on the operation of the criminal law, rather than on the causes or conditions of crime. It was unnecessary to think much about criminals per se, because they were, like other members of society, simply rational thinkers who could be deterred from crime through good policy. Indeed, some law reformers were at work even before the Enlightenment and the dissemination of classical penology. For instance, William Penn, the founder of Pennsylvania, drafted The Great Code (i.e., the Charter of Privileges) in 1701, which remained in force until 1776. In Europe, the French Code of 1791 and English legislative reforms drafted by Sir Samuel Romily in the early 1800s were derived from classical principles. Classical influence is also present in the American and French constitutions, particularly in their assignment of individual rights, many of which are now known as *rights to due process* or *rights of the accused.*

Just as some people today balk at the failure to take into consideration offender status or situational variables in sentencing (for example, whether the offender is an adult, is mentally competent, or is an otherwise successful contributor to society), the French Code of 1791 was considered too unbending to serve justice and had to be repealed in favour of law that distinguished between offenders on the basis of their status. The classical influence was generally eclipsed as specialists began to use scientific methodology to discover *criminals* instead of to prevent *crime.*

More recently, there is much classical influence in the proliferation of mandatory minimum sentences and in the use of sentencing tables. Mandatory minimums allow the judge a narrow band of discretion when sentencing an offender, even if there are mitigating circumstances. Sentencing tables allow only specific factors to be used in determining a sentence, including prior criminal history and aggravating circumstances of the crime, such as the use of a weapon. The judge has no discretion to select a sentence that is not indicated by the table. Both of these innovations are consistent with Beccaria's intellectual quest to increase the power of lawmakers over the power of judges.

The tide turned once again in the 1970s, when many criminal justice practitioners and researchers argued that many people choose crime of their own free will. Especially noteworthy were the findings of Lipton and associates in 1975, which reviewed the research on punishment from 1945 to 1967 and argued that correctional treatment in the form of rehabilitation had not reduced criminality. Martinson (1974) also surveyed rehabilitative interventions and concluded, somewhat overzealously, that "nothing works." Today, classical theory or classical penology continues to exert much influence in contemporary penology in arguments favouring incapacitation and "just desserts." It has also resurfaced in a number of criminology theories, including deterrence theory, rational choice theory, and routine activities theory.

## Deterrence Theory

**Deterrence theory** holds that people can be discouraged from committing crime by punishment and preventive measures. *General deterrence* refers to the use of punishment to inhibit crime rates or the behaviour of specific populations, rather than specific people. Essentially, general deterrence theory predicts an inverse relationship between crime rates and the certainty, celerity, and severity of punishment. *Specific deterrence,* on the other hand, refers to discouraging the activity of a particular individual through such steps as incarceration, electronic monitoring, or shaming. The specific deterrence effects of incarceration or other penal sanctions are measured through *recidivism rates,* or the chances of a person's returning to criminal activity upon release.

When we think about deterrence in terms of *certainty*, we can use the concept of the **tipping level** (Chamelin, 1991). By tipping level, we mean the point at which the probability of being arrested is high enough to act as a deterrent. For example, in the case of auto thefts, Chamelin (1991) found that a deterrent effect was reached when a clearance rate reached 40 percent. Tittle and Rowe (1973) concluded that a 30 percent arrest rate for all reported crimes would bring the crime rate down significantly.

Whereas auto thefts are understood as an *instrumental crime,* in which the criminal act is a means to another goal (Chambliss, 1967), contemporary theorists recognize that some crimes are not instrumental, but rather *expressive*. As we noted earlier, classical theorists argued that deterrence is of value when the actor is rational. It stands to reason that trying to get people to give up acts that give them pleasure is more difficult than trying to get people to give up a particular *route* to their pleasure (i.e., crime). With expressive crimes the illegal act itself is the "pleasure" that the individual pursues (Chambliss, 1967). Indeed, Jack Katz (1988) argues that crime can help to satisfy personal needs, such as the thrill of "getting away with it." If the crime itself provides pleasure, people who commit expressive crimes are likely to respond less well to the certainty of punishment than are those who commit instrumental crimes.

For some crimes, there is no doubt that *certainty* is also an obvious deterrent. If police in Windsor or Red Deer started enforcing every traffic law, they would probably add hundreds of thousands of dollars to the municipal coffers, and once word got around, traffic violations would decrease. For the vast majority, there is little pleasure in the offence itself and the behaviour can be countered by the pain of the punishment.

However, for expressive crimes, such as domestic assaults and underage drinking, the punishment is often too remote and the pleasure (in the crime) too immediate. However, recent neoclassical research has focused on these crimes, arguing that even in this hard test, deterrence still operates. We will take up a few examples momentarily.

The case for certainty is supported by both common sense and research. The case for *celerity*, or swiftness, is less clear. The principle that punishment must also be swift is captured in the aphorism "justice delayed is justice denied." In Canada, celerity is part of the constitutionality of the legal process, as entrenched in the Charter (section 11[b]: the right to be tried within a reasonable time). The Askov ruling in 1991 in Ontario threw out nearly 50 000 criminal cases because they had been delayed too long. But despite this constitutional protection, research testing the deterrent effect of quick punishment is hard to come by.

The final principle of deterrence is *severity*. It is argued that punishment must be proportionately severe. A stern lecture for a premeditated murder would be insufficiently severe to match the harm done by the crime. However, it is not yet fully proven that as severity increases, crime decreases. The case of capital punishment is an example. Although the research is somewhat divided, the strongest evidence repudiates the idea that capital punishment deters homicide. Some researchers argue that "brutalization" occurs when the state executes citizens—the state is in effect sanctifying or justifying, at the highest level, the relationship between violence and problem solving. In general, there is insufficient evidence to support the view that harsh punishments reduce the crime rate.

# Rational Choice Theory

Modern-day proponents of **rational choice theory** argue that some offenders, at least, are rational decision makers who seek to benefit themselves through their criminal behaviour. In the view of Cornish and Clarke (1987), offenders make decisions and choices in committing crime. Cornish and Clarke state that the distinction between actors is not *qualitative*, but instead is *quantitative:* everyone is a rational calculator and exercises free will, but some are limited in their ability to calculate.

Cornish and Clarke also argue that when we analyze the criminal choices of offenders we need to be crime-specific: rational choice theory has more promise, the authors say, by emphasizing the particular crime, rather than the general disposition to offend. In other words, how can we influence the choice to commit this particular type of criminal act? The processes are likely to vary greatly at different stages of the decision process and among different crimes.

Proponents of a rational choice model theorize that decisions to offend are based on the offender's evaluation of a situation. In fact, there are two steps to decision making in offending: the involvement decision (deciding to become involved or to stop participating in a form of offending) and event decisions (the tactics of carrying out an offence). Thus, rational choice theorists seek to evaluate the offender's decision making. They do this by seeing offences as having properties—including skill levels, payoffs, and costs—that structure an offender's choices. Rational choice theorists ask the question, What are the choice-structuring properties that are in play in a given offence? By **choice-structuring properties,** Cornish and Clarke mean the features of criminal opportunities that make them attractive to potential offenders, relative to time and place. It is through the manipulation of choice-structuring properties that a means of prevention is afforded; the constellation of motives, opportunities, rewards, and costs offered by each offence category may be manipulated. Therefore, rational choice, according to Cornish and Clarke, may assist in crime prevention.

One of the main arguments against the idea that rational choice may prevent crime is the problem of displacement. *Displacement* means that the site or target is replaced, but the agent of the crime in the offender remains the same. However, to counter the view that tinkering with a given crime through preventative efforts will merely shift the crime elsewhere, Cornish and Clarke argue that a frustrated potential offender may be just as likely to not seek another offending opportunity or may even seek a noncriminal solution. They argue that displacement is far from inevitable, but that we need to take a crime-specific focus in order to see this.

The authors give the example of suicide. Deprived of a more acceptable means of suicide, people will not always turn to less acceptable means. They cite a study in which detoxification of domestic gas accounted for a 35 percent reduction in suicides in Britain during the 1960s. They argue that by identifying the choice-structuring properties, researchers can compare different activities with the same goal—for example, different crimes may be committed with the goal of making money. Therefore, the researcher can trace displacement, should it occur, by looking to other relevant sites. It is evident that some activities will not have ready criminal alternatives once the activity is made unattractive.

The authors provide lists of choice-structuring properties for theft involving cash and for illegal substance abuse. They argue that these lists should be useful to criminologists in evaluating crime prevention initiatives by orienting the search for displacement sites. They acknowledge that their list concentrates on the opportunities, costs, and benefits of the various alternatives being compared. The offender may not necessarily be conscious of all the properties that may be structuring his or her choice.

## Routine Activities Theory

Rational choice theory provides a microlevel account of crime by focusing on choice-structuring variables. **Routine activities theory,** on the other hand, provides a macrolevel account because it explains changes in crime rates over time by considering social and economic conditions. However, while paying attention to structural variables, it nevertheless assumes that crime is opportunistic—by nature, people will, in the absence of deterrence, exploit illegal chances that come their way. In short, routine activities theory argues that we can understand changes in crime rates if we look carefully at changes in three distinct variables: suitable targets, capable guardians, and motivated offenders.

By *suitable targets,* Felson and Cohen (1979) are referring to the importance to criminal opportunity of perceptions of target vulnerability. In explaining the increase of crime at the same time as an increase of wealth after World War II, Felson and Cohen noted that there was a dramatic expansion in the production and proliferation of portable durable goods, like televisions, stereos, computers, and even large items such as automobiles. These goods were suitable as targets because they had value in the black market. All of a sudden, there was much wealth in the form of these goods, which could be targeted by those motivated enough to do the taking.

By *capable guardians,* Felson and Cohen are referring to the absence or presence of protection for targets. Something that is well guarded against theft or depredation is less likely to be targeted. Another sort of capable guardian is the family. As the nuclear family has replaced the extended family and, more often, both parents work during the day, there is greater opportunity for break-and-enter thefts because, in the absence of burglar alarms, there is no capable guardian defending the fort, so to speak.

By *motivated offender,* the authors are referring to the absence or presence of people who are sufficiently motivated to commit a criminal act. A number of motivators exist. In structural terms, motivation is more likely to be prevalent in societies that value wealth. When legitimate opportunities to gain wealth are scarce, people are also more likely to be motivated to commit criminal acts to satisfy this goal.

The combination of a motivated offender and a suitable target with a lack of capable guardianship thus produces a situation in which crime is more likely to occur. If you leave your bicycle unlocked outside a hostel, it is quite likely to be stolen. If you leave it unlocked at a family gathering on your brother's farm, it is more likely to be left alone, particularly if your family gets along.

Situational crime prevention theorists (Clarke, 1995) add to Cohen and Felson's arguments that certain lifestyle factors (shopping, leisure activities), the physical environment (defensible space), facilitators (guns, cars, and drugs or alcohol), and the presence or absence of offender "handlers" are also related to the chances of crime occurring (Osgoode, Wilson, O'Malley, Bachman, & Johnsston, 1996).

## An Evaluation of Classical Theory

The philosophy that human beings employ a rational calculus in decision making and are by nature predisposed to gratify innate wants that compete with the collective interests of society has been very compelling. Also influential has been the simple idea that crime prevention requires meaningful deterrence. Although much testing of general and specific deterrence and of the certainty, speed, and severity of punishment has yielded mixed results, the common sense of the argument has proved compelling to lawmakers in Canada over the past 20 years.

Similarly, the ideas that modern society has created more opportunities for crime and that there are specific features of situations, or "situational variables," that make for more or less crime, reinforce common sense expectations. Certainly, law enforcement practitioners have long been calling for more scholarly attention to the everyday features of the lived environment to root out strategies of crime prevention. This approach is followed by theorists like Clarke and Homel (1997), who describe crime prevention techniques flowing from research on situational crime prevention. These techniques include methods for increasing the risk and the effort involved with committing crime, as well as methods for reducing its rewards and inducing shame or guilt among would-be offenders.

However, there are a number of problems with the basic assumptions of classical theory. First, it is based on an inherently conservative view of social structure. The focus is on maintaining the distribution of goods and services in society. While Clarke (1995), for example, does allow that the socioeconomic structure is the base on which a "crime opportunity superstructure" is built, it is assumed that much tinkering with the superstructure will have the desired results in crime reduction, rather than the other way around. The social structure is considered to be out of the bounds of crime policy, despite the immense influence of economics on the distribution of wealth, poverty, and crime in society.

The view that humans are, by degrees, rational and passionate actors who choose their actions is involved in many of the arguments stemming from the classical school. The concept of a "limited rationality" preserves this perspective of an innate rational choice, much as the "reasonable person" standard in criminal law ensures the culpability of the majority of criminal actors. However, another way of acknowledging a limited rationality, like acknowledging a limited liability, is to say that some actions are partly determined by forces external to the actors or outside of their control. A second criticism, then, is that classical theory is not really concerned with the actor as a person, or even as a criminal, as a complex whole, but rather is concerned with the conditions of the act. Policies resulting from such a perspective, therefore, are likely to contribute to the dehumanizing of personal interactions and to the breakdown of trust relationships between individuals, as crime prevention efforts are likely to be directed by governments that may not always find a balance between honouring the social contract and respecting civil liberties.

# Positivism and Trait Theories of Crime

With the emergence of scientific methodology and the positivist school in the 19th century, thinking about crime and punishment turned toward examining the criminal and correction. *Positivism* was primarily a reaction to the Enlightenment. Whereas Enlightenment thinkers stressed the negative influence of traditional institutions—such as the Church and the class system, which granted only some people rights—the founders of positivism tried to reconcile reason and experience with traditional institutions like the Church. This philosophy was positive about and committed to positive change to the social system. It was committed to reconciling social traditions with emerging knowledge based on scientific evidence and methodology, and it allowed that individuals are determined rather than freely choosing. However, it also required that existing institutions adapt to scientific discoveries about the nature of humanity and society and acknowledge the leading role of scientific knowledge in societal evolution. The nature of human existence did not have to be taken as a given, but rather could be perfected through social engineering. In the main, **positivist criminology** took a narrow view of positivism, focusing on its methodology and its approach that the human condition is determined but changeable.

If people prone to committing crimes were not possessed by evil and were not simply rational actors who needed to be deterred, then what were they? The answer would spring from the method. Positivist scientific method involved deductive reasoning through systematic observation, accumulated evidence, and objective facts. When the "evildoer" became the "criminal" in popular under-standing, early Italian school criminal anthropologists like Cesare Lombroso, Enrico Ferri, and Raffaele Garafolo could set about discovering any unique traits to account for the deviation of this "class" of persons from the population as a whole. They did so, typically, by separating a sample of convicts from a control sample of soldiers or others representing the general population. They then set about distinguishing the two populations through systematic observation and sci-entific measurement. Thus, Lombroso "discovered" that criminals have more physical abnormalities than the general population; using Darwinian theory, he argued that these traits were "atavisms," or throwbacks to previous evolutionary stages of human development. Lombroso's later work and the work of the other Italian school positivists also explored the environment as a conditioner of crim-inal behaviour.

In the early 20th century, positivist criminologists studied various causes of criminality, including "feeblemindedness" and genetic or hereditary traits, body types, or somatotypes (Sheldon, 1949), psychological influences, and sociological influences (after Quetelet's work in 1831 on social statistics). For instance, fol-lowing Alfred Binet's invention of the intelligence quotient (IQ), many attempts were made to link criminality to inferior intelligence. With intelligence testing, governments could categorize people into distinct population groupings. A royal commission on the "feebleminded" was struck in Ontario in 1920 to look into the possibility of categorizing and institutionalizing these people. This work became problematic when better methodology found, for instance, that soldiers were at least as likely to be feebleminded as prisoners. *Eugenics*—social engineering through the controlled breeding for inherited qualities—thrived up until the 1920s in scientific circles and was enforced as late as the 1970s by the Alberta government.

While work dedicated to uncovering traits that separated criminal and non-criminal populations waned during the mid-20th century in favour of truly soci-ological approaches, which we will take up in the next section, the belief in the malleability of the criminal continued to inform penological studies. Correctional literature developed a treatment philosophy that thrived in policy documents until the 1970s. In recent years, a more conservative attitude toward crime and punishment has rejuvenated trait theory and the implication of bio-logical factors in criminal behaviour. Pierre van den Bergie (1974), Edmund O. Wilson (1975), and James Q. Wilson and Richard Herrnstein (1985), among oth-ers, revived the common sense assumption that biology is related to behaviour.

This approach includes biochemical theories related to hormones and diet, neuropsychological theories related to brain chemistry and structure, theories related to genetics, psychological trait theories, and sociobiological theories, which see crime as an offshoot of behaviour that maximizes the chances of an individual's genetic reproduction within environmental constraints. These theories are too many to be reviewed here, but a few noteworthy examples follow.

## Genetics: XYY Chromosome

Genetically normal individuals have 46 paired chromosomes, including 1 pair of sex chromosomes. The pair of sex chromosomes is called XX for the normal female and XY for the normal male. One deviation that can occur is the male may have an extra Y chromosome, forming XYY pattern. This infrequent deviation has been called *supermaleness.*

When compared with control groups of normal males, supermales, or XYY chromosome males, show a higher rate of criminal offending (Witkin, 1977). However, Witkin's study did not find a disproportionate tendency toward violence. The extra Y chromosome has also been identified with impaired intellectual or psychological functioning. In general, however, there is only an inconsistent relationship between XYY chromosome males and crime, and the courts have not accepted it as a defence for diminished criminal responsibility.

## Biochemistry: Hormones

There is much evidence that males are more aggressive than females, so the question has arisen, Are males more aggressive because they have higher levels of male hormones? The testosterone production of men over 30 is half that of men aged 17 to 29. This finding has led to speculation that testosterone is directly implicated in male criminality, and especially crimes of violence.

A self-report study by Olweus (1987) showed a substantial correlation between testosterone levels and self-reports of both verbal and physical aggression. There have also been findings that testosterone is related to precocious sexuality and substance abuse (Udry, 1988). Booth and Osgood (1993) found a significant to moderate relationship between testosterone and adult deviance. Testosterone is one of the factors, according to Booth and Osgood, contributing to a latent propensity toward deviance; its influence also moderates the relationship of social integration to adult deviance. The restraining influence of social integration is less necessary for men with lower levels of testosterone. Thus, increased testosterone affects temperament or self-control, which influences such factors as interpersonal attachments, which then influence propensity toward criminal activity.

In women, there have been findings that the fall in progesterone level and the relatively greater amount of estrogen during premenstrual syndrome (PMS) are linked to increased aggression, hostility, irritability, headaches, and other symptoms. These symptoms, in turn, are linked to an increased chance of engaging in illegal behaviour. A study by Morton, Addison, Addison, Hunt, & Sullivan (1953) found that 53 percent of violent crimes committed by a group of women occurred during the premenstrual week. More recently, Diana Fishbein (1996) found that menstruation is related to elevated female aggression. However, the data are still too unreliable to allow any firm conclusions. PMS has been recognized as a mitigating factor in women's defence at trial in many countries, including Canada.

## Neurophysiological Abnormalities and Aggressive Behaviour

Researchers studying animals have discovered a relationship between brain function and aggressive behaviour. Research has shown that the innate ability to inhibit and initiate aggression functions for the survival of species (sociobiology). Depending on the neural site stimulated, animals may either exhibit fierce rage or act passively and be unable to defend themselves from threatened assault. In humans, we tend to see aggression as an act of free will or as a response to the external environment. However, some neuropsychologists argue that we should not ignore the biological determinants of aggression, particularly when injuries to the neural structures can have an impact on people's behaviour.

The frontal lobe is the seat higher abstraction, judgment, planning, sustained motivation, and self-regulation. Its general functions are allowing decision making; providing continuity and coherence to behaviour across time; modulating affective and interpersonal behaviour so that drives are satisfied within the constraints of the internal and external environment; and monitoring, evaluating, and adjusting behaviour. The frontal lobe is the last area of the brain to fully develop, coming to maturity in the later part of adolescence, and its development moves us from childhood to adulthood. In short, the frontal lobe is essential to the individual's successful integration into society. The development of the frontal lobe depends on the psychological and cognitive environment, not just on the physical environment and DNA.

Frontal lobe damage, therefore, retards the ability to use knowledge to regulate behaviour; the ability to handle sequential behaviour; the ability to establish or maintain a mental set; the ability to monitor personal behaviour; and attitudes of apathy. According to the theory of frontal lobe function, frontal lobe impairment leads to aggressive behaviour because the brain loses the ability to maintain emotional balance and control.

As well as impeding the control of aggressive impulses, frontal lobe impairment impedes the individual's ability to empathize with others who are affected by the individual's loss of control. Empathy may also be associated with the higher socialization function of the frontal lobe.

Tests of the frontal lobe and other brain regions are done through various procedures, including CAT scan (computerized axial tomography) and EEG (electroencephalograph). A CAT scan uses X-rays to take cross-sectional pictures of the brain, and an EEG is a readout of the electrical impulses given off by the brain, reproduced as brainwaves. Studies using both CAT and EEG scans have found structural abnormalities in as many as 57 percent of aggressive patients (Volovka, 1987).

A study by Rosenbaum et al. (1994) found that batterers were two times as likely as nonbatterers (53 percent compared to 25 percent) in relationships of marital discord to have had a history of head injury. Where the relationship was without battery and was nondiscordant, only 16 percent of respondents had a history of head injury. These authors also found that in 93 percent of batterers with a history of head injury, the head injury preceded the first instance of battery.

## Policy Implications and Dilemmas

What are the implications to criminal responsibility under the criminal law of the view that behaviour is to some extent determined by biological factors?

Denno argues that "social science research has not yet demonstrated sufficiently strong links between biological features and criminal behaviour to warrant major consideration in determining criminal responsibility" (1988, p. 617). However, we have reviewed some of the vast quantity of research that has made strong links between biology and behaviour, and these links do have consequences for our firm positions on criminal responsibility.

There are some standards of providing evidence in the criminal law (such as in the state of Ohio) that may preclude the consideration of diminished responsibility or capacity even on medical or psychological evidence. Furthermore, the law requires the establishment of simple cause and effect, yet the social sciences now understand events as usually being contingent on multiple variables, where each has at best a slightly significant probability of having pushed forward an outcome.

In addition, courts are reluctant to accept statistical evidence brought forth by social scientists as fact, as was shown in the case of *McCleskey v. Kemp*. In this case, a U.S. court found difficulties in accepting statistical evidence of racial discrimination in death penalty sentencing. The lower courts in that ruling even contested the validity of social science research (Denno, 1988).

## Full and Partial Determinism

Absolutists in the positivist school argue for a full determinism position. *Full determinism* holds that perfect prediction of behaviour is possible, and it is possible without knowledge of the will of the individual. This position holds that even if we can account for only a portion of the individual's behaviour, such perfect prediction would be possible if sufficient research were done to discover all the determinants. The position argues that all behaviour could be excused or defended if all the causal factors were found.

The full determinism position is incompatible with the concept of criminal responsibility because fully determined behaviour is not the actor's responsibility, and it would be immoral to hold people responsible for actions that are determined by outside forces. But it would also be immoral to allow for *some* defences of, say, biological deficiency simply because they are the ones presently known to science. If we truly believe all behaviour is fully determined, we cannot excuse just the behaviour that we have come to know more about.

*Partial, or degree, determinism* is defined as allowing a degree of freedom of choice on a continuum from the hypothetically entirely rational, to the hypothetically pathologically determined (see Morris, 1982). Under a principle of partial determinism, it is the role of criminal justice to determine the point at which responsibility ends and excuse begins.

According to the principle of partial determinism, the role of the court is to consider physiological, environmental, cultural, educational, economic, and hereditary factors in determining whether a defendant can be justly held responsible for an act.

Degree determinists argue that a sliding scale could be used to assign measures of criminal responsibility. Some degree determinists, such as Morris, argue that excuses like insanity should be abolished under the premise that external influences are more influential than internal sources, such as psychosis. In this way, greater weight is given to the social than to the psychological. On the other hand, other degree determinists, like Bazelon, would merely extend the scope of all the behavioural impairments, both internal and external, social and psychological.

Degree determinism also takes into account graduations of responsibility, including predisposing, facilitating, and inhibiting variables. *Predisposing variables* will have a necessary but not sufficiently compelling relationship with the phenomena being studied. These variables might include genetic, psychophysiological, and neurological and social influences. *Facilitative variables* are those that in combination with the predisposing variable increase the probability that certain behaviour will occur. These variables include drug or alcohol use, victim provocation, the availability of weapons, and the environmental and social context. *Inhibiting variables* are those that in the presence of predisposing factors tend to decrease the probability that the behaviour will occur and may even prevent it from occurring. Examples are internalized norms, high intelligence, and socialization in acceptable behaviour.

Consider the example of two short-order cooks working in a busy restaurant on a very hot day. One of them has murdered the other in a violent rage. What were the circumstances?

1. *Predisposing:* Let us say that the cook who did the killing was a 20-year-old with exceptionally high levels of testosterone. Let us also say that this individual dropped out of school at age 12, that he had a frontal lobe impairment, and that his father solved problems by beating him and his mother.

2. *Facilitating:* Let us say that this young man was also on diet pills for an eating disorder, that he was told by the victim that he was "one big good-for-nothing," something that he was coincidentally often called by his father, and that he just happened to be holding a butcher knife for carving a turkey at the time of the incident.

3. *Inhibiting:* Finally, let us say that the young man was of moderate to low intelligence and would score quite low on testing of internalization of social-ethical norms.

Such an evaluation is then a *determination* of the degree to which this young man's actions were determined. It provides us with a picture of what we might call an accident waiting to happen. It puts the young man on the low end of responsibility. Legally, we would say that this individual had a diminished capacity to choose the moral wrong he committed.

Currently, we have in the books some incorporation of diminished capacity in the recognition of social, psychological, and biological factors. These factors include some genetic deficiencies, automatism, amnesia, Vietnam Stress Syndrome or post-traumatic stress syndrome, brainwashing, severe environmental deprivation, battered woman's syndrome, and premenstrual syndrome. Many of these factors are already very contentious inclusions as criminal defences.

A more worrying point for some in the allowing of evidence at trial for mitigated responsibility owing to biological impairments is the fact that some of the worst offenders will be the most suitable candidates. A study of 15 death row inmates found that all had histories of severe head injuries, and 12 of them had severe to less severe neurological problems (Lewis, Pincus, Feldman, Jackson, & Bard, 1986).

Another point is that mental illness and biological impairment are insufficient reasons to assume a lack of free will or responsibility for actions. The law of insanity defences is restricted to this idea of the ability to understand the moral nature of an act or to appreciate that an act is wrong. Ironically, psychopaths, who most clearly fit the description of legal insanity, are the least likely to be allowed the defence.

## Societal Responsibility

The balance of societal and individual responsibility is perhaps best expressed in the *societal fault model,* by which the judge or jury would be asked to determine the proportion of individual and societal fault, after being given information on the accused's social background. Where the accused can show that specific social institutions, such as schools, failed to discharge their duty to the defendant, resulting in his or her commission of a criminal offence, societal fault would be attributed.

What are the implications to policy development of the idea that criminal behaviour is to some extent a consequence of biological factors? According to Booth and Osgood (1993), findings of a relationship between biological factors, such as hormones, and crime in the main do not give the biological factors pre-eminence over social factors. As their study found, the social modulates the biological *propensity,* making the biological effect on crime indirect. Therefore, these explanations are biosocial, rather than purely biological, and so the policy implication includes governance of these social factors.

From a policy point of view, the findings are problematic, as there has been a division in the social sciences on the nature/nurture split. Although late in the 19th century and early in the 20th century the social sciences attempted to find the biological correlates of social phenomena, in the last half of the 20th century, the social sciences saw social phenomena as the consequence of acquired characteristics. The legacy of this later viewpoint is a reluctance to consider the biological basis of crime because of the implications such a relationship has for policy, especially where such policy depends on the notion of the free-willed individual.

One of the arguments in favour of policy that depends on the view of people as free-willed individuals is that society is better off acting on this assumption, even if it is not empirically proven. Under this argument, how we treat legal subjects has much to do with the fostering of people's responsibility for their actions in the first place. Under neoliberalism, governments promote the free will of citizens to avoid fostering dependent, irresponsible individuals under welfare state liberalism.

In terms of the response of the criminal justice system to offending, treatment is very much ensconced in sanctions. Offenders are required to attend treatment programs. Cognitive theory points out the thinking patterns of normative and non-normative individuals. It backs the cognitive behavioural approach to offender treatment or therapy. Cognitive theory really boils down in practice to interpersonal skills training and social skills training.

In general terms, whereas classical theory justifies applying formal sanctions, positivist theory justifies treating the behaviour of the offender once the sanction has been applied. This division in our response to wrongdoing can be described thus: first, we maintain a minimal responsibility on the part of all but very exceptional cases in the enforcement and prosecution through the Canadian justice system, and once we have applied the criminal sanction, we begin to mobilize the more determinist arguments in order to argue for policies that will help to change criminal behaviour. As we shall see in the next section, some middle ground between free will and determinism is offered by the social interactionists.

Where policy is directed at a treatment approach, there must be the political will to invest resources to improve the health of people who have caused others harm. To take the example of people with brain injuries, who may be more likely to demonstrate aggressive behaviour, a policy may be the longer-term treatment and rehabilitation of all people who experience brain injury (for example, from one to six months of treatment). Such a policy would demand the redistribution of monies to health care. In Canada, we have recently seen a shift from the welfare state, which makes such provisions, to the neoliberal state, which privatizes delivery, effectively cutting many users off.

# Sociological Theories of Crime

Thus far we have discussed criminal behaviour in terms of choice and determinism, rationality and biology, and deterrence and treatment. We have oscillated between finding causes in the individual or in human nature. What we have so far neglected is the whole range of causes in the relationship of the individual to society, to the social structure, and to various informal groups, such as family and peers. Although we may find it odd today, the intermediary organizations in which we spend most of our time were for a long time not seen as part of the puzzle of crime. The individual was seen as being born to commit crime or as choosing acts of deviance or criminality, and social relationships were not considered.

But we all live in a society full of complex relationships with other people and institutions. Those interactions shape us. They give or deny opportunity, reward or punish behaviour, and help to set our expectations of ourselves and of society.

In the last three sections, we divide the sociological theories into social process, social structure, and social reaction theories, a classification that is consistent with current texts (Brown, Esbensen, & Geis, 1998; Seigel & McCormick, 1999) and that helps to take us through causes of criminal behaviour to the behaviour of the criminal justice system, an approach that is key to any critical understanding of criminology.

# Social Process Theories

One of the first major events in the sociological understanding of crime was Edwin Sutherland's pronouncement in 1934 that criminality is normal, learned behaviour (learned in interaction with others). Although this was perhaps merely a restatement of what was already long-standing knowledge among penal reformers, it both brought into focus the importance of intermediary formal and informal institutions and rejected the idea of criminality as indicating innate abnormality or moral deprivation.

In his theory of *differential association,* or differential group organization, Sutherland argued that criminal behaviour is learned in interaction "with other persons in a process of communication" (1966, p. 81). It is learned within intimate personal groups, and the learning includes techniques for committing crimes and the motives, attitudes, and rationalizations that the groups use to favourably define the behaviour, even though it may violate the law. Simply put, the more time a person spends in the company of those who violate the law, the more a person learns of the techniques of crime and the more a person learns to see the activity in a favourable light.

**Social process theories,** like that of Sutherland, look at how people come to have beliefs and knowledge that predispose them to criminality. The idea that criminal behaviour is normal, learned behaviour was taken up by many other criminologists, who also looked into the dynamics of learning crime. For instance, *social learning theory* (Akers, 1985) proposes that people have different settings in which they learn values and beliefs and in which they are rewarded or punished for behaviour. Not all of us learn that acts defined as illegal are to be avoided. We may also have role models whose behaviours—some of which may be illegal—we come to imitate.

Another set of social process theories that owe a debt to Sutherland are *cultural deviance* or *cultural conflict theories* of crime. These theories begin with the premise that we live in a complex society in which there is disagreement about conduct norms, particularly among different levels of the class structure and across ethnic groups. Thorsten Sellin (1958) argued that members within a subculture have to adapt to the conduct norms of these groups, which may put their conduct in conflict with the conduct norms (and legal norms) of the dominant culture. Such conflict occurs, for example, with the Rastafarian culture, as smoking marijuana is part of Rastafarian spiritual practice, but possession is illegal in Canada.

Various cultural conflict and cultural deviance theorists (see, for example, Miller, 1958; Wolfgang & Ferracuti, 1967) looked at differences in values and norms between the dominant culture and subcultural pockets of inner city populations. In the main, they argued that these subcultures can be distinguished in their focus on machismo, honour, excitement, fate, autonomy, and street smartness and toughness. These values place their members in conflict with the dominant culture, because membership in the subculture sometimes require actions, such as defence of honour, that will be defined as illegal.

Social process theorists do not necessarily hold that society is at root conflictual. In fact, most hold that there is widespread consensus about the norms of society. Both learning and cultural deviance theorists generally believe that the dominant culture is also legitimate in establishing legal norms, as does another group of theorists known as social control theorists.

*Social control theory* takes up a classical view by asking not why people commit crime, but what prevents many from doing so. Their answer is that some people have been better bonded to society and thus have a greater "stake in conformity" (Toby, 1957). Not only do they have more to lose by drifting into criminality because of their *attachment* to others, which makes them sensitive to others' evaluations of them, but they also have less free time to commit criminal acts because they are *involved* in many conventional activities and have become *committed* to the conventional order through their relationship with conventional institutions, such as school and employment. In addition to attachments, involvement, and commitment, Travis Hirschi (1969) adds that people differ in their bonding to the conventional order in their *belief* of social values.

# Social Structure Theories

If we want to know what causes crime, we cannot ignore features of social organization. We have already summarized the argument of cultural deviance theory that cultural conflict can produce the criminalization of behaviour in one group. We have also seen the hypothesis of bonding theory that differences in how people are integrated into society will have an impact on their likelihood of becoming criminal. *Social structure theories,* however, seek explanations of criminality not so much in the relationship of the individual to social institutions, but in the characteristics of society itself. In this respect, social structure theory is macrotheoretical, because it focuses on crime rates, rather than on criminal behaviour (Williams & McShane, 1999).

## Anomie, Strain, and Opportunity

In Russia and South Africa today, crime rates are much higher than anywhere else in the world. Why? Do biological differences between Russians or South Africans and the rest of the world explain the higher crime rates? Is there more cultural conflict? Surely Russia has less cultural conflict than, say, Belgium or Canada. The answer to changes in crime rates must be found not by looking at determinants of individual variation, but instead by looking at changes in social organization.

In his study *Suicide,* Emile Durkheim (1897/1951) found that suicides were more numerous during periods of economic and political instability and crisis. He argued that a condition of social disorganization characterized by economic and political instability is one in which the norms of society are also no longer effective in regulating behaviour. This is a condition of normlessness, or *anomie,* to which suicide is a response. In addition to suicide, the absence of sufficient regulation in society also unleashes the passions and aspirations of individuals in other acts, some of which will be criminal. The collapse of Communism in Russia and the ending of apartheid in South Africa released aspirations for wealth attainment in both these societies, which, in the absence of legal opportunities to gain wealth and sufficient regulation, have produced skyrocketing crime.

Taking Durkheim's idea of anomie, Robert K. Merton later modified it and developed **strain theory,** which argued that societies stimulate aspirations as socially approved goals, but that the legitimate means to achieve these goals are unequally distributed (1938). Merton saw the relationship as involving a number of possible outcomes, depending on the fit between the values or goals of a society and the distribution of access or means to goal achievement.

The accumulation of money, as well as the status that results from material wealth, is the universal goal of Americans. There are also socially structured means for achieving this goal, such as schooling. However, the availability of the means is unevenly distributed in society. Some parents may force their children to work and may be unsupportive of their attending school, compromising their children's ability to meet societal goals through legitimate means. The gap between the goal of material wealth and the means of these children is wider than for children whose parents have a lot of economic, cultural, and social capital.

As Bernard (1987) argues, the theory is meant to be applied to the behaviour of aggregates in society, rather than individuals. As an example, where structural features create an uneven distribution of legitimate opportunities, there will be pockets of instrumental crime. However, many people have used the theory to explain individual-level action, such as conformity, innovation, and ritualism. They have looked not at groups that are blocked from achieving their goals and their behaviour, but at individuals who are blocked and their behaviour.

The individual who wants to achieve the cultural goal via institutionalized means has no problem in adapting and thus is a *conformist*. The individual who aspires to the goal but has insufficient means must adapt through *innovation* of means, which may be an innovation involving criminality. Other modes of adaptation are *ritualism,* in which the individual has no great aspiration for the cultural goal and so is content to follow institutionalized means—in other words, the individual goes through the motions. A *retreatist* is someone who neither aspires to cultural goals nor follows its prescribed means; a member of an alternative

FIGURE 4.2

----------------------------------------------------------------------

TYPOLOGY OF INDIVIDUAL MODES OF ADAPTATION

| Modes of Adaptation | Cultural Goals | Institutionalized Means |
| --- | :---: | :---: |
| Conformity | + | + |
| Innovation | + | – |
| Ritualism | – | + |
| Retreatism | – | – |
| Rebellion | +/– | +/– |

Source: R. Merton. 1957. *Social Theory and Social Structure*. Glencoe, IL: Free Press.

community is an example. Finally, a *rebel* seeks to substitute society's cultural goals with different ones, possibly through political revolution.

## Further Developments in Strain Theory

Missing from Merton's theory, in the opinion of Richard Cloward and Lloyd Ohlin (1960), was reference to the fact that illegitimate means are not equally available to everyone. These authors argue that while people may be strained in their ability to meet goals with the means at their disposal, people do not necessarily have access to the means of crime. They argue that just as there are legitimate opportunity structures, there are also illegitimate opportunity structures, which not everyone has access to. Perhaps there have been times when many of us would have joined a criminal gang, had it been available and accepting of us, but thankfully for law-abiding citizens, such access is not routinely available for most adolescents. This argument follows up Sutherland's fourth principle of differential association—that learning criminal behaviour depends on learning the techniques of committing the crime.

Albert Cohen (1955) also expands on Merton's theory. He argues that at least some crime attributed to people from lower-class backgrounds is committed by boys who act to show their rejection of middle-class values, which they cannot hope to measure up to. Some of them react through negativistic and nonutilitarian criminal activity in order to reclaim their status. Although stretching the definition of this motivation, an example is the two youths who shot thirteen fellow students at Columbine High in the spring of 1999, before turning their weapons on themselves, apparently in reaction to being unable to satisfy the status requirements of being a jock. The "Trenchcoat Mafia," which they are said to have been members of, was a subculture that existed in defiance of the mainstream cultural values at the school and served as an alternative source of status.

Cohen argues that a "middle-class measuring rod" consists of a number of values, including ambition, individual responsibility, cultivation of skills, respect for property, and deferred gratification. These values, Cohen argues, are more formidable challenges to people whose backgrounds have deprived them of various forms of capital (social, economic, or moral).

Steven Messner and Richard Rosenfeld (1994) have added to a growing list of theorists in the strain tradition by arguing that the "American dream" of material success attained through individual competition is a double-edged sword. Individual success often comes at a cost, and that cost is in other societal tasks that are not primarily economic in nature. Education, for example, once ideally an end in itself, is increasingly supported only where it can be shown to add economic value to individual and social life. Messner and Rosenfeld (1994, p. 68) argue that the American dream itself exerts pressure toward crime because it invites an "anomic cultural environment" where people adopt an "anything goes" attitude in the pursuit of personal goals.

This theory is much like *relative deprivation theory* (Blau & Blau, 1982), according to which much violence and crime are seen as the result of frustrations experienced by people who are relatively poor and who live near others who are economically advantaged. Elliott Currie (1998) also argues that market societies are particularly prone to violent crime because they chip away at informal support networks, withdraw public provisions, and force most people to make a hard choice between low-wage labour and unemployment. Much of this argument restates Willem Bonger's work, first published in 1916, in which he argued that the drive to economic success in capitalist societies pushes rich and poor alike into criminality.

## Social Ecology and Disorganization

In the town or city in which you live (assuming that you do live in one), you have probably noticed that certain areas are better maintained than others. If it is a city you live in, such as Toronto or Vancouver, you have probably noticed, as well, that there are different ethnic areas. There is a growing Chinatown in both of these cities, and there are dozens of other areas—Italian, Portuguese, Tamil, Somali, and Jamaican, to name just a few. Back in the 1940s in Chicago, Clifford Shaw and Henry McKay noticed this too. Building on the previous work of University of Chicago colleague Robert Park, they hypothesized a relationship between social disorganization and the movement of immigrant populations through Chicago. They also wondered if delinquency was something that did not belong to the group so much as to the place the group occupies on the map of Chicago.

Shaw and McKay (1969) pinpointed crime incidents over time on a large map of Chicago and found that crime was related to community variables, such as a decreasing population, a high percentage of foreign-born heads of families, and a low rate of home ownership. Using this data, they argued that delinquency was related to the social disorganization of place and to the physical structure of the city. Immigrants tend to move to areas of lower rents when they first arrive in a city, which in Chicago then, and in other cities still, is close to the central business district, in what they called *transitional neighbourhoods*. Because this zone is one in which people take up what they hope is temporary residence, the area lacks sufficient interest from residents in durable, formal, and informal social controls. People do not develop a stake in the community. Indeed, Shaw and McKay used various census data to confirm that there is an internal migration in the city from the transitional zone outward, and that crime rates also decline the farther into the suburbs a person moves.

# Social Reaction Theories

## Labelling

Much thinking about crime causation focuses on the biology, nature, and social environment of the individual. The individual chooses or is determined to commit criminal acts. **Social reaction theories** follow social learning inasmuch as they agree that criminal behaviour is learned. But they also place more emphasis on the interaction between social control agents, such as the courts, the police, and schools, and the individual. They remind us that what Sutherland calls "definitions" favourable to the commission of crime are followed by societal reaction to the criminal act. These reactions then help to shape the individual's identity. According to **labelling theories,** when a judge tells a youth, "You are first and foremost a thief," this formal, powerful reaction "labels" the youth, and the youth is more likely to act according to this label.

Howard Becker went even further than this, however. He broke from the consensus view of criminality by saying that "deviant behaviour is behaviour that people so label" (1963, p. 9). He argued that rather than focusing on how the individual is deviant, we need to recognize that there is no deviance until social groups create deviance by making rules "whose infraction constitutes deviance." Becker argued that much more attention needs to be given to the *social reactors* rather than to the individual designated by agents of social control as the criminal.

Labelling theorists like Lemert (1967) argued that in no small part the social reaction to the first act of deviance *(primary deviance)* imposes social penalties that cause further deviance, in a spiral that will eventually lead the individual to accord with the view of the social reactors that he is indeed, first and foremost, a deviant. This labelling effect, in which the individual accepts the social view of himself and acts accordingly, Lemert referred to as *secondary deviance.*

Labelling theory has influenced social policy. In the 1960s and 1970s, policies were launched to minimize the labelling of youths, including programs that sought to correct youths within the community. *Diversion* is a program that came straight out of labelling theory. This program allows youths to avoid the stigma of delinquency by giving those convicted of minor criminal offences the chance to be placed in informal programs at arm's length from the correctional system. Perhaps the most lasting influence of labelling theory on policy was the deinstitutionalization movement of the late 1960s and the 1970s. Liberals teamed up with fiscal conservatives to decry the warehousing of people who were mentally ill and also to restrict the use of prison to serious offenders. Although many mentally ill were released into halfway houses, incarceration rates for criminal offenders climbed.

## Conflict Criminology

While consensus theories are concerned with explaining the causes of deviation from social norms, **conflict criminology** is concerned with explaining how social control agents and agencies behave. The conflict perspective holds that there is an ongoing contest for power in society, and that the criminal law and the various agencies of law enforcement act, either directly or indirectly, in the interests of the powerful.

The central task of criminology from a conflict perspective is not to explain what causes criminal behaviour, but rather to explain the process by which certain behaviours and individuals are formally designated as criminal. For many consensus theorists, the social reaction to crime consists simply of actions that crime control authorities take to represent society's interests in being protected from crime. Conflict theorists argue that this social reaction is really an opportunity to consolidate power around specific interests and values that the powerful in society wish to uphold. While most conflict theorists would accept that there is widespread interest in peaceful coexistence, they believe that this interest ought to be distinguished from a consensus about the specific values and interests that an act is alleged to have threatened. There is much conflict in society about the distribution of resources to meet threats to peace and about the best program of intervention. In addition, conflict theorists argue that the norms, values, and principles that the law seeks to defend are politicized to serve the ends of the powerful. In this way, conflict theorists see the law as serving political interests in resource distribution by those who have more power in the shaping of public issues. They see the work of law making and of norm clarification zealously championed by powerful interests who are attempting to maintain and justify their special claims.

An example is the *individualization* of the crime problem by powerful conservative interests. These interests view crime as a social problem resulting from the deviant motivation of bad actors, rather than from the strained relations of dysfunctional resource distributions. The laws that are made and the norms that are clarified are those that attribute the problem to bad actors in the underclass of society, to lax social control in the lower and under classes, and to failures of individual motivation and personal responsibility. These laws and norms serve to maintain status quo distributions of social resources. Policies that were mindful of the real threats to

the underclass would, conversely, look at income opportunities, blocks to upward mobility, relative deprivation, social disorganization, and so on, as the real threats to security. But those in power persist in enforcing remedies that guarantee the further insecurity of the underclass. The social reaction to crime becomes a ritual condemnation of individual failing.

## Policy Implications

Social structure, reaction, and process theories all have similar implications for policy, although the more radical criminologists on the Left contend that a revolution of the market and productive or reproductive systems is needed. However, more typical reforms are changes to resource distributions to combat social disorganization and to produce less economic disparity. As for the operation of the criminal law and of crime control agents, equal representation of ethnic, class, and gender groups is advocated. A more equitable distribution of punishments for wrongdoing is also favoured. The economic and environmental crimes of corporate actors (often protected by the dispersion of responsibility in corporations), conflict and critical criminologists argue, must be punished according to a more representative view of the harm done. Regulatory resources devoted to these crimes must also reflect widespread concern with the state of the environment and with some semblance of balance in the administration of justice across class.

## Conclusion

Attributing criminal responsibility is by no means a straightforward undertaking. It depends on a view of the nature of the individual and of the individual's relationship with social institutions and forces. It depends on whether one thinks that there is a strong consensus of values and norms in society. It also depends on how one conceives of the nature of social forces and institutions that require intervention. This chapter has summarized in large brushstrokes some of the thinking that has been done to account for the causes and attribution of crime and criminal responsibility. Much of this theory has been tested, and at best, a single theory accounts for only a fraction of the total possible causes. Today, many theories are brought together in integrated theories of crime causation, which account for more of the difference between those who commit crimes and those who do not.

## Summary

This chapter has presented a brief overview of the history of crime theorizing. In general, there has been a movement between theories that argue that the criminal actor is a rational calculator, and theories that argue that the criminal is determined by social, biological, or environmental forces. We have stressed that despite the confluence of cause and responsibility in the actor of classical penal theory, there is an important distinction between attributions of responsibility and cause, which is recognized in social policy since the failure of first attempts to codify Beccaria's principles. In searching for causes of crime, we have seen that theorists have not only probed within the human body for evidence of abnormalities, but have also turned to contexts, including social disorganization and strain, and to the operation of the criminal justice system itself.

## Key Terms

choice-structuring properties (p. 78)

classical criminology (p. 73)

conflict criminology (p. 96)

deterrence theory (p. 76)

hedonistic calculus (p. 73)

labelling theories (p. 95)

positivist criminology (p. 81)

rational choice theory (p. 78)

routine activities theory (p. 79)

social process theories (p. 90)

social reaction theories (p. 95)

strain theory (p. 92)

tipping level (p. 76)

# Discussion Questions

1. Do theories of crime help us to determine legal responsibility for criminal behaviour? If not, why not?

2. Is social policy today more classical or more positivistic in orientation? Provide an example of recent legislation that illustrates your view.

3. Do you agree with social reaction theorists that how we formally react to crime may be at least as important as the fact that we react? Which social theorist has made the fact that we react central?

4. Why do you think biological explanations of criminal behaviour are becoming popular again?

# Weblinks

**www.soros.org/crime/research_brief__1.html** The Center on Crime, Communities and Culture offers an excellent resource brief on mental illness in US prisons. The site also offers links to studies on domestic violence and gun control.

**www.crimetheory.com/Reading/further.htm** The University of Washington offers a bibliography of criminal theory resources, some of which are online. Subject areas include labelling, race and gender issues, historical perspectives, and cultural conflict.

**www.ccsd.ca/cp/index.htm** The Canadian Council on Social Development has set up a Web resource in collaboration with the National Crime Prevention Centre, to explore issues of crime prevention through social development. The site offers statistics, news, and links to other relevant resources.

**wcr.sonoma.edu** The Western Criminology Review (WCR) is a forum for the publication and discussion of theory, research, policy, and practice in the fields of criminology and criminal justice.

**www.uiowa.edu/~030116/158/articles/dershowitz1.htm** Written by the famous American lawyer Alan Dershowitz, this article takes aim at the PMS defense. p. 99

# CHAPTER 5

# Law and Social Control

## Objectives

- To outline the methods by which the criminal justice system uses criminal law to control society and affirm the dominant societal values.

- To analyze the impact of special interest groups on the criminal justice system.

- To highlight the disproportionate number of Aboriginal peoples and other minority groups in the prison system as evidence of bias in the criminal justice system.

- To discuss the influence of the criminal law on social control and social change.

## Law and Society

What is the role of the law in society? How does the judicial system decide what is "wrong," and whose interests does the criminal law serve? When we examine the criminal justice system, we may conclude that Canada has made a deliberate policy decision to use the criminal law as an instrument to control Canadians' moral conduct and to affirm certain dominant moral values. However, many critics believe that using the law to promote morality is not only problematic and possibly futile, but also has major repercussions on our understanding of crime in Canada and our attempts to solve it. Hills (1971) believes that the consequences to societies that use the law to symbolize morality include overburden-

ing law enforcement and judicial administration. As well, when minor "morality crimes" are brought before the courts, the effectiveness of the justice system to deal with more serious crimes is compromised. Furthermore, by branding certain behaviours as criminal, the criminal justice system may actually encourage the growth of organized crime.

Larsen and Burtch (1999) state that the criminal law is the best example of an influential group's attempts to control the behaviour of Canadians. The law acts as an instrument of coercion by imposing **criminal sanctions,** or penalties to enforce obedience to the law, on behaviour that is considered threatening to the dominant group's values. However, while agreeing that certain types of behaviour, such as murder, robbery, and assault, are a threat to society, these authors believe that using the criminal law to control **moral behaviour,** or behaviour reflecting societal standards of right and wrong, is unacceptable. They argue that the state may inadvertently be contributing to problems of crime control by attempting to control moral behaviour in **victimless crimes**—crimes that are considered to have no victims because the participants are willing, such as drug use, prostitution, and pornography. By prohibiting the goods and services that the public demands, the criminal law may serve to inflate the price of the illegal product and encourage organized criminals to provide the demanded services. These prohibitions serve the role of creating monopolistic, strongly organized crime syndicates, whose huge profits allow them to expand and diversify. Of more serious concern is the fact that when the demand for the product is created by a physical addiction, such as drug addiction, high prices lead to the vicious cycle of secondary crime. Offenders commit crimes so that they can procure the money to purchase the illicit products.

Hills (1971) also believes that criminal sanctions against such victimless behaviours as gambling, sexual deviation, obscenity, drugs, or prostitution are almost unenforceable. Legislating private moral behaviour where the social danger is absent or difficult to assess can mean diverting the scarce resources of the justice system from those deviant behaviours that generate national consensus. In the absence of victims willing to testify in court against such crimes, the police often rely on informers and on contacts with the underworld. Recent judicial decisions have shown that Charter infringements on the legal rights of defendants, involving illegal search and seizure, false arrests, harassment, entrapment, and other illegal police practices, have been inordinately high in public morality crimes. Increasingly, critics have suggested that using the criminal law to prosecute victimless crimes provides the breeding ground for bribery and police corruption. Furthermore, because of the sporadic nature of law enforcement and the absence of any clearly definable social danger, these laws are violated with impunity, encouraging disrespect for the legal process and cynicism toward the criminal justice system.

When victimless crimes are prosecuted, judges often have to impose severe and mandatory sentences on offenders. As we saw in Chapter 3, the Supreme Court of Canada deemed as "cruel and unusual punishment" the sentence of seven years for marijuana possession. It is important for the Canadian judicial system to review the impact of the criminalization process for the wide variety of moral crimes. Would it not be more in keeping with the goal of moral and societal responsibility if the law were to concentrate on prosecuting possession and trafficking of hard drugs such as heroin and cocaine? Similarly, in terms of societal harm would it not be more responsible to focus on prosecuting purveyors of child pornography and child prostitution, rather than to use the present scattered gun and unenforceable approaches to the law?

It is clear that criminalizing morality diverts scarce law enforcement resources from the more serious crime problems, on which there is societal consensus. Crimes of violence, property crime, and white-collar crime pose a greater threat to the values of society. Relying on the law to deal with the public drunk, the prostitute, or the user of soft drugs such as marijuana is too often a repetitive process of arrest, short-term incarceration, and rearrest. The only outcome is a continuous overburdening of the branches of the justice system—the police, the courts, and the prisons. The final proof of the futility of the process is that in the history of prosecution for these offences in Canadian courts, very few of the major traffickers in gambling and drugs, and few, if any, of the producers of child pornography, are ever arrested and successfully prosecuted. As we move into the next millennium, Canada must seriously ponder the effects of overcriminalization and an overreliance on the criminal law to legislate morality. By arresting and convicting large numbers of people for such crimes as soft drug use, prostitution, gambling, or public drunkenness, the police and the criminal justice system are playing to the court of public opinion and to those who believe that such laws protect the moral standards of the community.

# Interest Groups and Law Enforcement

## Community Interest Groups

Increasingly, special **interest groups** (groups of people with a common interest or goal) are playing a role in the criminal justice system in Canada, in terms of both the development and the enforcement of criminal laws. Hills (1971) notes that the criminal law is a living, dynamic entity that takes its scope and meaning from its interpretation and application. Contrary to the rhetoric of justice officials, the enforcement and application of the Criminal Code is a highly selective process. For example, police officers decide which "suspicious" people to question and detain; judges decide whom to convict and the sentence to be attached to the conviction; and prosecutors decide who should be charged, the severity of the offence, and whether a plea bargain would be accepted.

The decisions by the police, the courts, and the judicial process in total are subject to the ability of interest groups to manipulate the system. A classic example of conflict between police and community groups is the attempt to control prostitution in our large cities. Because soliciting for prostitution is a relatively minor offence, most police forces would prefer not to devote their scarce resources to prosecuting this crime. However, in all our large urban centres, interest groups made up of business and residential owners bring immense political pressure on the police to control this social problem through legal means, even though their attempts have little impact. Since 1985, when Bill C-49 was proclaimed to toughen the law related to communication for the purposes of prostitution, the conflict has raged between interest groups. On one side are those who see the criminal law as a method for solving the problems associated with street prostitution, and on the other are the many civil rights groups who believe that the law is draconian, virtually unenforceable, and discriminatory against the street prostitute compared to other types of "sex for hire" workers. The failure of the legal system to control this form of behaviour in Canada reveals the problems that can result when law enforcement and the criminal law are driven by the needs of pressure and interest groups.

## Economic and Corporate Interest Groups

An example of the opposite impact of interest groups is the clearly biased interpretation of the criminal law in the nonprosecution of **corporate crime**—crime committed by businesses. Larsen and Burtch (1999) outline the ability of powerful economic and corporate interest groups to exploit human and natural resources, pollute the environment, form illegal monopolies, fix prices of goods and services, and manipulate the stock market, and yet to have all of these activities classified as legal behaviour. These authors believe that although corporate criminality is widespread in Canada, seldom are any of the activities clearly defined as Criminal Code violations, and thus are not prosecuted. Furthermore, if prosecution occurs it is usually through quasi-judicial tribunals, and fines are the major form of deterrence. Since these fines are paid out of corporate profits, the punishment fails to deter the deviant behaviour.

That corporate crime affects large numbers of Canadians is undeniable. Yet that those inappropriate behaviours are rarely defined and regulated by criminal law is also undeniable. Corporate interest groups often control and manipulate the law-making process and influence the legislators. The norm has been for special regulatory agencies, rather than the punitive criminal law, to handle morally reprehensible behaviour by the business class. Furthermore, although some of these behaviours may be classified under the criminal law, they are poorly enforced, reflecting the symbolic nature of legislation and enforcement. Larsen and Burtch (1999) believe that because of the immense influence of corporate interest groups on lawmakers, these interest groups are often involved in the process of defining inappropriate corporate behaviour.

Given the influence of these interest groups on law making, it is not surprising that street and property crime dominate Canada's Criminal Code. Corporate special interest groups protect their position of influence and power by attributing criminality to the powerless in society and using the criminal justice system as an instrument of coercion and force. It is clear that the individuals and groups who are most likely to be affected by law enforcement are those whose behaviours the dominant interest groups perceive as threatening. The danger in our society occurs when the values and norms of particular interest groups become incorporated into criminal law and the justice system. In our heterogeneous society, those who do not subscribe to these values and norms run the risk of being discriminated against by the legal system that was supposed to protect their rights.

If, in fact, the probability of being labelled deviant and subject to the criminal law depends on a person's social and economic position, then Canada's criminal law and justice system needs to be revised. When special interest groups use the legal system to maintain inordinate power and influence, the result is not only dysfunctional, but also conflictual. Unfortunately, in the court of public opinion, corporate crime ranks low on the scale of criminal behaviour. The public has accepted the belief that street crime is the form of crime that is most harmful to society and most threatening to the community. Therefore, street crime continues to attract the greatest public condemnation and most of the resources of the police and the courts. The public has bought into the idea that corporations are the purveyors of prosperity who keep the economy running and the Canadian people prosperous and economically satisfied. We have attempted to show that while many interest groups have successfully manipulated the law enforcement process, none has been as influential as the corporate interest group. Inevitably, the outcome of this influence is the compromising of the Canadian criminal justice system.

## The Experience of Minority Groups

Interest groups and law enforcement have played a role in the clear overrepresentation of minority groups in Canada's criminal justice system. Larsen and Burtch (1999) believe that the treatment of minority groups can be considered a test of the overall fairness of the legal system. Most modern Western legal systems embrace principles of equality before the law for all citizens. At the practical level, however, systemic discrimination in the justice system against racial and ethnic minorities is also widely practised.

In Canada, there are myriad examples of discrimination based on ethnicity, gender, and sexual orientation. But the greatest injustice, both in the past and today, has been the treatment of Aboriginal peoples by the Canadian criminal justice system. In terms of their percentage of the Canadian population, Aboriginal people are grossly overrepresented in all parts of the criminal justice system. Their treatment cries out for a major policy change in the Criminal Code definition and interpretation of criminal behaviour. The Canadian criminal justice system rests on the assumption that punishing deviant behaviour will increase compliance and assist in maintaining social order. However, it is the powerful interest groups in society that control the legislative process and decide what behaviour is normative or deviant. These interest groups also decide on methods to ensure compliance, such as imprisonment, fines, probation, or community service. Given the overrepresentation of Aboriginal people in the courts and prisons, it should be obvious to those who wield power in the criminal justice system that the correlation between punishment and compliance is not supported by the evidence. As Barsh and Marlor (1999) note, the disproportionate number of Aboriginal people in Canadian prisons has fuelled Aboriginal leaders' demands for an alternative approach to handling crime and punishment. These leaders suggest that through **community policing** (policing by officers who are part of the community), community control of sentencing, and greater interest group participation in defining criminal behaviour, more positive structural changes will result and incarceration rates of Aboriginal people will be reduced.

## The Challenge for the Justice System

Canada today is made up of a collection of interest groups representing myriad populations, be they social, economic, or political. To have one or a few powerful interest groups continue to define criminal behaviour using a homogeneous societal model is dysfunctional and, as seen by the experience of Aboriginal peoples, grossly unjust and unfair. The challenge for society, therefore, is to create a more inclusive legal system, one that allows for wider interest group participation in defining societal norms. As well, alternative mechanisms to obtain compliance are required.

To the objective outsider, it should be clear that the criminal justice system, in many respects, is an inefficient and dysfunctional system that is increasingly failing in its role of maintaining social order. Although the methods of alternative conflict management, such as healing or sentencing circles, may be inappropriate in urban Canada, they are worthwhile alternatives for Aboriginal communities in rural and northern Canada. In fact, negotiated justice is receiving increased attention in legal circles. The problem is that mediation, diversion, and

healing circles, while accepted as alternatives to traditional law enforcement processes, remain a weak junior partner to the established criminal justice system. Until alternative treatments and their proponents are given an equal role in the power structure and the legal system, their effectiveness will remain marginal.

The challenge for the Canadian justice system and law enforcement is to return power to the grassroots and remove it from powerful interest groups. Nergard (1993) believes that negotiated justice is a first step in this direction. The fact that judges in the North are increasingly using alternative sentencing practices and that the Supreme Court has advised judges to explore alternatives to sentencing when dealing with Aboriginal people are signs of positive change in our justice system. We must be aware, however, that powerful economic interest groups will not easily relinquish their hold on traditional justice in favour of alternatives that may, in fact, be more successful in obtaining compliance. Barsh and Marlor (1999) note that while negotiated justice holds out the hope that lawbreakers can be rehabilitated effectively and without incarceration, there is an increasing criticism of and backlash against programs that may be perceived as protecting the offender.

The onus is on the criminal justice system to represent the interests of all of Canada's people and groups. It has left itself open to criticism that minorities are not treated fairly by all branches of the justice system—the police, the courts, and the prison system. Countless investigations and inquiries bear this criticism out, and the evidence of systemic discrimination is overwhelming. Canada is today an amalgam of different ethnic and cultural groups, and our criminal law and justice system must eventually reflect this heterogeneity. To do otherwise will only continue to bring disrepute to the institution. To court the eventual breakdown of law and order through an inability to obtain the cooperation of disenfranchised groups is surely not the direction that our society should take.

Canada's culture, structure, and societal diversity have changed immensely when compared to the 19th century, when our nation was created. Today, our criminal laws create great strain and inequality for many individuals and groups, and we must be aware of the diversity of values and lifestyles in our midst. The increasing conflicts among various interest groups, the changing distribution of power, and rapid social and cultural change all point to a need for re-evaluation of the criminal justice system. By advocating inclusiveness in decision making by interest groups, a fair and just legal system can be created. As well, the justice system needs to address the following issues. A re-examination of the processes through which behaviour is defined as criminal, specifically in the light of Canada's multicultural society, is imperative. Furthermore, analysis of the impact that unequal enforcement and interpretation of the criminal law by police and the judiciary has on society, as well as of the effect of the criminal law process on both individuals and society, will provide the framework for a justice system that reflects our present norms and values.

# Criminal Law as a Mechanism of Social Control

## Informal and Formal Social Control

Rush (1994) notes that **social control** is the way in which societies encourage conformity. As a result of social control mechanisms, the majority of society's members accept the normative controls of the state; they know that supporting the legal norms will be rewarded and that nonconformist behaviour will result in sanctions, including fines and imprisonment. Social control operates on both informal and formal levels. *Informal social controls* are the unwritten codes of behaviour that the majority of small groups follow in everyday social interaction. While there is no formal sanction for failing to follow informal codes of behaviour, conformity is maintained through social pressure from other group members. *Formal social controls* are those that are legislated and form the written body of our civil and criminal legal codes. Statutory law, for example, dictates interpersonal behaviour through our highway traffic laws or behaviour related to business practices. When these formal social controls are violated, the negative sanctions can be severe.

Grana and Ollenburger (1999) note that the internalization of formal and informal social controls is an ongoing part of the socialization process. Through this process we learn who we are, how we should relate to society, and what our relationships are with others. Built into the socialization process are the control mechanisms that dictate how we learn skills and knowledge, how we can realize our aspirations, and how we can recognize our limitations. We also learn who in society occupies the positions of influence and power. Through socialization, the individual learns to accept, distrust, or reject authority and to admire, fear, or hate others in the society. For all of us, sanctions, whether they are positive or negative, are affected by our gender, ethnicity, and social status.

## The Effectiveness of Deterrence

Canada and other Western countries use criminal law to deter nonconformist or deviant behaviour, yet many social philosophers have questioned the effectiveness of deterrence in obtaining social conformity. Both Beccaria (1764/1963) and Bentham (1789/1988) noted that in early modern societies, deterrence was effective depending on the severity, the certainty, and the swiftness of the punishment. However, many modern criminologists have argued that deterrence may not be the most effective method of obtaining adherence to the criminal law. They believe that in prohibiting a behaviour, the state and the legislature are specifying a legal threat in order to obtain social control. However, the effectiveness of the legal sanction depends on the individual's response to it. Some people may conform as a result of the threat, others may change the style or frequency of the behaviour, and still others may refuse to accept that the behaviour in question is deviant. The point is that although deterrence is intended to eliminate certain behaviours that the state deems undesirable, its success is not overwhelming or guaranteed. Weinberg and Weinberg (1980) believe that the effectiveness of the criminal law varies depending on the personality and characteristics of individuals, as well as the social circumstances they face. For example, regardless of criminal sanctions, members of the drug subculture persist in using or trafficking in illegal drugs because they have failed to internalize society's attitudes toward drug use and believe that they will either not get caught or will be acquitted of the charge. However, as Grana and Ollenburger (1999) note, the majority of Canadians believe that the law is an effective means of social control, and that by attaching punishments to violations of our Criminal Code, we reduce **deviance,** or behaviour that does not conform with societal standards. The public perception is that legal sanctions at least serve as a guide as to right and proper behaviour, and at best they reduce the rate of crime.

But law can be useful to society as more than a means of controlling behaviour. Vago (2000) notes the importance of law as a means of conflict resolution and management in modern Canadian society. Dispute resolution can take many forms, including negotiation, mediation, arbitration, or plea bargaining. While most social conflicts may be resolved in noncriminal courts, using civil means of redress, plea bargaining is increasingly being used as a means of obtaining justice and settling legal disputes. However, many critics believe that the choice of either pleading guilty or going to trial is not a positive use of the criminal law. While bargain justice reduces the overcrowding of the court system, a major criticism of this approach is the view that there is no justice without a trial.

Vago notes that the criminal law is a highly structured means of social control. These laws define criminal behaviour and specify the sanctions to be imposed for violations. In both Canada and the United States, the law is increasingly being relied on to regulate behaviour. As we define more and more forms of behaviour as criminal, the various parts of the criminal justice system—the police, the courts, and the prison system—are more often formally involved in the process, and the percentage of the population labelled as criminals or deviants also increases. Therefore, in using the criminal law as a means of social control, we need to define criminal behaviour in the context of societal harm, rather than use it as an instrument to achieve the goals of a narrow, elitist power structure. We need to ask such questions as, Should we continue to invest the immense amount of financial and human resources to label and prosecute victimless crimes? In a heterogeneous society, should social norms be broadened to take into account cultural and social diversity? It is increasingly debatable whether social order is improved by criminalizing acts against public decency or morality, such as prostitution or gambling, when there is no consensus that these acts are actually criminal. As Vago notes, when these laws are enforced against lower-class and minority group members, the perception is reinforced among the power elite that the law is effective in prosecuting those who they insist are the real deviants in the society. More important, by staging frequent purges of immorality, the police receive the support of communities, which see the police acting to protect community moral standards. Yet the futility of using the criminal justice system to enforce special interest laws has not yet become apparent to our lawmakers and justice officials, and removing the criminal label and sanction from crimes of morality remains a highly controversial issue in our society.

# Criminal Law and Social Change

It is clearly documented that the criminal law has been used not only to obtain social control and compliance, but also to transform society. The colonization of Canada by the English and French in the 17th century is a classic example of the use of law to define the legal role and status of Aboriginal peoples. Through coercion, threats, and criminal sanctions, the colonizers forced Aboriginal people off their land and onto reserves. With the passing of legislation titled the

Indian Act, Aboriginal people became wards of the state and totally dependant on the federal government for the necessities of life. Caputo, Kennedy, Reasons, and Brannigan (1989) argue that colonizers used the law to deculturate and destroy the social and economic organization of Aboriginal people in Canada. Today, Aboriginal people have been left with an incarceration rate that is 10 times higher than for any other racial or ethnic group in Canada. This use of the criminal law to create subordinate and dominant groups is an example of the negative effects of using law to change society.

In some cases, laws can create positive changes in society. For example, as Grana and Ollenburger (1999) note, changing patterns of domestic relationships cause changes in divorce law, which also have an effect on society's view of marriage. The Canadian Charter of Rights and Freedoms has had a dramatic effect on criminal law and on the concept of justice in society. The fact that the courts could actually create laws, rather than simply enforce them, is creating a new function of the law as an instrument of social change. Vago (2000) notes both the positive and negative effects of using the law for this purpose. Because both criminal and civil law have the power to impose negative sanctions, they can encourage society to overcome its resistance to change. For example, if the law supports equal employment opportunities for designated groups, then employers, although they may be reluctant, will have to accept these legally sanctioned societal changes to avoid the negative sanctions imposed for noncompliance. This is a clear example of the coercive effect of the law. Because many people see the law as representing authority and believe that it is their obligation to obey it, they see the need for compliance. As well, because the law represents social order for the majority of Canadians, they accept its role in the socialization process and prefer consensus on issues rather than conflict. Legally dictated societal change, therefore, is accepted. However, when laws are created that further social ends, but that go against the social, economic, or moral principles of powerful interest groups, then conflict rather than consensus could be the outcome. For example, gun control laws in both Canada and the United States have met with immense opposition because these laws conflict with the views of many powerful interest groups. In this case, the effectiveness of the law as an agent of social change has been diminished. As Vago notes, the views of the powerful can negate the views of the oppressed or the majority.

Society also enacts public policy through the criminal law. In the past 25 years, major changes to public policy, including the legalization of abortion, the decriminalization of homosexuality, the abolition of capital punishment, and the enactment of gun control legislation, have been administered through the criminal law and the criminal justice system. The state is always attempting to control behaviour, and using the law is the most effective method of ensuring compliance. For example, without legal sanctions would the majority of Canadians wear seat belts or avoid drinking and driving? It is clear from examples such as these

that the criminal law can be a major means of societal change. If laws are presented as rational and fair to all groups, then acceptance will be positive. If enforcement is immediate and the criminal justice system is committed to the public policy, and if the positive or negative sanctions are clearly delineated, then compliance will outweigh resistance.

## Conclusion

Law is the major method of control in our society, and it uses punishment to regulate behaviour. Vago (2000) notes that Canada's highly structured and formalized criminal justice system uses elaborate techniques and methods to limit and control deviant behaviour. The Criminal Code, which contains all of Canada's criminal laws, incorporates the punishments for law violators, who are punished according to society's perception of the severity of the deviance. However, the use of the criminal justice system to control victimless crimes has generated considerable debate. Many critics believe that attempting to control crimes such as drug addiction, gambling, or prostitution through the legal system is not only expensive, but is also an ineffective method of controlling this type of behaviour. Critics also point to the minimal prosecutions for white-collar, corporate, or environmental crimes as evidence of manipulation of the legal institution by powerful interest groups. Yet the search for equity and justice for all groups in society, while a difficult task, is not without success in our institutional structure. A legal system that deals with crimes against society without favouring particular interest groups is on the track toward developing an equitable and fair society.

The basic premises of criminal law are that justice should be obtained by both the accused and the victim and that equity, fairness, and human rights should be guaranteed. Furthermore, as Caputo et al. (1989) note, the use of criminal law as a sanction should be invoked only as a last resort, when all other forms of social control have proved either inappropriate or ineffective. The law will be much more successful as an instrument of social change if this criterion is followed. Attempts to use the legal system to obtain social justice and social change should be seen as positive and applauded. The evidence is clear that when the law is designed to further the goals of social equity, has the support of important interest groups, and is in harmony with societal values, it will be a workable tool in the process of social change, while ultimately fulfilling its role as an agent of social control.

## Summary

This chapter has analyzed the role of law as a mechanism of social control. Individuals are socialized to behave in normative and societally accepted ways, and those who deviate from societal norms are subject to sanctions. These methods of social control can be either formal or informal. Informal social controls work best in small, face-to-face groups and in homogeneous societies. Because Canada's is a heterogeneous, complex society, with many interest groups, various racial and ethnic groups, a sophisticated division of labour, and differing adherence to mores, values, and ideologies, formal social control mechanisms are often necessary to ensure compliance among group members. Therefore, Canada relies on the criminal law as a method of controlling the moral conduct of Canadians and of affirming society's dominant moral values. The law acts as an instrument of coercion, but critics are increasingly questioning whether the criminal process should be used to control moral behaviour in victimless crime. Instead, they suggest that the police and the law should concentrate on the more serious crime problems on which there is societal consensus, such as robbery, sexual assault, murder, and fraud and embezzlement.

Increasingly, interest group manipulation of the criminal justice system is compromising its fairness and impartiality. For example, although corporate crimes are widespread in Canada, seldom are these activities punished as Criminal Code violations. Furthermore, discrimination against racial minorities is clearly documented in the criminal justice system. The challenge for the justice system and law enforcement is to create a system that reflects in its laws the heterogeneity of the society, that recognizes the strains that are present, and that re-evaluates the rationale for defining specific behaviours as nonconformist and criminal.

## Key Terms

community policing (p. 105)
corporate crime (p. 103)

criminal sanctions (p. 101)

deviance (p. 108)

interest groups (p. 102)

moral behaviour (p. 101)

social control (p. 107)

victimless crime (p. 101)

## Discussion Questions

1. Discuss the ways in which the criminal law acts as an instrument of coercion and social control.

2. Discuss the effect on the criminal justice system of special interest groups.

3. Describe the impact on ethnic minority groups of discrimination in the criminal justice system.

4. What are some of the positive effects that laws have on society?

## Weblinks

**www.ccla.org** The Canadian Civil Liberties Association (CCLA) is a non-profit lobby group dealing with issues of civil liberties. Their Web site offers information about CCLA's efforts as Canada's civil liberties watchdog, as well as CCLA history, news, and relevant links.

**home.istar.ca/~ccja/angl/aborit.html** This special issue of the Canadian Criminal Justice Association's Bulletin is on Aboriginal Peoples and the Criminal Justice System, and deals with the historic, demographic, social, political, and economic factors affecting aboriginal peoples in Canada's justice system.

**www.uncjin.org** The United Nations Crime and Justice Information Network (UNCJIN) is an electronic clearing-house coordinated by the United Nations Centre for International Crime Prevention, Vienna. The goal of the Centre is to act as coordinator and arbiter for the international exchange and dissemination of information on crime prevention and criminal justice issues.

**ssw.che.umn.edu/rjp/RJ-Sites.htm** The University of Minnesota's Center for Restorative Justice and Peacemaking Web site presents a great springboard for research on justice and social issues, with dozens of links to organizations and groups involved in criminal justice.

**www.lcc.gc.ca/en/papers/rapport/nathan/nathan.html** An academic study by York University's Nathanson Centre for the Study of Organized Crime and Corruption. The study considers how the concept of organized crime is used and misused in public discourse.

# CHAPTER 6

# The Police

## Objectives

- To describe the branches of law enforcement in Canada and their roles within the criminal justice system.

- To discuss the role of the police in crime prevention, law enforcement, public order maintenance, victim assistance, and emergency services.

- To portray both sides of the public debate over the issues of the powers, discretion, autonomy, and accountability of the police.

- To highlight the important initiative of community policing and the restructuring necessary to make this policy effective.

## Historical Development

Citizens in many other countries are often perplexed at how it is that Canada came to use a police figure as a national icon. In many other countries, including France, Jamaica, and India, the police could not serve to muster nationalistic pride. To understand how the Mountie has come to have this symbolic value, we need to talk a little about the history of Canadian policing.

In the 18th and early 19th centuries in Canada, policing was provided by four kinds of arrangements. First, there were regulations (called, interestingly, *police regulations*), which required householders to prevent disorder and crime. For example, they required that householders make available ladders and buckets in case of fire and keep basement entries to their houses locked to prevent unwanted

entry. Second, in towns there was often a nightly watch, which was staffed by able-bodied males as a duty of residency. Those on nightly watch would do set rounds, looking for suspicious activity or people and for signs of fire, and they would arrest and bring to a constable or a justice of the peace any person found breaching the peace or breaking the law. Third, there were amateur constables, appointed annually from the town or county rolls, who made arrests or carried out warrants on a fee-for-service basis (for example, getting a set amount for bringing a felon to jail). Fourth, in cases of public disorder or riot, there was a volunteer militia, which consisted of able-bodied men in the community who could be called on to suppress the affray.

Reformers of the day criticized these arrangements. They argued that the volunteer militia was a blunt and rusty instrument because of its sporadic use and lack of training. The watch was often subjected to ridicule for attracting fools and hoodlums, since the "better class" of men often deputized substitutes instead of doing their turn. The amateur constabulary suffered under a similar reputation in some parts of the country, as it was difficult to control and the men were viewed as either too inactive or too eager in collecting fees. Whether these charges were founded or not, in the 50-year period leading up to Confederation, a series of reforms took place at municipal, provincial, and federal levels, displacing the informal, voluntary, and part-time policing arrangements with full-time, publicly paid, uniformed police.

## Federal Policing

In the latter half of the 19th century, large tracts of land west of the Great Lakes were claimed by Britain but inhabited by Aboriginal peoples and eyed by expansionist Americans. Rupert's Land, an area of land extending down and west from Hudson Bay, was purchased from the Hudson's Bay Company by the federal government in 1870. The government felt an agency was needed to act as a liaison between settlers and Aboriginal people in order to prevent the sort of violent expropriation of Indian territory that was common in America, especially following the Riel Rebellion in 1869–70, when Louis Riel led the Red River Metis in protest against the takeover of their land by the government. The Dominion Police Force was created in 1858 by the federal government under the Act Respecting Police of Canada, but this force was limited to protecting federal buildings and to enforcing federal statutes, such as treason and sedition, and later to enforcing laws prohibiting counterfeiting. While it had jurisdiction for the whole of the country, in practice the police force served only central and eastern Canada. Consequently, in 1873 an Act of Parliament (the Act Respecting the Administration of Justice and the Establishment of a Police Force in the Northwest Territories) established the North West Mounted Police (NWMP). This force was modelled after the Royal Irish Constabulary and was mobilized with the tacit responsibility of easing adversities to settlers in the West, appeasing Aboriginal resistance, and deterring American colonization of British land.

Members of the NWMP faced great hardships both in trekking out to the area that later became Alberta and Saskatchewan (known as "The Great March") and in maintaining their spirits in the harsh, virtually unpopulated Northwest. A great number of the initial authorized 300 members deserted or were disciplined for drunkenness or insubordination. Nevertheless, the force gradually began to attract adventuresome young men of a high calibre who sought challenge in the harsh conditions and in their mission to "maintain the right." Soon, stories of great feats of heroism began to circulate and to define popular conceptions of the Mounties, who went to great lengths to "always get their man." The Mountie who travelled hundreds of miles criss-crossing the Yukon in search of the "Mad Trapper" is one such legend. In 1905, by royal decree, the NWMP became the Royal North West Mounted Police (RNWMP) and began taking up provincial duties under contract to provinces. In 1920 the Dominion Police were merged with the RNWMP to become the Royal Canadian Mounted Police (RCMP).

In the early years, it was unclear whether a federal police force was needed. The British North America (BNA) Act of 1867, which created Canada, provided under section 91 that law enactment be a federal responsibility and law enforcement a provincial responsibility. Although there was little or no parliamentary debate when the Act constituting the federal force was passed, many doubted the lasting need for such a force, given this distribution of authority and the temporary practical requirements for the colonization of the Northwest. In addition, provincial governments were up and running in the western provinces and (some argued) were capable of providing police services. Atlantic MPs, in particular, argued that there was no use for a federal force. The dual role of the federal force as police officers and magistrates in remote regions where magistrates were still not available was also criticized. Finally, some considered the Mounties' role in labour disputes at the Canadian Pacific Railway and during the Winnipeg General Strike ham-fisted. Between the late 1900s and the early 1920s, consequently, numerous attempts to have the force disbanded had taken place.

However, these storms were weathered with renewed support from federal governments in view, particularly, of worries about labour unrest and the popular belief in an incipient communist threat. In addition, Saskatchewan and Alberta had already established a precedent in the jurisdictional issue by contracting with the federal government for police services, beginning in 1905. Such contracting was extended to municipalities, beginning with Flin Flon in 1935. Opposition to RCMP expansion dwindled, and the force continued to expand in strength from its initial 300 in 1873, to 750 at the turn of the century, and to 1600 in 1920, when instead of being dismantled, it absorbed the Dominion Police.

During the Depression, the Force also grew by taking over policing duties from hard-pressed provincial forces. Since the 1950s, all the provinces except Ontario and Quebec (in addition to the Yukon and the Northwest Territories, Nunavut, and some 198 municipalities) have contracts with the RCMP to provide regular policing services.

Through the postwar years up until the 1980s, the force maintained its responsibility to counteract political insurgency—a role required by its absorption of the Dominion Police in 1920. Indeed, RCMP officers have infiltrated many political organizations regularly since World War I. However, this dual function of investigating political organizations and enforcing the Criminal Code became a source of widespread concern in the aftermath of the October Crisis of 1970, during which Prime Minister Trudeau passed the War Measures Act. After investigating RCMP wiretapping and counter-insurgency activity, the Keable Inquiry recommended that a separate agency undertake the role of intelligence gathering for national security. This is now the mandate of the Canadian Security Intelligence Service (CSIS).

Today the RCMP has a strength of some 15 000 women and men (excluding civilians and public servants). The RCMP's federal responsibilities are authorized under the Royal Canadian Mounted Police Act of 1959, according to which it is responsible for federal statutes, including excise and customs, narcotics control, the Indian Act, and federal properties. But RCMP officers also have the powers of peace officers. Members of the RCMP are required to enforce Canadian laws, prevent crime, and maintain peace and order. Finally, the RCMP also serves other police agencies in providing investigative and informational services, such as the Canadian Police Information Center (CPIC), established in 1972, which is a database available to police officials that stores criminal-related information entered by the country's police agencies.

## Provincial Policing

According to section 91 of the BNA Act, upon entry into Confederation the provinces were to enact legislation to assume responsibility for the administration of justice and the enforcement of laws. In 1858 the colony of British Columbia was the first to create such a territorial force, although Quebec is credited with establishing the first *provincial* force, the Sûreté du Québec (SQ), in 1870. Newfoundland established the Royal Newfoundland Constabulary in 1872. Ontario also had an abortive attempt to establish its force at the end of the 19th century, with the first provincial officer being hired in 1874 and legislation allowing the ad hoc appointment of provincial constables passed in 1877. It finally drafted a viable Act for a fully provincial force in 1909, when it passed legislation establishing the Ontario Provincial Police (OPP). Like the RCMP and other territorial and provincial forces, the OPP and its predecessor, the Niagara River Police, helped to secure the frontier, especially where precious metal deposits or the whisky trade made the frontier attractive to those seeking quick profits and relaxed social controls. Provincial forces established in Alberta, Manitoba, and Saskatchewan were short-lived. Saskatchewan and Alberta established their own provincial police forces by 1917, but the Saskatchewan Provincial Police was disbanded in 1928, in favor of a contract with the RCMP. Alberta's provincial policing was taken over by the RCMP in 1920. Today, only Quebec and Ontario's provincial forces survive. (The Newfoundland Constabulary no longer acts as a provincial service, but it still serves the communities of Corner Brook, Churchill Falls, Labrador City, and St. John's.)

The OPP enforces the Criminal Code in areas that do not have municipal or federal jurisdiction. Since 1945, it has provided policing by contract to municipalities that do not wish to institute their own forces. In Quebec, the SQ has jurisdiction over the whole province and may intervene in municipalities at the behest of the provincial government. In Ontario, the OPP may be called in when local police boards request additional policing or when the Ontario Civilian Commission on Police Services (OCCPS), the provincial body that oversees the

The Canadian Criminal Justice System

police forces, finds that a municipality is failing to meet the standard of service. Provincial police also oversee the delivery of policing to First Nations communities and are responsible for the policing of provincial property, such as the Legislative Assembly. As well, the OPP regulates private security in the province. In cases of labour demonstrations or political protests, the OPP may be called in to maintain order. Finally, the provincial police offer specialized services, such as marine, investigative, and tactical support services, to municipalities that are unable to maintain them.

# Regional and Municipal Policing in Ontario

The first municipal police force in Canada was established in Toronto in 1935. Soon afterward, London, Montreal, and Quebec City established municipal forces.

The responsibilities of municipal police forces in Ontario are set out in the Police Services Act, which was amended in January 1998. Every municipality is required to provide adequate and effective police services in accordance with its needs (section 4.1). Section 4.2 of the Act states that these services must include, at a minimum, crime prevention, law enforcement, assistance to victims of crime, public order maintenance, and emergency response. In addition, under section 4.3, the municipality must provide adequate infrastructure and administration to maintain these services, including vehicles, equipment, supplies, buildings, and communication services.

Also as per the Ontario Police Services Act, each municipality that maintains a police force is required to have a police services board. This board consists of a majority of municipal appointees depending on population size:

- Less than 25 000: 2 municipal, 1 provincial
- Regional and more than 25 000: 3 municipal, 2 provincial
- More than 300 000: 4 municipal, 3 provincial

It is noteworthy that the provincial/municipal split favours municipal control, rather than provincial control, as in the past. These police boards are overseen by the OCCPS, which ensures that all boards comply with standards and also conducts investigations and inquiries when there are substantiated complaints about the delivery of service. They may also make recommendations, or they may suspend the chief or the whole board, disband the police force, and require the OPP to take over policing if they find that the police service is unable to meet standards.

Throughout the 1960s and 1970s, the police were amalgamated in regional services, stimulated in part by requirements to provide specialized services, which are more expensive for smaller municipalities to deliver. Now, for instance, in the Greater Toronto Region, York Regional, Durham Regional, and

Halton Regional police forces provide regional service delivery. While having advantages, regionalization is also criticized for sacrificing local responsibility for more homogenized and standardized police delivery.

# Police Roles and Functions

Legislation compels jurisdictions in Ontario to narrow the terms according to which police services may be provided. According to section 42(1) of the Ontario Police Services Act, police constables have duties that include the following:

- Preserve the peace
- Prevent crimes and other offences and encourage crime prevention
- Assist victims of crime
- Apprehend criminals
- Lay charges and participate in prosecution
- Execute warrants
- Perform lawful duties assigned by the chief of police
- Enforce municipal bylaws (where applicable)
- Complete prescribed training

As noted above, the Ontario Police Services Act also requires that municipalities provide crime prevention, law enforcement, public order maintenance, emergency response, and, most recently, assistance to victims of crime.

## Crime Prevention

When Robert Peel drafted legislation in 1829 to institute a uniformed, full-time, publicly paid police force in Metropolitan London, he stressed a preventative role for his "Bobbies" or "Peelers," as they came to be known. Peel argued that his police should be judged by the absence of crime. Since then, the traditional role of the police has been crime prevention. But it has more recently been asked whether it is realistic to entrust this role to the police. After all, the causes of crime are multiple and varied, and neither the police nor any other single agency has the resources or the authority to sufficiently intervene into the lives of people to achieve this goal.

Are the police successful at crime prevention, and should we expect that they be? In many jurisdictions, the presence of more police has often been associated with more, not less, crime. Studies have also suggested that police presence is not a deterrent (see Kelling, Pate, Dieckman, & Brown, 1974). However, many criticisms of the ability of the police to deter crime focus on the relationship between police presence and crime absence. This relationship is often difficult to expose because the police themselves "make crime" in the sense that they are the ones who certify that an act is criminal. Police presence increases crime because more police means a greater penetration into the dark figure.

A counter-argument has often been that the absence of police patrol during police strikes, such as in Montreal in 1969, New York in 1971, and Stockholm in 1970, is associated with an escalation of certain types of opportunistic crime. Also, a recent study by Sherman and Weisburd (1995) finds that police presence in the form of increased patrols of "hot spots" does reduce reported crime. Much has also been made of the recent decline of major violent offences in New York City, following its much-touted "community policing" initiative based on the "broken windows" thesis of J. Q. Wilson and G. Kelling (1982). The program sought to reduce major crimes by displaying zero tolerance for minor acts of disorder, which are seen as creating a crime-permissive environment. Recently, Toronto has initiated "target policing" to deliver more resources to its own hot spots.

Most critics would acknowledge that much of the order-maintaining and peacekeeping work that police do retards some crime. Many police reformers who are seeking a more communicative, low-key police presence argue that crime may be reduced when police are more integrated into the communities they patrol. When police are problem solving or trouble shooting—for example, when they negotiate with leaders of a demonstration before the event rather than react to them after the demonstration has begun—they are doing crime prevention according to the broad view of their mandate. In this way, they prevent crime not by clearing criminals out of an area, but by disallowing the conditions that precipitate the criminal act.

Recently, crime prevention is not merely being asked of police—it is being required. In the case of Jane Doe in Toronto, the Metropolitan Toronto Police were sued by a woman who was sexually assaulted in her apartment in a neighbourhood and according to a pattern that was familiar to police working on a profile of the suspect. In this case, the police were accused of not doing their duty to prevent law violation because they failed to inform those who were likely targets.

## Emergency Service Provision

The police are, along with fire fighters and paramedics or ambulance services, one of the few public agencies available around the clock for emergency services. Many police activities are marshalled under the rubric of emergency services, from answering suicide and animal rescue calls to providing disaster relief, quelling riots, and responding to common criminal incidents. In much emergency work, the police are caught in a dilemma: if they restrict the scope of their availability to calls involving the need for law enforcement expertise, they can preserve and better define their professionalism in the most glorious of their functions. However, if they do narrow their services in this way, they also make themselves too inaccessible and push other service providers into their monopoly, which is law enforcement where legitimate force may be needed.

Periodically, governments have toyed with offloading some of the emergency response activities of public police to other service providers, especially where privatization and the rationalization of public services have been well developed. After all, do you need someone with police training and powers to rescue a cat from a tree or to direct traffic at an intersection because a traffic light is malfunctioning?

Thus far, the police have jealously guarded their response capabilities within the organization and have augmented them with civilian human resources. Perhaps they look at it this way: sure, we do a lot of grunge work that sullies us, but all that grunge work insulates us too, and at the core of the craft of what we do is law enforcement.

## Law Enforcement

Perhaps the role that the police themselves most identify with is **law enforcement.** Police officers often refer to themselves and are referred to by others, especially in the United States, as *law enforcement officers.* Of course, there are many kinds of laws and many kinds of officials with the duty of enforcing them. Officers of the Security and Exchange Commission enforce laws concerning the transaction of shares on the stock exchange. Officials at the Ministry of the Environment enforce, or oversee the enforcement of, regulatory standards and laws pertaining to levels of pollutant emissions from plants. Most people, however, think of uniformed public police officers first when they think of law enforcement officers.

Police officers enforce the Criminal Code, provincial statutes, and municipal bylaws (RCMP officers also enforce some other federal legislation). Law enforcement is both reactive and proactive. Police officers may anticipate the violation of the law in certain circumstances, and so they will proactively intervene. In fact, many law violations have such built-in presuppositions, including possessing tools for the purposes of breaking and entering and communicating for the purpose of prostitution. Much proactive enforcement of laws against drug trafficking is also anticipatory of future crime, which drug enforcement officers may facilitate while skirting carefully around legal prohibitions against entrapment.

Police officers enforce the law by identifying violators and bringing them before the appropriate judicial authorities for further disposition. In doing so, the police use their formidable powers to take personal freedoms away when they believe there are sufficient grounds to do so. If the violation is serious, the police may remand the offender in custody until a justice of the peace can hear the case. Police officers may also enforce the law by distributing information about law violations, issuing summons for court appearances, and offering warnings, by way of deterrent, when violations are minor.

## Public Order Maintenance

Enforcement of the law is complicated by the other roles of the police. If it were a matter of enforcing the law, and doing this alone, the police role would be more manageable, if still often controversial. However, the police also have the roles of **peacekeeping** and **order maintenance.** Police acting as peacekeepers take an active role in settling disputes and keeping them from getting out of hand. Order maintenance requires police to take a more passive role—their presence acts as a sufficient general deterrent.

Police spend a lot of time cooling tempers between spouses in domestic disputes, landlords and tenants, motorists, neighbours, and other potential adversaries. Many police researchers have noted that police use their discretion *not to arrest* where making an arrest is an option that can be legally justified. The Criminal Code indicates that a police officer *may arrest* an individual found committing an offence. However, much of the time, arresting one or more person is not the best way to handle a dispute in either the short or the long term. Major riots in both the United States and England have been caused by arrests that onlookers perceived as being unwarranted (for example, in Detroit in 1967

and Brixton in 1981). Police officers themselves have been attacked by wives whose husbands they arrested for assault. Order maintenance often means the restraint of law enforcement.

Police achieve their peacekeeping mandate in a number of ways. First, they are visible. Although in some cases, such as tense public demonstrations, too much police visibility can exacerbate the situation, in most cases in consensus societies, the presence of police brings a kind of official or state order. Second, although they may not be visibly present everywhere, their availability is known. The threat or promise of police attendance offers a form of peacekeeping-at-a-distance. Third, the police offer a form of state-funded dispute resolution. They provide 24-hour arbitration, a service that often prevents escalation in the dispute and thus avoids conflict resolution through the use of force.

## Victim Assistance

As many police officers will tell you much of modern policing is driven by complaints. Studies on police discretion have shown that the wishes of a complainant are important to the decision of whether to arrest. Reactive 911 policing depends on complainants' calls for service. Historically, the police and state prosecutors were mobilized to augment, and then to displace, with state interests, the role of the victim in the justice process for alleged wrongs suffered. The idea that the police and prosecutors stand in for the victim and through their intervention make the formal role of the victim redundant is one that is currently being reconsidered. As we shall see further in Chapter 11, victims, once marginalized in the formal process, are again assuming a role of importance.

Much of the current focus on the victim is a product of formal institutional neglect or indifference. But it is also the consequence of what may be a "recivilianization" or even a "reprivatization" of the criminal process. When the police begin to view their role as serving the victim rather than community or public interests, the historical rift between private prosecution and public prosecution may be closed. However, at present most police agencies have restricted themselves to informing complainants or victims of the progress of prosecutions against the accused.

## Conflict in the Roles of Police

Because police have such varied duties, role dilemmas inevitably occur. Should the police be more proactive in preventing crime? If so, how should they be proactive? Should they be more proactive in stopping criminals, or should they attempt to eliminate criminogenic conditions—the circumstances that offer opportunities of crime to motivated offenders? If they are to be more proactive in stopping criminals, then they are quite right to devote resources to organizing sting operations and to the infiltration and surveillance of criminal networks. If their proactivity is to be addressed toward eliminating the conditions or circumstances that attract criminal activity, then they may be better off devoting their energies to early interventions, such as diversionary or victim–offender reconciliation programs, and to problem-solving community policing interventions. Historically, there has been a shift toward more proactive policing on both fronts. But this is not to say that reactive policing is not alive and well. You have only to pick up the phone and dial 911 to confirm that it is.

As well, the police are a 24-hour service. But how much should they develop the role of meeting customer satisfaction, or of serving clients and markets? Would this orientation, set out in some recent policy documents, undermine their mandate to serve citizens under the rule of law?

But the most pressing and persistent role dilemma remains the one between maintaining order and enforcing the law. Much of the controversy surrounding police arises out of questionable decision making and mobilization. To stress again a central feature of the problem, the economic incentives to the individual officer derive mostly from arrests and the resulting overtime and court time that accrue. Peacekeeping and order maintenance, like much nonspecialist work, is seen for the most part as belonging to the larger question of the good arrest decision, rather than an end in itself. What is needed, as Robert Peel recommended in establishing the first London police force, is the rewarding of police for the peace they bring, rather than for the crime they solve or the people they arrest. Such a strategy for evaluation will by necessity make policing much more integrated with other mechanisms of local governance. To take a favourite example, police ridership on public transportation would be a crime prevention measure, because police presence reduces fear of crime.

## Police Powers

All police officers have the traditional power of the common-law constable, which refers to their right to seek an arrest and initiate a prosecution without a warrant. However, it should be noted that the capacity of the individual police officer to fulfill this common-law right is constrained by law, by the power and authority of other players in the criminal justice process, and also, more problematically, by political interference.

What are **police powers** in Canada? The police enforce warrants of the court, but they may also pursue warrantless arrests, under section 495(1)(c) of the Criminal Code. They have the power to preserve the peace and to arrest people when they have a good faith belief that a crime has been or will be committed, and they may enforce statutes and bylaws. Police may also search premises when they are in "hot pursuit" of a suspect, or when they have a search warrant under section 487 of the Criminal Code. They may install wiretaps or intercept communications under section 184, and they may obtain DNA samples under section 487.05.

Finally, police may use force under section 25. They are limited in their use of deadly force in situations where police officers perceive themselves or other citizens to be under immediate threat of serious bodily injury or death. Although section 25 does not restrict the officer from using deadly force in preventing the escape of a person when no other means exist to prevent that escape, section 37 limits the use of force according to an equivalency of "excessiveness"—the degree of force should not exceed the severity of the assault that it is intended to prevent. Also, police standards require investigation when an officer has discharged a weapon, and when an officer has killed or injured another person. In Ontario, the Special Investigations Unit (SIU) investigates such occurrences.

## Discretion

Just how much power do the police have? While we may talk of legal parameters on the use of force, real power is measured by the lack of constraints or by the autonomy to choose a course of action. **Police discretion** is the freedom of police officers to choose between two available courses of action. It has long been contended that the police enjoy what is called *low-visibility discretion*. This means that others, such as other officials, cannot readily review police officers' choice of action. The police make their decisions usually without the presence of respectable third parties, and they have the tacit sanction of superior officers. Police often use this power and the wide scope of the law in deciding not to arrest when an arrest is legally permissible. The fact that they have, in many instances, a full cartridge of statutory capacity at the ready gives the police the leverage to resolve matters without having to resort to enforcing statute, and to have these resolutions agreed to.

Let's take a simple example. Officer Joe comes upon you and a friend while you are firing beer bottle caps into a ravine from a park bench late one night, both of you with an open beer in your 18-year-old fists. Officer Joe is likely to approach you (depending on his professionalism) with an attitude of neutrality and firmness. You notice that he gives you and your friend a great deal of rope— Officer Joe might even be very friendly. But Officer Joe knows that there are at least three charges he can levy against you and your friend, including drinking under age, possessing an open container of alcohol in public, and littering. What he most likely wants to know is whether your attitude suggests that these transgressions are isolated and largely out of character, or whether you and your friend are serious deviants on your way to lengthy criminal careers. What Officer Joe will do is give you and your friend an "attitude test" to determine to which side of this equation each of you belongs. If you pass, Officer Joe can give you a warning and provide a form of informal social control in the garb of officialdom. By doing so, he will hope to bring you back into the fold of law-abiding and respectable citizens. The result is that order has been maintained, and it may also be said that he has enforced the law, but he has acted as a charismatic authority enforcing justice without the encumbrances of judge, jury, and legal process. The low visibility of the encounter is ensured because either you will fail the test and he will formally begin prosecution, or you will pass and be happy not to challenge his decision to not charge you.

It has often been noted that the distribution of decision-making power (or discretion) within police organizations is an inversion of that found in most other organizations. In most organizations, the decision to deploy the special capacities of the organization is reserved for the top echelons. But the nature of the special capacities of police work (such as legal powers and the right to use force) has kept much decision making with the front ranks. There is some suggestion, however, that new communications technologies may be changing this situation.

In the example above, what if Officer Joe were wired to a sophisticated miniature video and audio system that enabled sergeants in a monitoring and control station to observe the unfolding events and to call up data on you and your friend, leading them to suggest or insist on courses of action? It has at times been an administrative dream to know and see all from a distance, but even if such devices could routinely be used, the split-second nature of real-time interaction would still require that police work remain very much a matter of line officer discretion. As an analogy, many quarterbacks now have radio transmitters in their helmets so that coaches can instruct them on the play, and many on-air announcers are wired to take instructions from producers or directors behind the cameras. Even in these fields, we can see the limits of the human ability to balance the initiation of action and the taking of instructions. Often, we see television announcers and football quarterbacks caught in a stasis of indecision as they try to field two sources of input simultaneously. The terrible consequences of too much off-site discretion in policing have been seen in Ontario, where in 1988 an OPP Tactical Rescue Unit shot and killed an innocent, suicidal young man when the off-site commander issued an instruction to "take out" the suspect (Forcese, 1999).

## Accountability

Because the police enjoy awesome powers to take away rights and freedoms with low visibility, few discussions of the police will fail to mention **police accountability.** What are the mechanisms in place to ensure that police themselves follow the letter or the spirit of the law?

*Accountability* refers to the requirement among public servants to provide an account for actions taken or not taken. Police notepads, for example, belong not to the officer but to the department and are often entered as evidence. Police are accountable for what they write in these books.

Because there are several levels of policing in Canada, there are also different and sometimes overlapping mechanisms to ensure accountability. Unfortunately, for the most part, it has been impossible politically to make these mechanisms fully independent. Civilian review of police conduct has been successfully resisted. In Ontario, the closest approximation to a civilian review agency was the Public Complaints Commission, staffed in large part by lawyers and ex–police officers and disbanded in 1995. That being said, a police officer is liable for violating the policy and procedures of his or her department and can also be tried civilly or criminally.

Mechanisms to deal with police misconduct exist throughout Canadian jurisdictions; however, given the diversity in administration, procedures may vary somewhat across Canada. Currently, in Ontario there are three avenues for the redress of wrongdoing by a police officer. First, there is the internal investigation of complaints. Mid- to large-sized police agencies have their own internal affairs division, which investigates complaints about officer conduct. These investigations may be aided by external investigators called in from outside agencies, particularly when the complaint alleges a more organization-wide problem. Sometimes this practice is more commonplace, as in Montreal, where the Montreal police force regularly calls upon the Sûreté du Québec to look into matters of officer conduct. In Ontario, members of the public who are dissatisfied with the outcome of their complaint may appeal to the OCCPS.

Internal review processes have been criticized on a number of grounds. First, critics claim that the processes fail to promote structural changes because they take a case-by-case approach. Second, critics contend that internal reviews focus on protecting the organization from bad publicity rather than on protecting the public from bad cops. Third, critics claim that the practice of conducting background investigations of complainants deters potential and actual complainants from pursuing the process. Fourth, many consider the penalty structure of the internal process too lenient, as police officers are given small financial penalties, for the most part, for actions that many members of the public would condemn as illegal and irreconcilable with the status of a police officer.

A second review mechanism is external review by outside monitoring agencies. All provinces except Newfoundland have local or municipal boards or commissions that are authorized to oversee the delivery of municipal police services. Saskatchewan, New Brunswick, and Alberta also have police commissions that oversee provincial police forces. In Ontario, the OCCPS and the SIU are empowered to review police conduct. Indeed, the SIU does not require the initiation of a complaint, but instead investigates every case involving serious injury, sexual assault, or death that may have been caused by the actions of a municipal, provincial, or regional police officer. The agency operates directly under the attorney general and has the authority to decide whether charges are warranted.

Finally, there is civil procedure. Individuals can launch lawsuits against public police organizations for negligence in the provision of security. In 1998, Jane Doe won a 12-year-long case against the Toronto Police Service and was awarded $220 000 by a court in Toronto after the judge agreed that police tried to use her as "bait" to capture the balcony rapist.

Another unofficial but powerful mechanism of accountability is the local and mass media. In your daily newspaper, there is likely a story about police wrongdoing at least a few times a year in the mid-sized to large metropolises. These stories are provided in part to titillate, but they are also offered as part of the professional mandate of the media to act as a fourth estate in governance. While this function of the media as a watchdog on the police is far from neutral, as the media outlets select and present stories in formats and according to viewpoints that cater to powerful interest groups, it is another vehicle by which police may be held to account (see Ericson, Baranek, & Chan, 1987, 1989).

## Autonomy

The common-law office of the constable dates back to medieval England, where it was established in 1285 in the Statute of Winchester, and was imported to Canada in the Parish and Town Constable's Act of 1793. Just how much autonomy today's sworn police officers take from the historical autonomy of the constabulary office is much debated (see Stenning, 1983). It is also questionable just how much the decision-making authority of the office of constable is superceded by the authority of the chief of police.

There are both institutional and organizational factors that guarantee the police constable and the police function much autonomy. Institutionally, we in Canada distinguish ourselves from totalitarian regimes in that the executive function of government is institutionally separated from the judicial and legislative branch. There is a further separation between the police function and political authority. The controversy at the heart of the recent RCMP's Public Complaints Commission Inquiry into the influence of the Prime Minister's Office on the RCMP's handling of APEC security is the question of just how much political interference police officers in charge of APEC security may have been subjected to.

Institutional independence is also guaranteed in the convention that although political authorities, such as municipalities or provincial governments, may give direction on matters of policy, police forces retain decision-making authority over operations or how specific cases or even kinds of cases are handled. Such operational independence is bolstered by the fact that police monitoring bodies are often staffed by political representatives who, owing to their relative ignorance of policing, to the political constituency of their representation, or to their short duration as commissioners, are prone to deferring to police expertise (see Stenning, 1983).

Organizationally, constabulary autonomy is simply an expression of effective police work. The effectiveness of police as peacekeepers and law enforcers has long depended on optimizing each police officer's strengths within the police agency and jurisdiction. Subsequently, the agency reflects the peacekeeping and law enforcement capacity that each police agent can bring to bear, determining the basis of the term *police strength*. (However, under community policing initiatives, there has been much reinvigoration of unofficial agents in police provision.)

In addition, autonomy is supported because it is inconvenient for the entire police organization to be seen as directly responsible for the actions of its individual members. A police officer is personally and criminally accountable for her or his actions. The fact that the individual officer is mainly responsible for police wrongdoing can keep the organization as a whole relatively unencumbered when official actions draw criticism or legal action.

# Police Work

So you want to be a cop? Get in line. There are hundreds of applicants for each job in policing. This is not meant to depress or deter you, but it should alert you to the necessity of planning ahead. The role of policing goes some way to predicting the criteria for officer selection, but there are distinctive elements of the process of candidate selection and evaluation that reflect how role requirements may be ranked.

While this chapter on policing has spent relatively little time addressing considerations of law application and the use of force, these are the two areas stressed most strongly by formal police training. In police selection and training, both subjective and objective evaluation criteria are applied, and successful socialization to the job—as in many other professions where teamwork is essential—also depends on the neophyte's ability to absorb and adopt subcultural norms.

## Selection

The selection of police officers is at heart a complex undertaking because it involves a number of interests and dilemmas. There is a public interest in ensuring that public policing is representative of the community. There is a professional and occupational interest in ensuring that police officers have sufficient proficiency in those competencies that are crucial to their work. There is a further professional and occupational interest in demonstrating that the police tradition has always reflected the highest ideals and noblest intentions. However, in the transition to more representative policing over the past three decades, the greatest obstacles to progress have been the narrow interpretation of the core competencies of police work and the relative rigidity of those gatekeepers invested with decision-making power over entry and promotion. Police practitioners have overemphasized physical attributes, and those authorized to determine the candidacy and progress of police officers have too often been drawn from the ranks of the police.

The basic qualifications for employment as a public officer usually include the following:

- Canadian citizenship
- Minimum age (18 or 19)
- Physical and mental fitness
- Good moral character and habits
- Four years of secondary school

Normally, police agencies also require the candidate to meet a certain standard of visual acuity and to possess a valid driver's licence. In addition, Ontario, following the work of the Ministry of the Solicitor General's Strategic Planning Committee on Police Training and Education (Ontario, 1992) and its Police Constable Selection Project, has identified eight areas of core competency required of candidates for police constable:

- Analytical thinking skills
- Self-confidence
- Communication skills
- Ability to be flexible in dealing with diversity
- Self-control
- Facility for relationship building
- Achievement orientation
- Physical skills and abilities

It is worth noting that a criminal conviction does not by itself disqualify the applicant. Those with a criminal conviction on record may still be hired if they have received a pardon or if they have received a discharge and their record has been sealed by the RCMP.

```
BOX  6 . 1
```

-------------------------------------------------------------------------------

## POLICE SELECTION TESTING

In Ontario, police candidates secure qualification through Applicant Testing Services (ATS), a private agency contracted by the Police Learning System to provide constable selection services. The applicant must complete a GATB test evaluating problem solving and reasoning and must also pass a comprehension and communication test. The physical requirements of police selection under ATS and other selection services are still quite rigorous. In the following task, the applicant is tested according to "realistic training":

Pursuit Restraint Circuit: [candidate] will be evaluated by completing as quickly as possible a 25 metre circuit four times (total distance = 100 metres) while wearing a 9 lb. soft weight belt that simulates wearing a full equipment belt. During each rotation, a set of stairs are climbed and on the second and fourth rotation, a 4 ft. fence is scaled. Following completion of the circuit, the participant completes pushing and pulling on the "body control" simulator, performs two "arm restraint" simulations, then drags a 150 lb. rescue dummy a distance of 15 metres.

Source: ATS Web site. Available: www.applicanttesting.com

Controversy remains regarding how tests that distinguish between men can also be used to distinguish between women, particularly women of Asian descent who are of a slighter build. Even downgrading the physical requirements for women fails to address the more fundamental issue of how competencies are prioritized. On the one hand, it is stated that standardized tests are the only fair device of selection, but on the other hand, it is stated that the profession demands the widest spectrum of representation in order to match police service membership to communities. Tests still privilege physical characteristics—including physical strength—under the premise that certain abilities are a requirement for officer and community safety, but it is obvious that there can be no physical equivalency between the average Asian woman and the average European-Canadian or African-Canadian man. Stansfield (1996) found that physical skills were the primary consideration in police officer selection by the Metro Toronto Police Service; physical skills were evaluated at 74 percent, compared to 26 percent consideration for mental skills.

The acceptance of women into policing is not yet complete when women are still being evaluated according to antiquated, male standards focusing on physical strength. Multiculturalism is also an incomplete policy if distinctions between the innate proficiencies of various ethnic groups are not considered in police candidacy criteria. The focus on physical attributes stems in part from the nature of the job, in which a diverse range of physical and mental competencies come into play. However, the larger police services, in particular, are not served when focusing on physical competence if the selection process filters out candidates who may expand their typical officer profiles. In any event, services may still place additional requirements on officers who seek postings to work that require greater competency in measures of physical strength. We must consider whether all the energy put into selection is a consequence of the fact that although the service still has a great capacity to insist on standards of entry, the power of police associations has undermined the service's ability to maintain standards of performance once the officer has reached first-class status. It should be noted that studies evaluating the effectiveness of women in policing have found them to be just as capable as men.

The selection process usually also includes interviews (screening and board interviews) and is completed with a successful background check, which establishes such things as credit history, and interviews with people who may have knowledge of the applicant's character, judgment, values, and so on.

## Training

There are three forms of police training: recruit, in-service, and field training. *Recruit training* is the initial block of intensive exposure to law, policy, procedures, and skills development, which is now universally delivered at a specialized training facility like the RCMP's Training Depot or the Ontario Police College (OPC).

Most time spent in the basic training program is devoted to traffic law and accident investigation, criminal offences and provincial statutes, laws of arrest and evidence, and communications. The second largest block is devoted to firearms training, police vehicle operation, and defensive manoeuvres and skills development in executing arrests and in the use of force. There is also some instruction on race relations, police ethics, and general handling of stress, victims, and relations with the public.

During *in-service training*, individual services provide instruction in their forms, formats, policies, and procedures. This training can take anywhere from a few hours in smaller forces to up to eight weeks in the larger forces. Further in-service training is ongoing, such as in firearms recertification.

A key element of police training is *field training*, in which the trainee is assigned to a training or coach officer for instruction in the finer points of police duty, including how to work the on-board, computer-aided dispatch system and the protocols for handling the everyday workload.

## Composition of Police

Especially during the late 1980s and early 1990s, public police services were active in attempting to make the composition of police forces representative of

the communities served. However, much work is still to be done to make policing more representative. While visible minorities constitute 10 percent of the
employed labour force, they represent only 3 percent of police officers. While
there were no female full-duty public police officers prior to 1973, when new
labour legislation came into effect, women still represent only 13 percent of non-
civilian police today. However, greater representation of Aboriginal people in
policing has been achieved, at 3 percent of all police officers, nearly double their
1.7 percent representation in the total employed labour force (all figures for
1996 from CCJS, 1999b).

# The Cost of Policing

An evaluation of policing costs should take into consideration the wider impact
of decisions about resource distribution. Critical criminologists insist that the
costs of policing need to include the repercussion of more arrests on costs further down the justice system, as more court resources and more correctional
resources are used. Conservative criminologists would argue that the benefits of
prosecuting crime outweigh the costs to the system; in other words, human
resources and technology costs of policing should be measured against property
losses, higher insurance rates, and the pain and suffering of victims. Evaluations
of the impact of social policy decisions are still in their infancy. In the meantime,
most discussions about the costs of policing will be about the costs of police services, rather than about the relative costs of competing policy decisions regarding crime prevention.

Still, we should always be asking ourselves if we are getting the most out of
our public policy. The United States is often perplexing to European visitors
because, while it practises the most zealous accounting for the expenditure of
public monies, it also seems to have infinite resources for building prisons and
hiring police officers. Indeed, in California more money is now spent on putting
people in jail than in educating people.

*Juristat* reports that policing accounts for about 60 percent of the total money
spent on criminal justice, or nearly $5.81 billion out of $10 billion per year
(CCJS, 1999a). This is an annual cost to each Canadian of $196. Of this amount,
80 percent goes to salaries, wages, and benefits. Ontario and Quebec both pay
more per capita than the national average, while the maritime provinces pay the
least.

## Police Officer Numbers and Workload

The number of public police officers per capita in Canada has been dropping
since 1991 (*Juristat*, 1999). Table 6.1 shows the number of police officers in each

province and territory from 1994 to 1998. Although figures are not yet available, since 1999 many agencies have been doing new hiring, so we should expect increases between 1999 and 2001.

TABLE 6.1

NUMBER OF POLICE OFFICERS

| | 1994 | 1995 | 1996 | 1997 | 1998 |
|---|---|---|---|---|---|
| Canada | 55 859 | 55 008 | 54 323 | 54 719 | 54 722 |
| Newfoundland | 880 | 864 | 831 | 794 | 776 |
| Prince Edward Island | 193 | 191 | 205 | 204 | 203 |
| Nova Scotia | 1611 | 1611 | 1632 | 1624 | 1589 |
| New Brunswick | 1297 | 1298 | 1294 | 1304 | 1283 |
| Quebec | 14 712 | 14 163 | 13 780 | 13 768 | 13 603 |
| Ontario | 20 737 | 20 804 | 20 175 | 20 260 | 20 454 |
| Manitoba | 2130 | 2186 | 2215 | 2230 | 2226 |
| Saskatchewan | 1896 | 1868 | 1908 | 1872 | 1896 |
| Alberta | 4471 | 4420 | 4443 | 4478 | 4470 |
| British Columbia | 6383 | 6230 | 6420 | 6742 | 6865 |
| Yukon | 113 | 116 | 112 | 122 | 118 |
| Northwest Territories | 234 | 235 | 250 | 246 | 240 |

Source: CCJS, 1999b.

It is important to keep in mind that raw numbers by themselves do not tell us what we need to know about the relative strength of police officer numbers. To gauge their strength, we need to know how many police officers there are per population (see Table 6.2). Currently, per capita there are 181 officers per 100 000 population.

In the meantime, some have argued that the workload of police officers is getting too onerous, having doubled since 1963 (van Rijn, 1999). Workload is typically measured in Criminal Code incidents per officer. Table 6.3 shows that workload varies by more than a 2 to 1 ratio between major jurisdictions across the country, with Toronto having the relatively low number of 40 incidents per officer and Vancouver with the very high 89.48 incidents per officer. Needless to say, an officer assigned to the downtown core of Vancouver has a higher workload than one assigned to Montreal's downtown core. This higher workload also means that those officers are less likely to be engaged in activities more indirectly related to the administration of Criminal Code incidents, such as community policing.

## TABLE 6.2

POPULATION PER POLICE OFFICER

|  | 1994 | 1995 | 1996 | 1997 | 1998 |
|---|---|---|---|---|---|
| Canada | 520 | 534 | 546 | 548 | 554 |
| Newfoundland | 653 | 657 | 675 | 697 | 700 |
| Prince Edward Island | 694 | 706 | 664 | 670 | 671 |
| Nova Scotia | 575 | 576 | 571 | 577 | 589 |
| New Brunswick | 579 | 579 | 582 | 578 | 586 |
| Quebec | 490 | 511 | 528 | 531 | 539 |
| Ontario | 522 | 527 | 550 | 555 | 558 |
| Manitoba | 528 | 517 | 512 | 511 | 513 |
| Saskatchewan | 533 | 543 | 534 | 547 | 541 |
| Alberta | 605 | 620 | 626 | 633 | 652 |
| British Columbia | 577 | 607 | 605 | 588 | 585 |
| Yukon | 266 | 266 | 285 | 264 | 268 |
| Northwest Territories | 278 | 283 | 270 | 277 | 283 |

Source: Statistics Canada, CANSIM, Matrix 301.

## TABLE 6.3

POLICE OFFICER WORKLOAD, BASED ON CRIMINAL CODE INCIDENTS

|  | POPULATION (1997) | OFFICERS PER 100 000 | CRIME RATE PER 100 000 | INCIDENTS PER OFFICER |
|---|---|---|---|---|
| Winnipeg | 677 291 | 181.6 | 10 281 | 56.6 |
| Regina | 198 845 | 173.5 | 14 500 | 83.57 |
| Montreal | 3 384 233 | 172.6 | 7531 | 43.63 |
| Toronto | 4 511 966 | 163.5 | 6549 | 40.05 |
| Halifax | 349164 | 150.6 | 9388 | 62.33 |
| Edmonton | 899 466 | 147 | 8836 | 60.11 |
| Vancouver | 1 927 998 | 145.6 | 13029 | 89.48 |
| Calgary | 885130 | 135.7 | 7796 | 57.45 |
| Hamilton | 663 587 | 135.3 | 7608 | 56.23 |
| Ottawa-Hull | 1 045 249 | 133.8 | 7827 | 58.49 |

Source: van Rijn, 1999.

These numbers notwithstanding, police numbers (or strength) are often bolstered not according to a need represented by a rise in crime statistics, but rather according to the prevailing political viewpoint on the importance of law and order in government policy. In Ontario, for instance, Premier Mike Harris has courted public opinion using the American-style "tough-on-crime" approach. Despite an eight-year decline in the violent crime rate, at the time of this writing, many politicians have learned that a law-and-order platform still wins votes, and such policy often includes the promise of more police hiring, even if, as we have seen thus far, much of that new hiring is in fact swallowed up in force replenishment.

In the meantime, it may shock you to learn that even in the busiest sections of major cities at any one time, the actual number of officers on patrol is startlingly low. Approximately 15 percent of the strength of a police department is on duty during the peak 4- to 12-hour shift. This strength is distributed across the entire city, often leaving sizable gaps in coverage. Consequently, there may only be one or two cars registered as "clear" at any particular time in a busy downtown sector. In Toronto, the Toronto Police Association found in a snapshot study of the numbers of police on the streets during the graveyard shift between 11 p.m. and dawn, that there were only 164 officers in 82 cruisers—3.2 percent of the total 5000 uniformed officers (van Rijn, 1999). This distribution would seem to pay insufficient attention to crime patterns, given that crimes against people peak between 6 p.m. and 2 a.m. Although the study was neither scientific nor unbiased, it does underscore the importance of the distribution of human resources in policing. The real challenge is staffing according to need while setting a shift rotation that satisfies officers and that does not aggravate the already high levels of stress-related dysfunctions that can result from police work (for example, family violence, alcohol and drug abuse, and suicide).

# Community Policing

From the first fleet of automobile patrol cars in the early 1910s to the proliferation of fleets of patrol cars equipped with two-way radios from the 1930s to 1950s, police organization was driven toward a model of reactive, call-for-service patrol. This model meant that in the first half of the 20th century, police organizations were changing their mandate from peacekeeping to law enforcement. Although the typical police officer in the 1950s was not unavailable to keep the peace, in the larger urban centres he was more likely to be seen only when someone placed a service call to the station or when he noticed something happening while en route between such calls.

But in the organization of reactive patrol, police had forgotten much of the legacy of Robert Peel's principles, in which crime prevention, rather than clearance of Criminal Code violations, was to be the best goal and measure of policing. In fashioning themselves more as impartial servants of the law, they had also distanced themselves from local problems that required peacekeeping and order maintenance expertise. In short, while police organizations between the 1920s and 1960s modernized themselves with sophisticated communications, command and control, and intelligence-gathering systems, many had also lost touch with the communities they policed.

This distance became obvious in the many urban riots in the United States in the mid-to-late 1960s, in which police practices were cited by the Kerner Commission as a major precipitator of the riots (Peak, 1997). Many of the police incidents were deemed discriminatory or racist, but this finding only confirmed that the police had become out-of-touch with the interests and concerns of the large constituencies they were accountable to. They came in, made arrests, and left, leaving a wake of dissatisfaction. Added to these findings was a famous study by George Kelling and colleagues (1974), which found in a controlled experiment of random patrols in Kansas City that increasing the number of patrol cars in a test area failed to decrease crime in that area. This finding suggested that police patrol had little effect on crime.

By the early 1970s, many police organizations had responded with isolated programs. These programs included training in race relations; unit beat policing, whereby police officers are assigned regularly to the same beat; and public relations liaisons with schools. In the late 1970s and early 1980s, however, a distinct and positive philosophy of community policing began to emerge. It was touted by its advocates as a reinvention of the way police would deliver services. Among those credited with bringing a philosophy of community policing to life are Robert Trojanowitz, Herman Goldstien, George Kelling, and James Q. Wilson.

## What Is Community Policing?

Community policing can be defined as a return to the principle that policing is accomplished by the community as a whole, rather than one specific agency of government. When you think of policing, you probably visualize the police, including the uniform, weapons, technology, and various cultural idiosyncrasies associated with the police personality. Policing, however, is more than the modern organization that most of us have come to depend on for problems related to personal security.

Because professional police organizations have become so central to our understanding and expectations of policing delivery, community policing is mostly understood as a partnership between the local professional police organization and various other agencies, be they voluntary, private, or public.

Community policing also involves change to public police organizations. Recent changes to the OPP, for example, have altered its organizational structure to enhance the appearance, at least, of an organization dedicating resources to front-line delivery. Thus, reorganization according to community policing often includes the following changes:

- Decentralizing decision making (becoming less paramilitaristic)
- Reducing bureaucracy
- Rewarding nonconventional initiatives in crime prevention
- Reducing specialization or creating a generalist orientation (e.g., focusing on problem solving)
- Instituting practices of the "learning organization"

For the most part, it has been a tall order for Canadian police organizations to follow through on the restructuring that community policing calls for. Two of the biggest forces, the RCMP and the OPP, have done much restructuring but are still labouring under the vestiges of central command, large bureaucracies, traditional rewards (for law enforcement), and specialization. Reforms face resistance from the line officers, and community policing also competes for resources with traditional, reactive law enforcement. At budget time across the country, the police often remind the public that the community policing programs it wants can come only through greater financial investment.

# Conclusion

How policing will look as we enter this new millennium is impossible to predict. However, certain patterns and key developments may be worth noting and watching, whether you yourself will be a participant or an observer.

One trend, of course, is the continual development of technology. The capacity of technology to reduce the human labour required to perform specific tasks is too often overestimated. In police work, new technologies have often been credited with awesome improvements to service delivery. Telegraph, fingerprinting, radio-cars, Canadian Police Information Centre (CPIC), and DNA profiling have each in their turn promised revolutions in the capacity of the police to perform. Closed-circuit television or video surveillance allows a form of virtual patrol.

Another trend is the growth in private security. In your daily life, you are more likely to come across a private security officer than a public police officer. Private security outnumber public police in Canada by a ratio of 2 to 1. The public police are said to be able to perform a smaller relative share of the policing role; the RCMP, for example, have been reducing their capacity to police economic crime and are increasingly ceding this responsibility of law enforcement to private security and intelligence services.

There is further a trend in which, despite long-standing efforts at prevention, police organizations are developing a number of tiers. No longer is it possible to see public police officers as the generalists that early versions of community policing supported. Rather, we see in other nations, such as the Netherlands, new subconstable ranks and private and volunteer patrols, in which the most visible policing is no longer the full-duty constable, but rather a hybrid of public and private or lay and professional service providers. The responsibility of public police in the area of patrol may be one of community safety coordination or "beat management," rather than direct enforcement (see the Salinas Police Department Web site at www.salinaspd.com/cops_st.html). Here, the police are seen as accreditors and coordinators of patrol, rather than as those who provide that patrol themselves. This kind of "governing at a distance" may happen to other areas of traditional delivery, as well. More and more in advanced democracies, specialists are required for effectiveness, from crime scene investigations to strategies of crime prevention, yet local authorities can no longer afford front-line patrol by full-duty police officers, and volunteer and private delivery is filling the gap.

This brings to bear a third dynamic, which is the relative power of local versus extra-local and national versus transnational police authorities. As the information age causes increased globalization, more crime and criminal deprivations occur via the information and exchange channels we use. Patrolling and securing these new channels of communications requires strategies oriented to a different version of jurisdiction than has typically been the case. Policing the global marketplace requires "global cops," or police with outstanding connections and agreements with other forces in faraway places.

What all this means is that policing is changing dramatically and quickly. What we have been able to expect for many decades may no longer be serviceable by the role and resources of the public police as we know them today.

## Summary

In this chapter we have highlighted several important features of Canadian police organization, history, and administration. First, we showed that Canadian police history is unique in that it developed with aspects of both British colonial and American municipal policing. Canada's federal police were important emissaries of the advantages of British rule and have maintained much legitimacy, despite periodic doubts as to the need for a federal force. We also reviewed police powers and responsibilities, and noted the influence of community policing. Finally, we reviewed some of the selection and training methods and practices and offered some brief remarks on possible future issues facing police work.

## Key Terms

law enforcement (p. 122)
order maintenance (p. 123)
peacekeeping (p. 123)

police accountability (p. 127)

police discretion (p. 126)

police powers (p. 125)

# Discussion Questions

1.  What are the three levels of public police jurisdiction in Canada?

2.  What is meant by community policing?

3.  Why was the NWMP established as a federal police force?

4.  List some of the functions or services provided by the public police. Which do you believe take precedence? At times of budget cutting, which do you think are likely to take the first hits?

5.  What might be expected of the future of public policing? Do you believe that the public police are endangered by increasing privatization?

# Weblinks

**www.rcmp-grc.gc.ca/** The RCMP has a thorough and informative site with links to information on their forensic services, the national DNA databank, peacekeeping, and recruiting info, as well as the latest news releases.

**www.sgc.gc.ca/whoweare/aboriginal/eaboriginal.htm** The Aboriginal Policing Directorate is responsible for administering the First Nations Policing Policy and providing national leadership regarding the delivery of policing services for Aboriginal people off-reserve.

**www.salinaspd.com/cops_st.html** The Web site of the Salinas Police Department, outlining their Community Oriented Policing model.

**www.interpol.com** The Web site of Interpol, the international police force, provides fascinating information on international crime issues such as trafficking in human beings, terrorism, drug trafficking, and internationally wanted criminals.

**www.theiacp.org/pubinfo/** The International Association of Chiefs of Police site offers links to police training information, legislation and policy, research initiatives, and publications.

# CHAPTER 7

# The Court System

## Objectives

- To illustrate how the court system establishes guilt or innocence, imposes sentences, and maintains social order and control.

- To examine the roles and functions of the provincial courts, the federal courts, and the Supreme Court of Canada.

- To analyze the processing of a criminal trial through the court system and the roles of judges and juries.

- To examine the Young Offenders Act and outline its positive and negative features.

## The Criminal Court Structure

Cunningham and Griffiths (1997) liken the court system in Canada to a byzantine labyrinth that few understand. However, it is through this labyrinth that the courtroom search for truth must occur, and the outcome of the criminal trial, which pits the resources of the defendant against those of the state, should be about both truth and justice. The courts are central to the Canadian criminal justice system—through the process of the court, we establish guilt or innocence, impose sentences, and maintain social control and order. Because the court system is established to protect the rights of those charged with a criminal offence, it monitors other branches of the justice system, specifically the police and the prosecution. It is that dual role of protecting the accused from abuse while controlling and punishing the guilty that makes the court the hallmark of our democracy.

Friedenberg (1985) notes that the introduction of the Canadian Charter of Rights and Freedoms has placed even greater responsibility on our courts to protect individual rights from the tyranny of the state. Furthermore, the concept of judicial independence is embodied in the principles of fundamental justice, and Canadians expect their cases in the courts to be heard before a judiciary that is fair, impartial, and not subject to political pressure from any branch of the government.

The courts of Canada can be divided into three sections: the provincial courts, the federal courts, and the Supreme Court of Canada. The provincial and federal courts both have a trial and an appellate wing, and at the top of the heap is the Supreme Court of Canada, which serves as the appeal court of last resort for both systems. Canada has a national legal structure in the sense that the Supreme Court of Canada is accepted as the final arbiter of disputes from across the land by federal and all provincial governments.

## The Provincial Court System

Most criminal trials are heard in the **provincial courts.** The BNA Act of 1867 allowed for each province to establish a system of courts responsible for both civil and criminal cases, ensuring that the provinces would retain authority to set up a general system of courts. The Act allowed the provinces to establish lower-level and appellate courts, but it gave the federal government the power to appoint and pay judges for higher levels of courts. Only in lowly magistrate courts could the provinces appoint the judges. Furthermore, responsibility for creating criminal law and statutes was delegated to the federal government under the Constitution Act of 1867, while the provinces were mandated to enforce the law and to conduct criminal prosecutions in court. Schmalleger et al. (2000) note that in the last two decades the court system has been greatly simplified—every province has a provincial court as the central criminal trial court and has a superior court. Ontario is making noises that court reform should create two courts, one trial and one appeal. Although this proposal sounds logical, the major impediment to reform has been the truncated division of responsibility over criminal law and courts, as set out in the Constitution Act of 1867. In a typical Canadian balance of power politics, the struggle over the appointment of the judiciary and division of authority remains ongoing, and the solution of creating a simplified provincial and appeals court process seems unattainable.

The workhorse of the court system is the provincial court. All criminal and civil cases enter a provincial court, and the vast majority of less serious cases are tried there. Within the provincial court system are separate divisions, including small claims, family, youth, traffic, and criminal courts. The criminal division deals with all offenders charged who are over 18 years of age, and the youth court handles offences committed by those under age 18. The provincial governments appoint provincial court judges and pay their salaries.

The most serious criminal offences, such as first degree murder cases, are tried in provincial **superior courts.** As stated earlier, under the Canadian Constitution, the federal government appoints and remunerates judges of the courts of appeal and the superior courts.

The role of the provincial court is to arraign the accused, set bail, ensure that the Crown makes proper disclosure of evidence, determine the amount of bail, decide on the method of trial, and, 90 percent of the time, conduct the criminal trial. If the defendant pleads guilty or is found guilty after a hearing, the judge in provincial court also imposes the appropriate sentence. Schmalleger et al. (2000) note that provincial courts do not hold jury trials; instead, the presiding judge is empowered to interpret both fact and law. In most instances the goal is swift and decisive justice, with informal and uncomplicated jurisprudence the expected outcome. Because of the great number of cases and the need for swift justice, only the provincial superior courts use the complete extent of the justice system—the  juries, prosecutors, defence lawyers, witnesses, and expert witnesses that we have all been exposed to in courtroom dramas and movies. This formal procedure can be long, expensive, and difficult, involving many legal eagles and expert witnesses, as illustrated by the Paul Bernardo murder case. While there is a place for both the formal procedural model and the more informal hearings in the courts of the nation, the overload of the court system is creating pressure for cases to be quickly resolved and for decisions to be based on uncomplicated issues of law and fact.

All provinces have **courts of appeal** as part of the superior court system. The appeals court usually consists of a panel of judges. At this level there are no juries present; instead, three to five judges examine the evidence and the findings of the original judge, and they extensively question the defence and prosecution lawyers, who appear before them. The appeal court usually renders a decision after long and extensive debate and discussion in private. This decision, often made in writing, can be a majority with minority dissent, or it can be unanimous. In split decisions, the verdict is that of the majority. The role of the appeal court is to review the transcript of the lower court to ensure that the hearing was fair and in accordance with statutory and case law. Brockman and Rose (1996) note that most convictions are reaffirmed on appeal. However, sometimes the appeals court will find that the trial judge erred in his or her decisions in terms of allowing or not allowing certain evidence to be heard. As well, the judges may determine that the statute relating to the case was improperly interpreted. Should the appellate court find these aberrations in law or fact, many options are possible, all within the premise that the original verdict will be set aside. Some of the options include sending the case for retrial or overturning the conviction and acquitting the defendant. Depending on the nature of the offence and the statute in dispute, decisions of provincial appeal courts can be further appealed in the court of last resort, the Supreme Court of Canada. The Supreme Court will usually review the cases that are appealed to them and decide which cases they will hear and which decisions of the appeal courts they will rule as final. However, in split decisions of the appeals court or on questions of law, a Supreme Court appeal is almost always granted.

## The Federal Court System

Side by side with the provincial court system, is the **Federal Court of Canada,** divided into a trial and an appellate division. This court is not involved in criminal cases, but instead deals exclusively with legal actions brought against the federal government and federal agencies. Appeals from the decisions of the trial division can be made to the Federal Court of Appeal and finally to the Supreme Court of Canada.

## The Supreme Court of Canada

The **Supreme Court of Canada** is an immensely powerful institution. Because of its ability to review all decisions of the provincial and federal courts, it has the power to define which lower-court decisions reflect best the laws and the Constitution of Canada. Schmalleger et al. (2000) believe that the evolution of the Supreme Court is a classic example of institutional development in Canadian history. In its earliest years it was not influential in developing legal doctrine, but today it is a system that wields great legal power in most aspects of Canadian life. Its influence has grown owing to its willingness to confront social change and the resulting legal ramifications. As well, it acts as an alternative to the arbitrary decisions of the lower courts, and it counters manipulation of the justice system by provincial and federal governments. The Canadian Charter of Rights and Freedoms, created in 1982 as part of our constitution, delegated the Supreme Court as the repository of judicial review of government actions and laws. The Court has willingly accepted its role as the arbiter of Charter-protected rights, and consequently its workload and importance have increased. When the Court agrees to hear a case, it reviews the records and invites written and oral presentations from all parties involved in the case. While the Court gets hundreds of requests petitioning for appellate review, only about one hundred cases are actually selected to be heard annually, and these cases usually involve some aspect of case or statute law or an issue of national importance. As is the case with other appellate courts, a majority decision is the decision of the court, and in most instances both written majority and dissenting opinions are provided. The federal Cabinet may also request an opinion from the Supreme Court on a matter of constitutional importance. This special role tends to further the power and influence of this court with respect to law and the political structure of Canada.

# Trial and Case Resolution

Cunningham and Griffiths (1997) note that there are countless rules of procedure and evidence governing criminal prosecution in the court systems. One of the most important principles is the *presumption of innocence,* whereby the defendant is considered innocent until either convicted or acquitted. As well, it is the role of the Crown to prove guilt—it is not the role of the accused to prove innocence of the charge. Two further tenets of our justice system are that a person cannot be held criminally responsible for an act committed owing to a mental disorder, and planning or attempting to commit a crime is a criminal offence punishable by law. Crimes are also divided into two categories. **Summary conviction offences** are less serious types of crimes, and **indictable offences** include more serious crimes, such as murder, robbery, sexual assault, kidnapping, or fraud.

## The Decision to Go to Trial

In most provinces the police lay the criminal charge, and under the discretionary clause, the recommendation is to proceed only if there is a reasonable prospect of conviction and if pursuing the charge is in the public interest. Although the police usually lay the charge, that decision will normally be either ratified or rejected by the **Crown attorney,** the prosecutor who acts on behalf of the government in prosecuting an indictable charge. The police officer lays out the information pertaining to the charge before a justice of the peace, outlining the alleged infractions of the Criminal Code that the accused has committed. Should the justice of the peace accept the bona fides of the charge (that the charge is made in good faith), then several options are in place to ensure that the accused will appear in court for the trial. In the case of less serious offences, the justice of the peace issues the accused an appearance notice to appear in court and defend the charge. In more serious cases, the police will issue an arrest warrant. After arrest the decision must be made whether to release the defendant on bail or detain him or her in police custody. The Charter of Rights protects Canadians from arbitrary detention and presumes that release from police custody after arrest will be the norm. Only if the police have reasonable grounds to believe that the accused will fail to appear in court or that it is in the public interest to detain the accused, will detention withstand a Charter appeal on the grounds of arbitrary detention.

The Bail Reform Act of 1976 established a legal framework to provide for the release from custody of the accused. Bail is considered to be an urgent necessity for the accused, as otherwise they could lose their jobs, leading to the financial ruin of themselves and their families. Furthermore, when submitted to lengthy pretrial incarceration, defendants will have more difficulty retaining legal services or assisting in preparing their defence. The literature is replete with evidence that pretrial incarceration creates a presumption of guilt and a self-fulfilling prophecy, with conviction and prison the inevitable outcome. As a result of these reforms and Charter protections, the majority of those arrested for Criminal Code violations today are granted some form of bail. However, if the suspect fails to attend the trial, the security will be forfeited, and a warrant will be issued for the suspect's arrest. While continued detention without bail is no longer the norm in the court system, the Supreme Court has upheld the right of the Crown to object to bail when the suspect has been charged with an indictable offence after having been previously released on bail for a separate indictable offence. Furthermore, the Court has ruled that the onus is on the accused to establish that they should be granted bail when they have been charged with trafficking in or importing narcotics.

For summary conviction offences the Criminal Code sets out clear rules for trial and conviction. Accused persons should appear in person before a judge, but they may have a legal representative appear and plead on their behalf. The vast majority of these offences are heard in provincial court, and Hann (1973) notes that because of an extremely crowded court docket, these cases are proceeded with "swiftly and summarily." More than 75 percent of all cases examined in the Toronto provincial courts were dispatched with three or fewer court appearances, with sometimes no more than five minutes for each court appearance. In fact, **plea bargaining,** whereby the accused pleads guilty to a lesser charge agreed on by the defence and the prosecution in order to obtain a lighter sentence, and assembly-line justice are becoming the norm for summary conviction offences in the provincial court system. Critics of this trend are suggesting that due process is often lacking in the legal outcomes of these decisions, and that the justice system is being severely compromised because of heavy court workloads.

The Criminal Code states that unless specifically expressed by law, those accused of indictable offences should be tried before a judge and jury. However, as Griffiths and Verdun-Jones (1994) have noted, exceptions provided in the law have become so common that it is today rare for an accused to be tried by a judge and jury. In the main, indictable offences fall into three categories. In the first category are the most serious offences, including murder. The Criminal Code allows for persons charged with these offences to be tried by a Superior Court judge without a jury, provided the judge and the provincial attorney general both agree on this approach. The least serious of the indictable offences in the Criminal Code, including theft, fraud, or embezzlement, are heard by the judge alone. Finally, with a catch-all category of offences, including armed robbery, sexual assault, attempted murder, and dangerous driving, the accused has the option of choosing trial either by judge and jury or by judge alone.

All those accused of an indictable offence first appear in the provincial court. If the offence falls into a category to be tried in provincial court, it continues there to its conclusion. Others will be moved to the superior court, depending on the severity of the offence. However, it is important to note that before these cases are forwarded to the superior court for trial, a provincial court judge must conduct a **preliminary inquiry** to determine whether there is sufficient evidence to warrant a committal of the accused for trial. The preliminary inquiry is an important phase in our criminal court process. The purpose is not to establish the guilt or innocence of the accused, but rather to find out whether the Crown has sufficient admissible evidence to result in a guilty conviction when presented in a trial. Both the Crown and the accused have the right to call witnesses and to cross-examine witnesses. However, while the Criminal Code provides for an elaborate mechanism under which a preliminary inquiry can be conducted, the actual preliminary is usually a perfunctory examination of the case; Holmes (1982) notes that witnesses were called in less than half of the cases. Furthermore, in more than three-quarters of the cases, the inquiry lasted for less than a day. The judge conducting the preliminary inquiry has two options at the conclusion of the hearing. Based on the evidence presented, the judge can order the accused to stand trial for the offence charged or can substitute another charge. As well, the accused can be discharged if the judge believes that on the basis of the evidence, the Crown has presented an insufficient case. The goal of the Crown is to make a prima facie case (one with enough evidence to make a judgment), not to prove the guilt of the accused in the preliminary trial. As a result of evidence provided at the inquiry, the Crown can change the nature or severity of the charge, illustrating the power of the Crown in our justice system.

## The Criminal Trial

The actual criminal trial before a judge and jury is a well-choreographed affair. Both the Crown counsel as prosecutor and the **defence counsel** make an opening statement to the judge and jury, in which they outline their position and evidence. While no evidence is presented at this stage, the goals of the defence are to poke holes in the Crown's case and to present support for the defendant's alibi or character. The presentation of evidence is the centrepiece of the trial, and the Crown counsel martials the prosecution's case. The Crown counsel's purpose is to prove the guilt of the defendant, and the evidence can be of two types, direct and circumstantial. **Direct evidence** is factual evidence, such as wiretaps, videos, photographs, or testimonial evidence by eyewitnesses. **Circumstantial evidence** is not as clear cut, and the judge and jury will have to evaluate its veracity. Unlike real evidence, such as physical material, weapons, fingerprints, or recorded confessions, circumstantial evidence includes such circumstances as a witness who saw the accused running from the scene of the crime or a witness who heard the accused threatening the victim on a previous occasion. In today's modern criminal trial, DNA evidence is becoming a major tool of forensic detection in connecting the accused to the victim, even though eyewitnesses may be lacking.

Judges have the important role of deciding which evidence a jury will hear. In making this decision, they also need to ensure that a jury will not be biased as a result of the content or presentation of evidence. An error in allowing or disallowing the use of evidence can be grounds for appeal of the jury's verdict, particularly by the defence in guilty verdicts. Schmalleger et al. (2000) note that witness testimony is the major tool by which evidence is introduced in court trials. Witnesses can include victims, investigative officers, the defendant, and, in today's courts, experts in certain fields. Whether to call the accused as a witness is a major issue for defence lawyers. The defendant's right to remain silent and to refuse to testify is protected under both common law and the Charter of Rights. Furthermore, the Supreme Court of Canada has ruled that if a defendant refuses to testify, prosecutors and judges should refrain from commenting on this fact, other than to instruct a jury that silence does not equal guilt. It is the duty of the Crown to prove its case, with or without testimony from the accused. All witnesses can be cross-examined by the other side, and the purpose of the cross-examination is to verify the witness's credibility and memory of the events. The hope of the lawyer conducting the cross-examination is to poke holes in the testimony of the witness and to discredit the evidence that is being presented. In some instances, witnesses perjure themselves or make untrue statements in the courts, leaving themselves open to criminal prosecution. Furthermore, if perjury is proven in the court trial, the witness can damage the case in the eyes of the jury and affect the outcome of the trial.

# The Jury Process

At the conclusion of the criminal trial both sides make their closing arguments. This is a process of summation, review, and analysis of the evidence. For the prosecutor, the purpose is to hammer home the evidence presented and prove the guilt of the accused. For the defence counsel, the purpose is to discredit the prosecution evidence and case and cast doubt in the minds of the jury members. If the accused has not taken the stand, the defence also must convince the jury that this should not be perceived as reason for a guilty verdict. In cases of circumstantial evidence, the defence has to show, as well, the lack of direct proof of the accused's guilt. Finally, before the case goes to the jury, the judge's role is to outline the main evidence as presented and to remind the jury of their duty to be objective and impartial in reviewing the evidence. In his or her charge to the jury, the judge will also outline the various verdicts that the jury can return, the burden or proof that the Crown must show, and of the need to return a unanimous verdict. Juries, after receiving their instructions from the judge, often retire to the jury room and begin their deliberations. They can from time to time request additional transcripts of the evidence or further clarification of the rules of evidence or legal issues from the judge. While in most instances juries return their verdicts within hours or days, in more complex cases this process can last weeks. If a jury, after a long period of deliberation, informs the judge that it is unable to reach a unanimous verdict, the judge can discharge the jury and order a new trial. Judges have also been empowered to attempt to break deadlocks by using every persuasive technique to clarify the evidence for jury members who cannot accept the reasoning of their colleagues. However, the Supreme Court of Canada has stated that while judges can attempt to prevent hung juries, a juror should not be coerced to change his or her mind simply to conform to the majority opinion.

Critics of the legal system point to the jury system as one of its main weaknesses. They believe that the ability of the jury to sort through the evidence and accurately determine a defendant's guilt or innocence is questionable. These critics assert that when faced with increasingly complex legal issues, many jurors not only do not understand trial court language and practice, but may not even understand the instructions or charge from the judge. Furthermore, in highly publicized cases, it is difficult to separate emotions from fact. With today's increasing use of technical evidence and expert witnesses, it is not surprising that jurors could be lost as to the importance of legal technicalities or could fail to comprehend the expertise of expert witnesses. The calling into question of jury members' impartiality was brought home to the public by the recent obstruction of justice trial of Gillian Guess, in which it was found that while part of the jury for a murder trial, she was having a sexual affair with one of the accused. Moreover, fellow jurors told the court that Gillian Guess bullied and badgered her colleagues into bringing in a not guilty verdict.

Alternatives to the present system could be to hold the trial before a panel of judges or to use professional jurors, who would be trained in the necessary skills, such as due process, objectivity, and observation. However, the concept of a "trial by judge and a jury of one's peers," which comes from centuries of British jurisprudence, is difficult to eradicate. As well, this right is enshrined in section 11(f) of the Charter. While there is room for improvement in the selection, training, and maintaining of the quality of jurors, our view is that the system does protect society from arbitrary justice and bias.

## Appeal

At the conclusion of the trial and the finding of guilt or innocence, either the prosecution or the defence can appeal the court's decision. Appeals can involve questions of law or fact, and there are different appeal procedures for summary conviction and indictable offences. Cunningham and Griffiths (1997) note that an appeal court has various options when a case is appealed before it. If it believes that there is no merit to the appeal, it may decide to not hear it. Alternatively, it can hear the appeal, discuss it, and direct that the offender be acquitted or order a new trial. In most appeals, it is not the conviction that is appealed, but the sentence. In this case, the appeals court could uphold the sentence, reduce the sentence, and in rare occurrences increase the sentence. In some instances, it could substitute a lesser conviction and commensurate sentence. In many cases, the appellant will apply for bail while the appeal is heard. Because in the bail hearing the appeals court examines the sentence and evidence, frivolous appeals for bail solely to avoid incarceration are uncommon in the Canadian court system.

The final arbiter of the appeal system is the Supreme Court of Canada. The Criminal Code provides for appeals to the Supreme Court of the decisions of the lower courts of appeal. The right of appeal must relate to a question of law, and it is automatic if a judge of the court of appeal has dissented in the judgment. As well, the accused can obtain the permission of the Supreme Court to appear to argue a question of law. The Crown can also use these same grounds to appeal a decision of the appeals court.

# Juveniles in the Court System

No other part of the criminal justice system has been as subjected in the last few years to criticism and harsh judgment from both the public and law enforcement agencies as the **youth court** system. Schmalleger et al. (2000) note that in the last decade, the increase of senseless youth violence among both young males and females has reached epidemic proportions. As well, statistics show that firearms were involved in a higher percentage of violent crimes among youth than adults. An example of a case that has provoked public outrage for youth offences is the 1997 case in Victoria, British Columbia, where eight teenaged boys and girls without provocation verbally and physically attacked and murdered 14-year-old Reena Virk. Social critics suggest that large numbers of youths are alienated and neglected, emotionally or physically brutalized, and abandoned by a society in which members are too selfishly concerned with achieving their own goals. Given this neglect, many youths eagerly embrace criminal activity, and a significant proportion of crime today is committed by youths. While the majority of this crime—over 50 percent—is property related, including theft, breaking and entering, and motor vehicle theft, an increasing percentage is violent, including assaults and robbery. A major concern is the doubling of the rate of female violent crime in the past five years. Because of the strong correlation between youth crime and later adult criminal behaviour, it is important that we analyze the causes of youth crime, as well as the youth justice system through which it is processed.

Since Canada was formed as a country in 1867, there have been many approaches to handling the problems of youths who choose not to follow the norms of society. The reform school movement in the 1860s focused on delinquent youths who were involved in serious criminal activities. This approach emphasized traditional values and duplicating a family environment, which was intended to instill discipline and authority. Schmalleger et al. (2000) note that this method of rehabilitation soon foundered as environments were overcrowded and institutional structures, rules, and procedures were too routinized. In 1894 Canada's Parliament passed the Juvenile Delinquency Act, which allowed state intervention in the arrest, trial, and imprisonment of juvenile offenders. The rationale was the belief that youth offenders should be treated separately and differently by the court and that their behaviour could be changed. The belief was that nurturing could protect youths from the stigma of being labelled criminals, and youth courts would protect the identity of juvenile offenders. The guiding principle of this Act was that youth should be rehabilitated, and the use of non-criminal procedures would ensure that the needs of the child would always take precedence. Finally, the Act stated that juveniles who committed serious offences that merited incarceration should be detained in separate juvenile detention centres, rather than be housed with adult criminals.

The Juvenile Delinquency Act, while a laudable and pioneering piece of legislation aimed at rehabilitation, was increasingly criticized over the years for its failure to reduce juvenile delinquency or to rehabilitate offenders. As well, the power of juvenile courts to enforce punishment that was often harsher than in adult court also brought criticism. During the 1960s and 1970s, two opposing models of handling juvenile delinquents were debated. The welfare model, which was the basis of the Juvenile Delinquency Act, had as its premise the introduction of intervention methods that could be individually worked out to meet the needs of the offender. The hope was that with proper resources, youths could be rehabilitated and accept societal rather than deviant norms. The opposite school was based on the thinking of the classical school of criminology, which believed that young offenders made a deliberate choice to choose deviant behaviour because it brought them more pleasure and rewards. Therefore, it was the role of the state to ensure that youths were accountable for their actions. As well, this model proposed that youths should be offered the same legal rights as adults. In the midst of this debate came statistical evidence that youth crime was on the increase, along with rising public support for a "get tough" attitude on youth crime. The result was the **Young Offenders Act (YOA)** of 1984, which was a compromise between the benevolent welfare model and the "get tough" law and order model favoured by the police and some justice officials. The YOA standardized the age of young offenders at 12 to 17 years, defined criteria and procedures for diversion from court, mandated the use of legal counsel, and permitted the youth courts to issue only determinate sentences.

## Youth Courts

The youth courts have jurisdiction for all offences falling under the Criminal Code, as well as for provincial offences. However, some provinces give jurisdiction for prosecuting young offenders to either the social services or correctional services ministries, depending on the age of the offender. Griffiths and Verdun-Jones (1994) note that given the less serious nature of most youth offences, the police have great discretion in determining the methods for handling complaints. In all provinces, it is expected that in keeping with child welfare laws, children under 12 will be diverted from the criminal justice system in cases where they have committed a criminal offence. However, with older offenders and when the offence is more serious, the police will file a formal report to the Crown, who reviews the evidence and decides whether to use alternative measures, such as diversion, or to proceed to the youth court.

The goal of the YOA is to ensure that in court, the youth is allowed full equality before the law, including legal counsel. The trial is held before a judge, without a jury. If the offence is of a serious indictable nature and the offender is 14 years or older, the case can be transferred to adult court. As in adult court, the

youth and Crown counsel both have the right to appeal a judge's decision. In cases where the judge has ordered detention, sentences are automatically reviewed after 12 months, and in no case can the sentence be increased.

Because of immense public criticism levelled at the Young Offenders Act, the Canadian government has made a series of amendments to the Act. Most of these amendments are geared toward toughening the sentences and improving the operations of justice officials. For example, provisions are now included to publish the identities of young offenders who are deemed by the state to be a public danger, as well as to empower the police to apprehend youths who violate their parole. In general, the purpose of the amendments is to increase the enforcement process and to shift toward a crime-control model of youth justice.

While the Act standardized the procedures to be enacted in the courts, such as the rights of the accused and the role of the Crown and defence, probation officers or judges have much discretion. Judges must now issue determinate sentences, but they still have wide latitude in sentencing, and the result is that different judges use different approaches and often come up with widely differing sentences for identical offences.

Caputo et al. (1989) note also that judicial decisions in youth court can be seen as shifting to a punitive rather than paternalistic and rehabilitative model. More young offenders are being sentenced to closed- and open-custody facilities and to sentences of longer than three months. This trend has been noticed across the country, with Ontario's per capita rate of custody among the highest in the

The Canadian Criminal Justice System

nation. The majority of youths found guilty of a criminal offence receive a community-based, noncustodial sentence. This sentence can include community service, a fine, payment of compensation or restitution, and probation. Winterdyk (2000) notes that probation designed to provide supervision of youth offenders in the community is the most frequently used method of punishment. There is considerable criticism of community-based programs by those who advocate stricter justice for young offenders. For example, while the role of probation officers in providing supervision and counselling to troubled youths is critical, some people see only high recidivism rates for those on probation or parole, rather than the success stories of young offenders who go on to become full participants in the normal codes of behaviour. Some also believe that institutionally based programs can be more effective than those based in the community.

Custodial sentences are usually meted out for the most serious offences, and the court can specify whether the sentence must be served in an open or a closed facility. Open-custody facilities can include group homes or community residential centres. Secure-custody facilities, such as youth detention centres or boot camps, are operated by the provincial governments. Since 1997, when Ontario opened its first boot camp, this model has become the norm for the province, and by 2005, it is expected that all youth detention centres will follow this model. These are privately run centres, where harsh discipline and shock incarceration are the tools of treatment. While the goal is still to rehabilitate the offender, the method is harsh realism and a physical regimen of exercise, discipline, and skills training. Although the effectiveness of this approach is unknown at this time, the method is gaining public support. There are various proposals to amend the Young Offenders Act, with most of the changes relating to methods for handling more serious criminal offences and in general toughening the penalties for youthful offenders. We should be careful, however, that in attempting to improve the system, we do not lose sight of the goal of rehabilitation. As well, replicating the deterrence and punitive model of the adult criminal justice system by itself will provide no long-term reduction in youth crime.

# Diversion and Alternative Measures Programs

The purpose of alternative measures and **diversion programs** is to facilitate the reconciliation of victim and offender, to compensate the victim, and, most important, to avoid a formal hearing in youth court. The goal is to allow the young offender to be rehabilitated in the community and to avoid the stigma of a criminal label. All alternative measures programs across Canada are designed to allow young people to take responsibility for their criminal behaviour, to meet with their victims, and to work out mutually satisfactory methods for restitution. This process also allows offenders to perform community service and to attend counselling and treatment programs. As well, early intervention programs have as their goal the prevention of criminal behaviour in youths who may be at risk but who have not committed a serious criminal offence.

Jaffe et al. (1985), in attempting to assess the effectiveness of diversion and alternative measures programs, note that the major objectives of these programs are to reduce the number of cases that come before youth courts, to bring about a positive change in the attitudes of young offenders, and to lower the rate of youth crime and recidivism. The authors' comparison of the records of young offenders in Ontario who had been exposed to alternative measures programs with those who had no exposure showed no clear differences in terms of recidivism rates or attitudes toward crime and victims. Fischer and Jeune (1987), however, note that in their comparison of the two groups of youth offenders in western Canada, some notable differences did occur in terms of attitudes toward recidivism and restitution. As well, these programs cost less than the court process. Because these programs have been operating for less than a decade, it is imperative that society allow sufficient time for evaluating their operations. Reverting to a more punitive and deterrent model for youth will have in the long run a negative impact on rehabilitation, and it will hinder the re-entry of youthful offenders into the norms of the wider society.

Jones and Krisberg (1994) note the complexity of problems facing our youth today. Broken homes, poor parental supervision, poverty, low self-esteem, poor interpersonal relationships, and peer group pressure can all be contributors to delinquency and later adult criminality. Research has also shown that one of the key variables is the relationship between problem families and juvenile delinquency. To deal with this variable, programs are being developed that involve all parts of the community, including schools, social service professionals, neighbourhood groups, law enforcement personnel, and community help centres. Further research on street kids in Canada has suggested that physical and sexual abuse can lead children to leave abusive homes and fall into a pattern of drug abuse and violence. It is clear that a home environment where parents and children share emotional involvement and common values is the best option for reducing delinquency. These research reports point to the importance of the family in the socialization process and in the teaching of societal values and morals. This is not to say that in today's complex society, other influences, such as peer groups, the media, or the Internet, may not be as important in affecting the behavioural choices of our youth. The bottom line, however, is that a problem exists in society, and it is necessary to use all the tools at our disposal to find solutions.

# Conclusion

The issues discussed in this chapter occupy a central role in an analysis of the Canadian criminal justice system. The criminal court and trial are the basis of our democratic principles of fairness and justice. The adversarial process that pits the Crown against the defence, with a judge and or jury being the final arbiter of justice, is based on centuries of jurisprudence. While there are weaknesses in the court structure and process, nothing that has been advocated can improve on the peer-based, fact-finding process of our judicial system.

That our youth have special status and courts to adjudicate their deviant conduct is as it should be. In our changing society, with increasing challenges to established institutions and norms, it is not surprising that deviant and criminal behaviour among youth has been increasing. The easy availability of drugs, the decline of the family as the major socializing agent in the society, and the increase in family violence, abuse, and breakdown have all contributed to deviance in the society. Faced with increasing youth crime rates and with more serious violations by youth of the Criminal Code, the justice system has been forced to reconsider its goals and purposes in terms of youthful offenders. A historic philosophy of rehabilitative justice embodied in the Young Offenders Act has been roundly criticized by law enforcement agencies and other critics for coddling deviant youth, and immense pressure is being placed on justice officials to adopt a more punitive model for handling youthful offenders. Diversion and other alternatives to custody measures are being criticized as failing to reduce recidivism rates among delinquents. While recognizing that the challenge to find answers to increasing rates of violent behaviour among youth is daunting, we believe that the only long-term method for success must remain rehabilitation. Closed custodial incarceration only exacerbates the institutionalization process, creating a social system based on violence, exploitation, and a subculture of learned deviant behaviour. A punitive approach may appease public opinion, but it fails to address the underlying causes of non-normative behaviour in our young people.

# Summary

The Canadian court system is a complex network of provincial and federal trial and appellate courts, and at the apex is the Supreme Court of Canada. Provincial courts are located in every city of the nation, and they have the power to hear all criminal cases, as well as small claims, business, and family disputes. The superior provincial courts hear more serious criminal cases. Federal courts hear cases that come under the Federal Court Act and that usually involve tax, immigration, and administrative tribunal matters. Each of these courts allows appeals to the appeal division, and the Supreme Court of Canada can decide to hear cases from any of these jurisdictions if they pertain to a constitutional or legal interpretation issue.

Whereas the police lay charges, it is the role of the Crown attorney to review the evidence and decide if the evidence justifies prosecution. The Charter of Rights and Freedoms protects all citizens from arbitrary detention and provides for the right to bail and a fair trial. Because of the crowded court docket, plea bargaining is becoming increasingly common. In this process, the Crown and the defence together decide on a common plea and sentence, which they present to the judge. However, in the case of serious criminal offences, a judge and jury trial is still the norm. In this situation, it is the duty of the Crown to prove the defendant guilty, and it is the role of the defence counsel to poke holes in the prosecution's case. Regardless of the verdict, the decision can be appealed to the higher court, either on grounds of law or fact.

Juveniles have always been treated differently in the courts of Canada, and today the Young Offenders Act is the guiding principle for the administration of juvenile justice. The goal is the rehabilitation of the offender and diversion from the formal court system. For more serious offences, the youth is allowed full equality before the law, including legal counsel. As in most situations involving criminal justice, there is continuing debate as to whether youthful offenders should be punished more severely, such as by long periods in detention centres. The public pressure is for increased enforcement and retributive justice. However, because of the complexity of the causes of youth deviance, any policy that hinders the re-entry of offenders into the wider society will be counterproductive.

## Key Terms

circumstantial evidence (p. 149)

courts of appeal (p. 144)

Crown attorney (p. 146)

defence counsel (p. 149)

direct evidence (p. 149)

diversion programs (p. 155)

Federal Court of Canada (p. 145)

indictable offence (p. 146)

plea bargaining (p. 148)

preliminary inquiry (p. 148)

## Discussion Questions

1.  Plea bargaining is an increasingly important part of the court system. Discuss the pros and cons of this practice.

2.  Discuss the success of alternative measures programs for young offenders.

3.  What are some of the factors that have led to calls for a review of the present jury system?

4.  Discuss the various stages in a criminal jury trial.

## Weblinks

**www2.lexum.umontreal.ca/bv/classification1.cfm?categorie=7&classement=1&lan=En** This site, hosted by the Law Library of Canada and Quebec, provides links to Canadian judicial Web sites including the Supreme Court, the Federal Court, and provincial courts.

**www.rand.org/publications/MR/MR699/** RAND, a public policy research institute, has posted the complete text of their report "Diverting Children from a Life of Crime: Measuring Costs and Benefits." The report is conveniently posted as separate chapters, and with figures and tables also provided as a separate file.

**canada.justice.gc.ca/en/ps/yj/index.html** The Department of Justice hosts a Youth Justice Web site, with links to relevant legislation and articles on the topic.

**www.acjnet.org/capcj/en/law/publications/judicial.html** This article, written by a University of Calgary professor and entitled "The Canadian judicial system: What do people know about it?" looks at the level of information ordinary Canadians possess regarding our court system.

**www.firstlinelaw.com/indexfl.html** The First Line Criminal Law Information, a Web resource provided by a Canadian private firm, offers articles on such topics as being arrested and charged under the Criminal Code and dealing with police searches and seizures.

# CHAPTER 8

# Corrections

## Objectives

- To acquaint readers with the criminal justice process in Canada from charge to trial to sentence.

- To outline the principles that underlie sentencing decisions in Canada.

- To describe the plea-bargaining process and its objectives.

- To explore the trial process, including the role of the prosecution and defence attorneys.

## From Charge to Trial

Once a crime has been committed and a suspect apprehended, the police lay charges. In Canada, charges are laid by the police, rather than through the office of the district attorney, as in the United States. The police conduct an investigation of the crime and then propose to charge the suspect with one or more offences. It is quite common for police to "upcharge" or to "overcharge" suspects. Upcharging means charging a suspect with a more serious crime. In cases of homicide, for example, the police may upcharge in order to be able to negotiate when a plea bargain is appropriate, and if the evidence does not support a charge of premeditated murder they can switch to the lesser charge of manslaughter. It is much more difficult to charge a person with a more serious form of a crime once an initial charge has been laid. Overcharging can also involve adding a series of charges to the offence(s) with which the person is

being charged in order to ensure that a conviction will be possible on at least some of the charges. It is also advantageous to the Crown in plea negotiation to have numerous charges with which to construct a deal, as the Crown may decide to drop some charges in order to focus on others.

Television viewers are familiar with the guarantee of rights, referred to as the *Miranda warning*, which is issued to suspects upon arrest in the United States. Police officers are compelled at the point of arrest to warn suspects that they have certain rights, including the right to remain silent, to contact an attorney, and to have an attorney appointed if the suspect cannot afford one. The rights of Canadians who are charged by police are contained in the Charter. Fundamental among these rights is the right to life, liberty, and security of the person. All Canadians have the right to know the reasons for their arrest or detention. They also have the right to counsel. Police must inform suspects of the specific charges being made against them. Further rights guaranteed by the Charter include:

- The right to have a trial conducted in reasonable time
- The right to avoid self-incrimination
- The right to be considered innocent
- The right to obtain a jury trial
- The right to not be denied bail without just cause
- The right to avoid double jeopardy (being tried twice for the same offence)
- The right to not be submitted to cruel and unusual punishment
- The right to have an interpreter during the trial

In Britain, recent legal amendments have removed the right of the accused to remain silent. The courts in Britain now interpret silence to mean that the individual is revealing guilty knowledge of the crime committed. The right to silence is important because accused often give incriminating information to the police in the hope that the charges will be dropped if they just "explain" everything. For some accused, this offering of information reflects their nervousness at the time of being charged and the human desire to communicate, even when it is not in their interest. Peter Demeter, a Mississauga contractor who murdered his wife, hired a leading criminal attorney to handle his case. The lawyer requested a $10 000 retainer and then indicated that he would give Demeter $10 000 worth of advice. That advice was simply to say nothing to the police. However,  Demeter thought himself more clever than the police and invited detectives into his home for drinks, all the while "cleverly" talking about his relationship with his wife and his theories about the crime and how it might have been committed. Eventually, he managed to talk himself into a life sentence in prison for her murder.

Following arrest, most people are released until the date of their first appearance before the court; thus, the individual is generally free to remain in the community for several months. For the small number of offenders who are charged with extremely violent crimes or who present a substantial risk of fleeing from the jurisdiction, the court will require remand to a jail or detention centre. Accused are given a notice to appear, which states the time, date, and place of the trial. As well, accused must present themselves at a police station before their court appearance to be fingerprinted. If the police decide not to arrest the person at this time, they may still do so at a later date by asking a judge to issue an arrest warrant or a summons to ensure that the individual will be in court on the appropriate date. If the individual fails to appear for the court date, an arrest warrant is issued, which allows the police to pick the person up and bring him or her to a jail pending a hearing.

Some offenders are brought before a justice for what is termed an *initial hearing*. This is an opportunity for the charges that are being laid to be read to the accused. The initial hearing is a short process and is adjourned until the accused can obtain legal counsel to assist him or her in the case before the court. When counsel is present at the initial hearing, a number of courses are open to the prosecution:

- In cases of a summary or a minor indictable offence, a plea from the accused may be taken.
- A trial date can be set when a plea of not guilty is registered.
- A preliminary hearing may be set for more serious charges.
- The accused is required to select the manner of trial, either before a judge sitting alone or before a judge and jury. If the accused elects for a trial before a provincial court judge, he or she can make a plea at this time. If the accused chooses a trial before a superior court judge, sitting either alone or with a jury, a preliminary hearing date must be set.

## Preliminary Inquiry

Under Canadian law, in cases of serious offences a preliminary inquiry must be held before proceeding to a full court trial. The preliminary inquiry serves to determine whether the prosecution can produce sufficient evidence to warrant proceeding to a full trial. This process has two functions: it eliminates the need for costly trials when there is flimsy evidence against the accused, and it protects the right of the individual not to be subjected to a full criminal trial with all its stresses when a strong case cannot be made. The process is surprisingly similar to a full trial. The prosecution presents evidence to demonstrate to the judge that there are sufficient grounds for a full trial. As in a full court trial, the prosecution also will call all relevant witnesses.

The role of the defence attorney is also the same in a preliminary inquiry. This procedure allows the defence to cross-examine the witnesses, understand the strengths and weaknesses of the prosecution's case, and evaluate the quality of the witnesses and evidence that will be brought to bear against the client. This evaluation of the evidence is important if it is obvious that a trial is warranted, since it allows the defence to formulate a trial strategy. The accused's attorney also presents witnesses and evidence. While accused have the right to take the stand in their own defence at this hearing, they rarely do so. Unless the accused can provide an ironclad alibi—for example, "I was in England at the time; here is my plane ticket, hotel bill and other receipts, and pictures of me in front of Buckingham Palace with the Queen on the 24th"—it is usually wise to observe silence until the trial. Hearing the evidence against them and witnesses for the prosecution may assist the accused in giving evidence at the full trial, where it will have the greatest impact and may come as a surprise to the prosecution. At the conclusion of the presentation of the evidence, the judge must determine whether there are sufficient grounds to commit the offence to a full trial or whether the defendant should be discharged. Any case can be committed to a full trial without going through a preliminary inquiry at the discretion of the prosecutor.

# The Criminal Trial

Jury trials are rare in Canada. A jury trial is a costly process, particularly when the case is before the courts for an extended period of time. While the O.J. Simpson case was instructive in some aspects of the criminal trial process in the United States, it would be atypical in Canada. Plea bargaining is the most common way of resolving charges in the criminal justice system (see the discussion later this chapter). Cases that proceed to trial typically involve contentious issues of evidence, a higher level of complexity, a truly innocent accused, or the prospect of lengthy jail time when there is no plea bargain available or offered.

Juries are selected randomly from the tax assessment or voter registration lists of communities within the court's jurisdiction. Once chosen, jury members are sent a notice by the sheriff's office to register for jury duty or to provide sufficient reasons for why they cannot serve. Certain professionals are excluded from jury duty, including police officers, criminology professors, and members of the clergy, reflecting the fact that they may be in too powerful a position to influence other jury members' decisions.

A jury in Canada consists of 12 people. Those selected for jury duty are examined to determine their suitability. The prosecution, the defence, and the judge question prospective jurors to ascertain their willingness and ability to sit in judgment. A person who admits to being prejudiced against the accused, to having already formed an opinion for any reason, or to being unable to judge the case on the evidence put before them in the court is dismissed. When a case is

An artist's sketch of a jury. Most Canadian courts do not allow photographs to be taken during the proceedings.

highly controversial and has received a great deal of pretrial publicity, the defence and prosecution may issue a considerable number of challenges before they select a jury. Many lawyers now employ specialists who advise them of jurors whom they believe would be more sympathetic to their clients or might find in their favour. Attorneys may base their challenges on the information these experts pass on to them. This portion of the criminal trial is known as *voir dire*.

## The Courtroom Proceedings

Once a trial commences, it takes the form of a complicated human drama governed by strict rules of procedure. Television dramas like *Perry Mason, Matlock,* and *Law and Order* have given Canadians a perspective on criminal trials that is not grounded in reality. Trials are rarely sensational, as courtroom observers may attest to. Although the evidence given, such as in a murder trial, may be shocking, the trial is typically formal and dry. The prosecution is required to present a full case against the accused and to prove guilt beyond a reasonable doubt.

The trial is an adversarial process, rather than a truth-seeking forum, despite the protestations of Johnny Cochrane and Marcia Clark during the Simpson trial. The prosecution brings witnesses to the stand and presents evidence and any other materials that may be legally placed before the court to secure conviction. The defence attorney is required to provide the best possible defence short of breaking the law for his or her client, according to Edward Greenspan (1987), one of Canada's most eminent criminal attorneys. The defence attorneys will cross-examine witnesses, challenge testimony or witnesses where appropriate, and do essentially all that is within their legal powers to secure their clients' release by creating a reasonable doubt. "Beyond a reasonable doubt" implies not that all doubts of innocence are erased, but rather that the evidence before the court is sufficient to find the accused guilty.

There are few surprises in the conduct of a criminal trial. There are no last-minute confessions from the stand, no manipulation of the process by judges, no speeches by the defence or prosecution when cross-examining witnesses. The judge ensures that due process and fair play are observed by both sides. Failure to follow simple rules of procedure will result in the judge's ordering that evidence be struck from the court record and the jury ignore the evidence presented, or it may result in a mistrial. A mistrial results when procedures are severely flawed, the evidence is insufficient to warrant a defence being made, or evidence has been misleading, making it impossible to reach a fair verdict. After the judge declares a mistrial, a new court date may be set by the prosecution if sufficient grounds for proceeding still exist.

## Opening Statements

Both the prosecution and the defence present opening statements to the judge and jury, if present in the trial. In their opening statements, both sides hope to present an overview of their cases and alternative theories of what actually occurred. The opening statement is key because if it is not followed through in the trial, serious consequences may ensue in the form of an unexpected verdict. The O.J. Simpson trial is a model of how *not* to present either a defence or a prosecution case. Vincent Bugliosi, a prominent criminal trial attorney who prosecuted the Manson family (and hundreds of murder cases in Los Angeles), demonstrates in his book on the case, *Outrage* (1996), that in his opening statement, defence attorney Johnny Cochrane promised to present a number of witnesses and pieces of evidence that were never delivered. The prosecution neglected to point this omission out in its summation. In most trials, this failure of the defence to follow through on the opening statement could easily have resulted in doubt being placed in the jury's mind. A key witness who was promised is never called. Does this mean that the witness did not want to testify? Was Mr. Cochrane not being truthful? Does this mean that he is not truthful about other matters? Did this witness have evidence that would have shown the accused's guilt? Questions such as these reveal how central a good opening statement is to a successful case. Judges and juries want to be shown a road map and to be led down it. Only poor preparation makes the opening statement unreliable.

The opening statement is an opportunity for the attorneys to red flag certain evidence or testimony as crucial. If an attorney states, "Watch for Mr. X—his testimony provides a solid alibi for my client," you can bet that the jury will perk up when Mr. X is called to the stand. If, on the other hand, he never takes the stand, doubts may be created. The opening statement also provides the defence with an opportunity to remind the jury that the burden of proving guilt is on the prosecution and to instruct the jury on how they can acquit the defendant. The prosecution is likely to emphasize the serious nature of the offence and the responsibility of the judge and jury to see that justice is done.

## The Calling of Witnesses

The prosecution case consists of the calling of witnesses, usually police officers, experts, and witnesses who can provide information on various aspects of the offence that is under consideration by the court. The prosecutor questions the witnesses on what they have witnessed directly or have heard directly. Information about someone that a person hears from another party is considered hearsay and is not permitted to be entered into evidence. As well, the opinions of most witnesses have no place in a criminal trial. However, experts with proven credentials in areas of specialization, including psychiatry and forensics, may present expert opinions to the court, as long as the opinions are based on direct scientific inquiry, on an interview with the accused, or on physical evidence that has been examined. Examples of expert opinions include blood-splatter analysis, crime scene analysis, and firearms testing.

After the prosecution has directly examined each witness, the defence attorney engages in cross-examination. For people who have never appeared at trial, this is a most stressful and anxiety-provoking experience. The defence has the task of trying to clarify or "shake" the witness's testimony through a series of carefully considered questions. Following the preliminary hearing, the defence should be aware of the witnesses they will confront and of the points that the witnesses were unclear or seemingly unsure about. Skillful cross-examination can "tie a witness in knots" and thus cast doubt upon his or her testimony. Witnesses who are considered unreliable, including criminals, drug addicts, alcoholics, paid police informers, and people who have been granted special consideration for their testimony, will receive rough treatment, at least verbally, from a skilled attorney.

Once the prosecution has presented its case in full, it "rests" its case, and it is now the turn of the defence. The defence calls witnesses to build its case in a parallel manner to the prosecution's. Following the presentation of the defence's case, the prosecution may present rebuttal witnesses. These witnesses are intended to refute the testimony or evidence presented by witnesses for the defence. For example, if a witness claims to have been with the defendant at the time of the crime, the prosecution can present a rebuttal witness who knows that the witness is lying. The defence may, of course, also examine these witnesses.

## Closing Arguments

Following witness testimony, the prosecution and the defence present closing arguments. Both sides restate their cases, either for innocence or for guilt, presenting the evidence in a way that is most favourable to their arguments. The defence presents its arguments first, followed by the prosecution. During these statements, the attorneys are prohibited from commenting on any evidence that was not presented at court. It is at this point that they can make a powerful statement to the jury if there is a chain of evidence to support their contentions. Juries respond well to cases that are presented in an orderly and logical manner, in which the opening remarks, evidence, and closing arguments are closely aligned. This presentation requires a great deal of thought and planning on the part of the attorneys. A measure of the research required to present a compelling defence is Edward Greenspan's assertion that when asking a question of a witness, one should always know the answer in advance (Greenspan and Jonas, 1987).

At the conclusion of the case presentation, the judge will give instructions to the jury. These instructions may relate to the type of charges that the jury is to consider, complex legal issues that the jury needs to understand, or the type of evidence and standard of proof that are required as proof of offences. The judge's charge to the jury must not prejudice its decision, however, since that would leave the verdict open to appeal. The judge will normally discuss the burden of proof that the state's case must meet and the meaning of "reasonable doubt."

The jury now retires to deliberate on the case. This process may take a few hours or days. The judge will normally call the jury back to the courtroom to inquire about their progress if there is a substantial delay. Members of the jury may ask to view evidence in order assist their decision making. In a long trial, the jury may be sequestered. When sequestered, jury members are usually lodged in a hotel either for the entirety of the trial or for the period of deliberations. If they are allowed to return home in the evening, they are cautioned not to discuss the case with anyone.

If it cannot reach a decision, the jury is considered to be "hung." At this point, jury members are discharged from their duties, and the onus is on the prosecution to either bring or drop further legal action against the defendant.

As of June 2000, convicted people will immediately be sampled for their DNA in the court's holding facilities. Before sentence is passed, normally a period of time transpires during which presentence reports are constructed to assist the judge in finding an appropriate sentence. This stage normally takes place within a few weeks of the conclusion of the trial. Convicted people have the right to appeal the decision of the court. Usually, the appeal process is lengthy and may involve the appeals court, and if a significant legal issue is being decided, the Supreme Court.

In the next section we will explore the process of sentencing and its underlying principles in the Canadian criminal justice system.

# Sentencing Options

## Incapacitation

One approach to sentencing in Canada, **incapacitation,** involves imprisonment of offenders. Through separating offenders from society, protection is provided to law-abiding citizens. In some parts of the world, incapacitation many mean execution or amputation of a hand to prevent pickpocketing or similar punishments to prevent the repetition of a crime. A new form of incapacitation is electronic tethering or monitoring of offenders, who are confined to their homes. The philosophy guiding incapacitation is that confined prisoners will be unable to commit further crimes because they are isolated from society.

Historically, the British government took the issue of incapacitation one step further by removing criminals not only from civil society but also from the country itself. Under the transportation policy, convicted criminals were shipped to Australia, Africa, and America either to serve a term of imprisonment or to toil as indentured servants for five to seven years. This approach punished prisoners

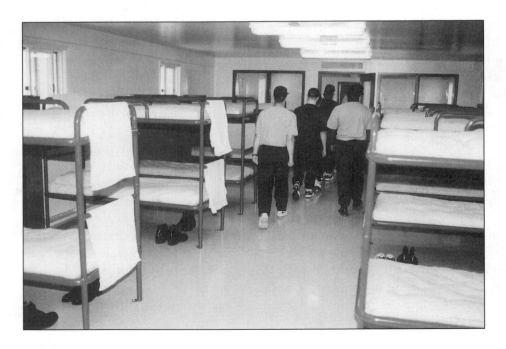

by taking them from their families and loved ones and moving them into environments that the British considered uncivilized and primitive. Transportation to America ended with the American Revolution and the severing of ties with England, particularly in matters related to the dumping of "undesirables" into the new republic.

## Deterrence

**Deterrence** is the attempt to prevent crime by imposing penalties that are constructed to convince potential offenders that they will lose, rather than benefit, from committing criminal acts. Two forms of deterrence are general and specific deterrence. General deterrence refers to discouraging criminal acts through penalties, which induce in people the fear of punishment. Specific deterrence refers to inflicting punishments on specific individuals to deter them from future criminality.

Under this approach, it is assumed that people will be deterred after they rationally consider the potential punishment that awaits them. However, given the influence of drugs and alcohol and the frequent spontaneity of the decision to commit crime, it is unlikely that most criminals weigh the consequences of their actions. Furthermore, given the variability in sentencing decisions in Canada, it is also unclear how the criminal justice system could determine, in advance, the penalty to be imposed. As well, although repeat offenders may be familiar with criminal law and the sentences typically handed down for specific crimes, deterrence appears to have little effect on first-time offenders.

With serious crimes, there is little doubt that individuals recognize that a severe penalty will follow apprehension. But does this knowledge affect their decision to commit crimes? Canadian homicide statistics, for example, clearly demonstrate that the death penalty or the lack of it is not a deterrent to potential murderers (Fleming, 2000). As a deterrent, the death penalty has two disadvantages: first, it does not work, and second, it is irreversible. However, despite the knowledge gained from criminological analysis, a majority of Canadians, and certainly most policing agencies, support the reintroduction of the death penalty. Given the evidence, the death penalty can serve only as a retributive measure. It appears that the ideas of Jeremy Bentham were correct—that is, there must be a certainty that punishment will be imposed in order it to be effective. Yet because sentencing is variable and extralegal factors may affect judges' decisions in imposing sentences, this end cannot be reached under current Canadian law.

## Rehabilitation

**Rehabilitation** is intended to provide opportunities for offenders to change themselves and thus avoid future involvement in crime. This approach involves training, education, and treatment programs that encourage offenders to develop a socially acceptable, productive, and law-abiding lifestyle.

The rehabilitative movement arose in concert with the increasing medicalization of deviance and crime after 1900. There can be little doubt that for some offenders rehabilitative programs work. However, it has been argued that high recidivism rates indicate the failure of this approach. In Canada, over two-thirds of offenders are estimated to reoffend following incarceration. Some critics have argued that no matter how high the quality of such programs, the community is structured in such a way to promote failure for many ex-inmates. A more radical hypothesis would suggest that society views certain individuals and social groups, particularly those drawn from the lower socioeconomic strata of society, as "social junk" to be constantly recycled for criminalization and imprisonment.

## Just Deserts/Retribution

Another goal of sentencing is to punish offenders for their crimes. The previously discussed sentencing approaches focus primarily on what the offender might do in the future or on the effect that various forms of sentences could have on them. The **just deserts** approach, however, focuses on the act or events that led the individual to be convicted. The underlying philosophy is that the criminal has benefited from the crime and now must pay society back for his or her misdeeds, presumably to make things "even." Under this principle, large financial penalties would be imposed for the crime of engaging in fraudulent business practices. In this way, the financial gains that offenders made from their illegal acts would be far outweighed by the fines imposed by the courts. However, while this measure appears on the surface to be reasonable, there are sentencing discrepancies that undermine its effectiveness. If our focus shifts to the area of environmental crime, the problem with this sentencing approach becomes apparent. Brady (1990), in examining the sentencing of individuals versus corporations for such environmental offences as dumping toxic chemicals into waterways and improperly disposing of toxic waste, found that individuals paid penalties roughly equivalent to those of corporations charged with similar offences. For corporations, therefore, the fines are merely a token amount. In cases such as these, the principle of just deserts may be better applied to individual criminal offenders than to corporations.

## Restorative Justice

**Restorative justice** places the victim more centrally in the criminal justice system by focusing on the harm that the offender inflicts not only on the community but also on the victim. Victims have traditionally expressed dissatisfaction with the police and with the handling of their cases in court. For victims, crime is deeply felt and emotionally charged, and they often view their treatment by the criminal justice system as a second form of victimization. Victims report frustration at the failure of police to inform them of the status of their cases. They also often find it difficult to address the complex emotional and psychological issues that arise from their victimization. Since they have generally been unable to confront the perpetrators outside of the courtroom, they often report a sense of being denied justice.

The process of healing and closure for victims was finally addressed in recent Criminal Code amendments that permit victim impact statements (VISs) to be used in court (see Chapter 11). These statements allow victims the chance to directly confront offenders with the suffering their crime has produced and to influence sentencing options. Victims' rights have become an important element in Canada's justice system through a variety of programs, including the following:

1. *Victim-witness assistance programs.* These programs assist victims and witnesses in their journey through the criminal justice process.
2. *Victim funds.* These programs require offenders to pay into funds that compensate victims for medical expenses, physical or psychological damage, and wages lost as a result of victimization.
3. *Restorative programs.* These programs allow offenders to meet with victims. Restorative programs are useful in helping victims to deal with psychological trauma and in assisting criminals to understand the extent of the suffering they have directly inflicted on victims.

The judge and/or jury may consider all of the sentencing approaches listed above when imposing sentences. Historically, each approach has enjoyed a brief period of ascendancy. In the 1960s and 1970s, rehabilitation was a primary goal of sentencing. Rising crime rates in the 1980s and the perceived dissatisfaction with the rehabilitative movement led away from rehabilitation toward a more repressive model of punishment. Today, with the focus on the baby boom cohort, concerns over crime and fears of crime (whether grounded in reality or not) may come to dominate sentencing goals. In an era of conservative approaches to law and order, strict adherence to principles of punishment and responsibility will continue to be championed.

# Sentencing Dispositions

In Canadian courts, there are generally five types of sentences or dispositions that the judges may impose upon conviction of offenders:

1. Fines
2. Suspended sentences
3. Probation

4. Incarceration

5. Capital punishment

Fines are typically awarded in criminal cases involving minor crimes. Fines are also frequently combined with another sentencing alternative, such as probation. A **suspended sentence** may be imposed in cases where the court perceives that the offender needs treatment, rather than confinement. Under this form of sentencing, a sentence is handed down, but it is unenforced provided the offender commits no further crimes. Not only is it more effective and positive for some offenders to remain in the community, but also costs to the justice system can be reduced. Offenders who run afoul of the law because of persistent intoxication in public places are often granted this form of sentence, since jails are considered inappropriate for people who are considered to suffer from a recognized medical illness (Fleming, 1974). Supervision is rarely imposed upon the person; instead, failure to obtain proper treatment or rehabilitative intervention can result in the offender's committing a new offence, which will bring him or her back before the courts. At this point the judge may order the offender to serve the original custodial sentence that had been suspended. Similarly, the judge may impose **probation,** commonly referred to as community supervision (discussed in full in Chapter 10). Under probation orders, the individual is required to regularly report to a probation officer for supervision and to abide by certain conditions in order to avoid returning to court. Incarceration, or imprisonment, removes the offenders committed of serious crimes from the community in order to ensure its protection. Capital punishment is no longer an option in Canada, having been abolished in 1976.

# The Imposition of the Sentence

Imposing sentences is one of the key duties of judges. Juries do not have sentencing authority, but administrative tribunals may impose sentences in non-criminal cases.

In felony cases—that is, cases dealing with serious crimes—sentencing is related to a wide variety of information that is available to the judge. One of the most important sources of information is victim impact statements, which emerged in the 1990s as a response to victims' rights advocacy. However, there is little evidence to support the idea that victim impact statements have a demonstrated effect on increasing sentences, owing to the strictures of law and the limited number of possible sentences that are open to judges. Instead, the process provides the victim with a form of active intervention and the offender with an opportunity to learn.

In considering the type of sentence that should be imposed, judges will often review a presentence report. These documents include the social, criminal, and personal history of the offender. Presentence reports also attempt to evaluate the individual's suitability for various treatment programs.

The imposition of sentence often involves conviction on more than one charge. The convicted person is sentenced on all charges. When the sentences are **concurrent,** they commence on the same day and end following the serving of the longest term imposed. For example, if an offender receives three years for carrying a concealed weapon and ten years for armed robbery, after serving the ten-year sentence (less parole eligibility), he or she would be freed from confinement.

Another form, the **consecutive sentence,** is typically much more ominous than the concurrent sentence. In this case, the offender referred to in the above scenario would serve the three-year sentence first, followed immediately by the ten-year sentence. The full length of the term if served would be thirteen years. However, consecutive sentences are rare—they are usually reserved for offenders with a long record of serious crimes against people or for those who have committed several heinous crimes at one time. Given recent medical advances that have extended people's lives, some judges sentence particularly dangerous felons so that they will be held until the end of their natural (or extended) lives.

# Factors Considered in Sentencing

Sentencing does not simply involve applying a fixed penalty to the offender. All Criminal Code offences carry maximum sentences. Misdemeanour offences carry a maximum sentence of two years less a day in confinement, served in a provincial institution, and/or a fine of up to $1000. Felonies typically invoke longer sentences of from two to twenty-five years, depending on the crime committed. However, it is rare for an offender to receive the maximum on being convicted for a first offence. A mandatory minimum sentence is imposed for several crimes: first degree murder and drug trafficking. In some U.S. states, mandatory minimums are imposed for possession of even a very small quantity of drugs. Michigan, for instance, imposes a mandatory life sentence on people found in possession of little over an ounce of cocaine. While it could be argued that mandatory minimums have a powerful deterrent effect, it could equally be argued that they fail to take into account mitigating circumstances in sentencing. So, if a first-time cocaine user happens to buy slightly more than an ounce for personal use, believing it to be only an ounce, the judge would be forced to impose a life sentence with no possibility of parole. Many countries have strict prohibitions against possession of illegal drugs, and life sentences and the death penalty are common sentences.

At the time of sentencing, the judge is called upon to consider a number of extralegal factors. These factors may be grouped into two broad categories: mitigating factors and aggravating factors. *Mitigating circumstances* may be defined as factors that when considered individually or together justify a more lenient sentence. These factors diminish an offender's responsibility for a crime. For example, first-time offenders deserve consideration, given their lack of a criminal record. An offender who has performed community service, been responsible, and acted selflessly may be granted a lesser sentence. Old age or a pre-existing medical condition that requires monitoring also may influence a judge's sentencing. For example, the late Harold Ballard, a well-known businessman and former owner of the Toronto Maple Leafs hockey team, received what many consider a lenient sentence for fraudulent business practices because he was ill at the time of sentencing. More frequently, the submission of a guilty plea results in sentence reduction, since a costly trial is avoided (Beddoes, 1989).

*Aggravating factors* are those that can increase a sentence. Obviously, a previous criminal record can have a negative impact on the sentence if the current offences are consistent with those committed in the past. For some offences, the judge seriously considers evidence of the offender's deliberation and planning, since these qualities reveal that the crime was not an impulsive action. Judges also may view particularly violent or prevalent crimes in their communities as warranting lengthier sentences. A recent Toronto case involved the carjacking of a prominent attorney and his wife. The assailants severely beat both victims. The judge handed down lengthy prison sentences of sixteen and eighteen years to the two perpetrators in order to deter others from committing similar crimes. Since carjackings are rare in Canada but common in many U.S. states, the judge determined that an effective way to dissuade others from engaging in this behaviour was to be extremely harsh in sentencing.

# Plea Bargaining

Plea bargains have been compared to game shows: they invite the offender to "make a deal." But are plea bargains a good deal for everyone? Do they circumvent the judicial process in allowing the Crown attorney to determine sentences, instead of requiring a formal hearing? These are important questions, since society depends on the judicial process to provide due process to every person charged with a crime. Plea bargains are employed in as many as 90 percent of the criminal cases that come to the courts (Klein, 1976). It is a sad reality that most people charged with offences are, in fact, guilty. On the advice of defence counsel, they may opt to plead guilty in return for a reduced sentence.

The plea-bargaining process involves consultation between the defence attorney for the accused and the Crown attorney representing the state. The defence, typically meeting in the Crown's office, will suggest an appropriate sentence in private consultations. Viewers of the television series *Law and Order* will be

The Canadian Criminal Justice System

familiar with the plea process. Almost every episode of the television drama contains one or more scenes in which a defence attorney offers a plea bargain to the prosecutor. A period of negotiation follows until a sentence agreeable to both parties is decided on. At court, the accused enters a plea of guilty, after which the Crown offers a sentencing recommendation. The judge normally accepts the Crown's recommendation but is not strictly required to do so. Since judges, Crown attorneys, and defence attorneys work together in court from day to day, tacit cooperation is required to ensure the smooth flow of cases through the justice system. Accused people also benefit from providing evidence or testimony that results in another crime being solved and another person subsequently being convicted. While the criminal underworld considers turning a fellow criminal in a serious offence, the practice is quite common among career criminals. CrimeStoppers and TIPS programs, which allow individuals to benefit financially from anonymously turning in offenders, also have been highly successful.

The most famous plea bargain in Canadian criminal history was granted to Karla Homolka, the former wife of multiple murderer Paul Bernardo. Homolka benefited from her willingness to provide information as the only living witness to the torture and murders that she and Bernardo committed together. Rather than receiving a life sentence, which would have confined her to a prison cell for a minimum of 25 years for her part in three homicides, she was convicted of the lesser charge of manslaughter and received a 12-year sentence (which is reduced by parole eligibility). By late 1999, having served seven years of her sentence, Homolka was being considered for transfer to a halfway house in Montreal, the first step toward re-entering civil life. Her imminent release set off a series of public and political debates about the support for Homolka's release plan provided by the Elizabeth Fry Society, an organization dedicated to helping women re-enter society from prison.

Most experts and the public view sentencing as being differentially administered across Canada. Similar offences committed by relatively comparable offenders can produce widely varying sentences. Some criminologists believe that a movement toward structured sentencing would create both uniformity and fairness. Under this model, judges would have no discretion in the sentencing process. Crimes would have set penalties. Extralegal factors would have no relevance in the process. This form of sentencing appears appropriate for very serious crimes. There are, however, serious drawbacks to its use. First, it does not allow for rehabilitative progress to result in early earned release. Without incentives such as early release programs, it may prove difficult or impossible to motivate prisoners to engage in treatment or educational programs. Second, this form of sentencing denies consideration of the person's contributions to the community and lack of previous criminal behaviour. Third, given the size of the prison population in Canada, authorities would quickly be overwhelmed with prisoners whose release date could not be shortened for any reason.

# Capital Punishment

Death is the most serious sentence that can be imposed on an offender. Capital punishment is no longer a sentencing option in Canada. The last executions in Canada took place at Toronto's Don Jail in 1962. Hanging was often employed in cases of capital murder between Confederation (1867) and the repeal of hanging in 1976.

The repeal of the death sentence in Canada can be traced to several cases of wrongful execution in England and Canada. In Canada, both the Coffin and Truscott cases were central to this debate (see Chapter 10). One book in particular, *A Calendar of Murder* (Morris & Blom-Cooper, 1963), was instrumental in demonstrating the often slim circumstantial evidence that could result in a death penalty. These two eminent researchers underscored the true nature of most homicides as tragedies of human weakness and frailty, rather than coldly calculated acts. The authors produced a short vignette on the details of each murder committed in England during 1960. Rather than displaying the ingenuity, callousness, and cunning of the homicidal foes of Sherlock Holmes, the average murderer acted spontaneously out of a fairly repetitive range of motives. These motives, including jealousy, sexual infidelity, and greed, have also been documented by Canadian criminologist Neil Boyd (1989). Offenders and victims in homicides are frequently under the influence of illegal drugs, alcohol, or a mixture of several chemicals. Since most murders are committed in the heat of passion, spontaneously and without deliberation, it rapidly became apparent to researchers that death was an inappropriate sentence.

# Conclusion

The principles of sentencing have remained relatively stable through countless centuries of the administration of justice. However, the principle of retribution, which once figured prominently in the sentencing process, has gradually given way to more informed and humane principles that more broadly serve societal interests—specifically, deterrence and rehabilitation. This move away from retribution is symbolized by the abolishment of capital punishment in Canada.

The trial process in Canada includes both informal and formal interactions between the defence and the prosecution, with a view to resolving issues of guilt and innocence and determining sentencing. Plea bargains are common in the court process in Canada and represent a trend toward minimizing the use of formal trial procedures in determining sentences.

# Summary

In this chapter, we have explored the correctional system, focusing on the issues behind sentencing and sentencing determinations. We have analyzed, in terms of their goals and effectiveness, the principles underlying sentencing in the Canadian justice system and their role in sentencing decisions. As well, we have discussed the goals of sentencing, including deterrence and rehabilitation, and have examined plea bargaining as a central component of the administration of justice in Canada.

# Key Terms

concurrent sentence (p. 173)

consecutive sentence (p. 173)

deterrence (p. 169)

incapacitation (p. 168)

just deserts (p. 170)

probation (p. 172

rehabilitation (p. 169)

restorative justice (p. 170)

suspended sentence (p. 172

# Discussion Questions

1.  What is the purpose of the criminal trial?

2.  How should sentencing goals be weighted in determining an appropriate sentence?

3.  Which of the goals of sentencing is most important to society? Why?

4.  What societal factors might be associated with the decline of the rehabilitative movement in sentencing?

5.  What are the purposes of plea bargaining?

6.  Should plea bargains be permitted in Canadian courts?

# Weblinks

**www.canadalegal.com/gosite.asp?s=1457** Written in plain language and with all legal terms explained, this article, by a Nova Scotia law firm, provides information on how an adult gets sentenced for a crime.

**www.acjnet.org/capcj/en/law/publications/07sentencing.html** The Canadian Association of Provincial Court Judges provides a link to articles on sentencing issues, with topics such as sentencing reform and dangerous offenders.

**www.chebucto.ns.ca/Law/PLENS/sentence.html** The Public Legal Education Society of Nova Scotia, committed to "helping Nova Scotians understand the law," provides a clear, easy-to-understand overview of what is involved in sentencing.

# CHAPTER 9

# The Prison System

## Objectives

- To outline the historical development of prisons in Canada.

- To compare Canada's rate of imprisonment with that of other countries.

- To examine federal corrections in Canada.

- To distinguish between various security classifications in Canadian prisons.

- To describe life inside prisons and the inmate subculture.

- To look at various issues concerning Canadian prisons today and in the future.

- To examine issues confronting women in prison.

The problem of how society will deal with those convicted of criminal offences in Canada is one that confronts judges across the nation. One of the most frequent sentences for offenders is imprisonment in a provincial or federal institution. Increasingly during the past 200 years, the justice system has embraced prisons as receptacles for the unwanted in Canadian society. However, a number of criminologists have questioned the continued and increasing use of prison as the first choice among sentencing options (Morris, 1997). The "punishment industry," by which we mean the entire range of activities within corrections, is well funded and seems to have an almost infinite capacity for expansion, in the view of some writers (Culhane, 1985, 1987). By 2000, Canada had built over 60 federal prisons and over 100 provincial facilities—in fact, there are more prisons than colleges and universities in this country.

For many Canadians, prisons remain an enigma. Some view prison as a place purely reserved for punishment, while others stress its rehabilitative potential. It is a widely held belief that prisons are similar to social clubs where prisoners live a life better than many average citizens. The ability of convicted murderer Karla Homolka to pursue a university degree in prison is one issue that angers many Canadians, who feel that prisons may reward criminal behaviour. They cite their own inability to afford a university education in condemning the opportunities offered to prisoners.

In reality, the majority of Canadians know little, if anything, about prisons. Few want to become educated about prisons, preferring to see them to be apart from society. The majority of prisons are located in isolated rural areas far from major cities. Prisons, therefore, not only remove prisoners from society but also take them far from their communities, creating double isolation for prisoners. Since our prison population is drawn in large measure from the poorest in society, the location of prisons in hard-to-reach locations means that many prisoners' families have difficulty visiting them.

What little Canadians know about prison life has generally emerged from television programs or movies that focus largely on prison life in the United States. The popular A&E documentary series *American Justice,* for example, has provided viewers with a view of American prisons and interviews with men and women, from minor offenders to those awaiting execution on death row. One dramatic view of prison life in Canada was provided in the training video shot by correctional services personnel when quelling a disturbance at the Kingston Prison for Women in 1995. This disturbing video featured naked women being beaten by male guards and left wet and virtually naked on cold prison floors. It was a vision that shocked Canadian sensibilities regarding the nature of imprisonment in their country.

In this chapter, we will examine the components of the correctional system in Canada. We will begin by focusing on the history of the prison system and its underlying philosophies of correction and control. Next, we will analyze the current population of the prison system and explore the key issues that face prisoners, including the prison subculture, violence, and suicide. Although men overwhelmingly form the largest portion of the prison population, we will also discuss women in Canadian prisons. We will then consider emerging crises in the prison system, including the housing of prisoners with HIV/AIDS and the difficulties that the growing geriatric prison population present. We will discuss next the challenges of prison privatization and its relation to prison conditions. Finally, we will suggest alternatives to prison that have emerged in recent discussions among prison reformers, inmates, and criminologists.

# The Evolution of Prisons in Canada

The first large houses of confinement to Canada were designed on the model of British institutions. Prisons were meant not only to physically confine those who required punishment and removal from society but also to symbolically represent the severity of punishment through the austerity and the sheer enormity of their scale. Few visitors or innocent passersby could fail to be forewarned of the severity of punishment upon viewing the first federal prison, opened in Kingston, Ontario, in 1832. Designed to accommodate long periods of confinement as the preferred method of punishment, it stood as a silent but ominous monument to the consequences of crime. Punishment had by this time largely moved from the public square into the privacy of the institution, prisons provided an ideal location for attempting to transform those who failed to abide by the law.

According to Curtis and Blanchfield's (1985) illustrated history of Kingston Penitentiary, in May 1849, George Brown, editor of the *Toronto Globe* (later *The Globe and Mail*) undertook an investigation of the conditions in the penitentiary. What he discovered was an institution where violence and human degradation were everyday events. Brown's investigators severely criticized the practice of corporal punishment, or whipping, which was inflicted on children who were incarcerated at the prison. Curtis and Blanchfield report the cases of two children that are illustrative of the approach of the prison to discipline:

> Convict Peter Charbonneau [was] a ten-year-old serving seven years. The punishment book noted that Charbonneau's prison offences were of a trifling nature, like staring, winking and laughing—behaviour one would expect of a young boy. But for this he was stripped of his shirt and publicly lashed fifty-seven times in eight and a half months.

> There was also the case of Antoine Beauche, sentenced to three years in November 1845. The report notes that this eight-year-old received the lash within a week of his arrival and was given no fewer than forty-seven lashings in nine months.

> Women convicts were not spared ... One fourteen-year-old, Sarah O'Connor, was flogged on five occasions during a three-month period. Another, Elizabeth Breen, aged twelve, was flogged five times in four months. (1985, pp. 42–43)

The food in this early prison was kept intentionally routine and dull. The food purchased at the local market was typically unfit for human consumption. Most meals were soggy and flavourless, as they were cooked in steam boilers. Bread was the staple of all diets but was reported to often be mouldy. Brown also reported on the numbing routine prisoners were subjected to:

"Silently and obediently, day after day, week after week, year after year, the inmates at Kingston were supposed to shuffle along the corridors to their work every morning, their heads inclined at an angle that would prevent them from looking at the man ahead, work all day at a bench without making the slightest gesture to anyone around them, shuffle to the mess hall and eat meals that were calculated to keep them alive without appealing to 'luxurious' tastes and not communicating with anyone." (Curtis & Blanchfield, 1985, pp. 42–43)

Early prisons were home to all kinds of criminals and "misfits," mixing men, women, children, the mentally ill, and syphilitics together with dire results. Societal members viewed prisons in much the same way as they had previously viewed leper houses—as a holding place for all those who were "bad" and "evil." The first French prisons, for example, had been located in former leper colonies. It is little wonder that prisoners became the new "untouchables" in our society. Prisons were places invested with mystery and terror, designed to instill fear and also to ward off public interest and criticism.

Over the first hundred years of its existence, the federal prison system expanded with the construction of 8 more institutions. Between 1950 and 1990, 16 more were built, double the number built in the first hundred years.

North American prisons were based on two significant approaches to punishment and correction in the 19th century. The first approach is referred to as the **Pennsylvania system.** Prisoners were relegated to small cells, where they were to read the Bible. They were allowed to exercise in a small yard for less than one hour per day. Heavily influenced by the Quakers, this approach to imprisonment kept prisoners on their own, in a form of solitary confinement. While more benevolent than modern forms of complete segregation, this approach was also strongly connected to religious and moral ideals: inmates were supposed to contemplate their acts and repent.

The second major approach to imprisonment in the 19th century was referred to as the **Auburn system.** The architects of this system believed that hard labour was the path to reform of the convict. Prisoners were put to work performing jobs necessary to the functioning of the prison. They also worked in animal husbandry and agriculture to produce food for the inmate population. The Auburn system has also been referred to as the silent system, since prisoners were forbidden to speak to one another at any time. *The Birdman of Alcatraz,* a film depiction of the life of Robert Stroud, contains scenes depicting the "no talking" rules. Similarly, in *White Heat,* actor James Cagney breaks the silent system by screaming and smashing the lunchroom (and the heads of several guards) when other inmates whisper to him the news of his mother's death.

What also distinguishes this second system is that unlike earlier prisons and jails, the institution was built with *tiers* or *blocks:* multiple floors containing individual cells stacked one on top of another. This design was adapted from the original concept of a British 17th-century philosopher and writer, Jeremy Bentham. He proposed the construction of the **panopticon,** a circular, multi-tiered institution that would require few guards to maintain control. Tiers permitted guards to "lock down" segments of the prison, whole tiers, or individual cells. The tiers also allowed more prisoners to be housed in one building, as they were stacked rather than spread out. The Auburn-style prison was the model eventually adopted for the first Canadian federal prison in Kingston.

# Prisons in Contemporary Canada

## Rates of Imprisonment

Canada has a high rate of imprisonment among Western nations (see Figure 9.1). The **incarceration rate,** which is the number of people jailed per 100 000 population, was 129 in 1997. The incarceration rate has been rising consistently since the opening of the first prison in Canada. Rising rates of imprisonment in Canada may seem to make sense. It could be argued that the increasing population in Canada and our increasingly criminal society, as perceived by Canadians, fuel ever-higher rates of imprisonment. But comparisons with other countries

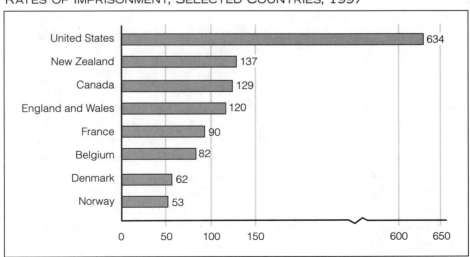

FIGURE 9.1

RATES OF IMPRISONMENT, SELECTED COUNTRIES, 1997

Source: U.S. Department of Justice; Canadian Centre for Justice Statistics, Statistics Canada; Council of Europe; and Ministry of Justice, New Zealand.

indicate that rising rates of imprisonment have little to do with crime rates; rather, they reflect a country's policies toward dealing with crime.

Norway and Denmark incarcerate 62 people and 53 people per 100 000, respectively. These rates are less than half the Canadian rate. Does this mean that residents of these countries are less criminal that Canadians? Research would suggest that there is little difference in the respective levels of criminality in both countries; instead, the differences may be attributed to very different approaches to punishment. Countries with high incarceration rates have chosen through legislation and penal policy to use prisons as the major form of social control. The United States, for example, imprisons 634 people per 100 000.

It would appear that there is an almost limitless capacity for societies to create and fill prison spaces. However, the question of what kind of society a high rate of imprisonment produces is troubling. If there are few alternatives to prison, rates will climb accordingly. Similarly, some criminologists would argue that the ever-expanding number of prisons has produced a prison industry. This industry is a huge employer of thousands of prison employees and tens of thousands employed in support industries. Criminals are thus the raw product required to keep the industry working and growing, if we accept this line of thinking. Rising incarceration rates in Canada over the past century also reflect the view of many small communities that prisons are a permanent source of jobs, prosperity, and community stability when few other economic opportunities exist.

A high rate of imprisonment leads to a considerable number of Canadians having criminal records. In 1998, Canada had an adult population of 23 086 400 (adults are persons over 18 years of age). By 1998, 2 617 380 Canadians possessed a criminal record. This is approximately 10 percent of the adult population, or one in ten people. According to the Correctional Service of Canada (CSC), the average number of adults imprisoned at any one time in Canada during 1997–1998 was 32 951. According to the CCJS, there were over 37 000 inmates on register in Canada's 151 provincial/territorial institutions and 48 federal facilities on October 5, 1996. Those who were between 20 and 39 years of age were overrepresented in this one-day snapshot of corrections. Interestingly, inmates were more likely to be unmarried, to have fewer years of education, and to be unemployed than the general population of Canada at the time of their admission. Most inmates had a previous record of conviction, with 83 percent of the individuals in provincial/territorial facilities falling into this category and 72 percent having served a previous term of incarceration in a provincial/territorial prison. In terms of offences, 73 percent of federal inmates were serving time for an offence against the person, in particular homicide/attempted murder and robbery. In provincial/territorial prisons, 33 percent of offenders were in prison for crimes against the person, particularly sexual assault and robbery. Table 9.1 profiles the total male inmate population in 1998–1999.

TABLE 9.1

----------------------------------------------------------------

PROFILE OF THE FEDERALLY INCARCERATED MALE INMATE POPULATION, 1998–1999

| | NUMBER | PERCENT OF MALE INMATE POPULATION |
|---|---|---|
| Age 20 to 34 | 6 100 | 49 |
| Serving a first penitentiary sentence | 6 489 | 52 |
| Length of sentence | | |
| Under three years | 2 241 | 18 |
| Three to six years | 3 832 | 31 |
| Six to ten years | 2 066 | 16 |
| Ten years or more | 1 866 | 15 |
| Life or indeterminate | 2 527 | 20 |
| Offence | | |
| Murder—first degree | 636 | 5 |
| Murder—second degree | 1 593 | 13 |
| Schedule I (violence) | 8 245 | 66 |
| Schedule II (drugs) | 1 498 | 12 |
| Nonscheduled (nonviolent) | 1 742 | 14 |
| Sexual* | 2 223 | 18 |
| **Total number of male inmates** | **12 532** | |

*Sex offences have been presented separately from the violent category to illustrate their proportion in the inmate population.

Source: CSC, 2000.

# Security Classifications

Prisons in Canada exist primarily to confine lawbreakers. Therefore, it is crucial, from a management perspective, that the risks associated with each prisoner be assessed at the time of their entry into prison through **security classifications.** The initial classification will likely be at a higher security level, and later, as a prisoner approaches release, a lower level of classification may be appropriate. Incoming prisoners are assessed for classification according to the risk they pose for escaping, for being a danger to other inmates or correctional officers, and for breaking the rules of the prison. Another factor might be the assessment of the harm offenders could pose to the community if they were to escape. A serial killer might show little interest in escape, for example, but if he or she were to escape, the danger to the community would be great.

Classification occurs after the parole officer assigned to the case reviews the details of the crime. The parole officer also reviews the offender's past record of offences and institutional behaviours (for repeat offenders). Upon the offender's entry into the institution, a placement officer conducts an interview with the new prisoner to assess the appropriateness of the institutional classification to the prisoners' needs. The placement officer reviews the inmate's previous record of behaviour (where it exists) and decides on specific programs, if any are available at the institution, that would benefit the inmate. People who require treatment for sexual offending can be directed to a prison that might not match their security classification but that would provide necessary treatment.

According to Ekstedt and Griffiths (1988), the CSC has developed specific definitions for three security classifications and a fourth, "mixed" category:

1. *Maximum security.* The prisoner is likely to attempt or complete an escape and poses the threat of committing serious harm in the community.

2. *Medium security.* The prisoner is likely to attempt escape but does not pose a risk of behaviour that would cause serious harm to the outside world.

3. *Minimum security.* The prisoner poses little risk for escape. If the prisoner were to escape, he or she would not cause harm.

4. *Multilevel.* The prisoners are from two or more categories and are mixed owing to space constraints and to a need to encourage positive role modelling.

Table 9.2 breaks down the security classification of male and female inmates in 1998–1999.

TABLE 9.2

SECURITY CLASSIFICATION OF INMATES, 1998–1999

| SECURITY | MEN | PERCENT | WOMEN | PERCENT |
|---|---|---|---|---|
| Maximum | 2 708 | 22 | 96 | 31 |
| Medium | 7 560 | 60 | 129 | 42 |
| Minimum | 1 481 | 12 | 29 | 10 |
| Not yet classified | 783 | 6 | 51 | 17 |
| Total | 12 532 | 100 | 305 | 100 |

Source: CSC, 2000.

By 2000, the CSC, which is responsible for the operations of federal prisons, had 52 institutions in its system, of which 10 were maximum security, 21 medium security, and 14 minimum security. A further 7 are multilevel facilities. Reflecting the concentration of Canadians in large urban centres, prisons are generally more numerous in provinces with larger populations (see Table 9.3). Currently, 5 prisons are open in the Atlantic region, 12 in Quebec, 14 in Ontario, 13 in the Prairie provinces, and 8 in B.C. It is interesting to note that the three

Prairie provinces share roughly the same number of prisons as Ontario despite their smaller total population. Several criminologists have pointed out that Aboriginal Canadians make up a disproportionate number of inmates in the Prairie system (Hylton, 1983).

TABLE 9.3

-----------------------------------------------------------------------------------

REGIONAL DISTRIBUTION OF PRISONS IN CANADA, 1998–1999

| SECURITY LEVEL | ATLANTIC PROVINCES | QUEBEC | ONTARIO | PRAIRIE PROVINCES | B.C. | TOTAL |
|---|---|---|---|---|---|---|
| Maximum | 1 | 3 | 3 | 1 | 2 | 10 |
| Medium | 2 | 5 | 5 | 5 | 4 | 21 |
| Minimum | 1 | 3 | 4 | 4 | 2 | 14 |
| Multilevel | 1 | 1 | 2 | 3 | 0 | 7 |
| Community Correctional Centres | 4 | 6 | 3 | 3 | 1 | 17 |
| Total per region | 9 | 18 | 17 | 16 | 9 | 69 |

Source: CSC, 2000.

The number of inmates that each prison can hold varies from a low of 78 to a high of 501. The average capacity of institutions is 259 people. Minimum security facilities are smaller, since there is an emphasis on preparing the prisoner for imminent re-entry into the community. There is a greater need at this juncture to monitor the inmate's behaviour. Minimum security institutions house 121 people on average, while medium and maximum security facilities house 379 and 235 respectively. The majority of institutions are between 10 and 50 years old. Only 6 prisons that are over 50 years old are still in operation.

## Prison Architecture

The four levels of prisons have very different physical structures. The architecture of each structure reflects the level of security required to ensure confinement of prisoners and their progress toward freedom in the community.

Minimum security prisons have, at least outwardly, the appearance of college campuses. It is rare that any form of fence or wall surrounds them. Security levels are very low because inmates are near the point of return to the community. They have a lot to lose by attempting escape at a time so near to release. Few offenders are tempted to escape. The promise of light at the end of the carceral tunnel becomes, itself, a form of self-imposed wall. Prisoners do not even wear special clothing. Visitors would find that prisoners and staff are dressed similarly. While formal cells are not evident, prisoners are allocated private or semi-private rooms.

The emphasis at minimum security facilities is on preparation for return to the community. Prisoners are encouraged to engage in life skills courses, which are designed to assist them in reintegrating into the community. Life skills classes focus on seeking employment and accommodation following release and on fundamentals for living on the outside. Given the subculture of prison life, with its own specific rules and argot, this is a time to relearn how to live in the outside community and to "shake off" the "joint." In other words, prisoners require time to adopt the language and interpersonal skills that will lead to success in the community.

Mixed institutions combine both minimum and medium security inmates. The mixed institution is an interesting and potentially positive development in correctional approaches. The advantage of a mixed institution is that it allows medium security prisoners to observe what awaits them as they move to minimum security status. Give the influence of prison subcultures, there is the potential to create more positive outcomes for prisoners. The more positive aspects of the minimum security designation can be seen as an inducement, perhaps, for inmates to focus on developing acceptable behaviours and on working toward their own release, as they can view release becoming a reality for other prisoners. This sense of the possibility of release prevents inmates from being further entrenched in the inmate subculture, which has little relationship to success upon release.

Mixed and medium security institutions are enclosed by chainlink fences topped by barbed wire and razored wire. Prisoners have greater freedom in these facilities are than in maximum security facilities and may have access to educational programs, as well as treatment courses.

Maximum security prisons are built with a focus on preventing escape. To deter escape, these prisons have high brick or wire fences and are equipped with electronic surveillance systems designed to prevent escape from the inside and rescue attempts from the outside. Prisoners' movements are highly supervised and monitored. Cell counts are conducted at various points throughout the day to ensure that all prisoners are on site and accounted for.

**Protective custody** units are also a part of maximum security prisons. Often prisoners have to be protected from other prisoners because of the crimes that they have committed. Serial killers, including Clifford Olson and Paul Bernardo, are held in special sections of the building. Members of the general population of inmates are not allowed into these special units, which require more correctional officers in order to guard the prisoners. Inmates who require protective custody include those who have been or would be the targets of sexual assaults, serious assaults, or even murder attempts if they were to remain in the general population. Sex offenders are universally reviled in prison society because inmates have families outside of prison who are vulnerable to sex offenders. Rapists and pedophiles are at the greatest risk in prison.

Inmates who are "rats"—that is, who cooperate or give evidence against other inmates to the authorities—also require protective custody. In protective custody, they are safe from other prisoners but must spend 23 hours a day locked in their cells.

**Solitary confinement** is used in maximum security prisons in order to punish prisoners who fail to obey institutional rules or who commit violence against others. There are strict rules concerning the use of solitary confinement as a form of punishment. However, Canada has had a poor record of abuse with this form of prisoner control. Several cases brought to the courts by prisoners have demonstrated correctional officials' willingness to place prisoners in "the hole" for periods of hundreds of days (Jackson, 1983).

Maximum security prisons are holding places for people serving life and other long-term sentences for serious offences against persons and/or property. Treatment programs aimed at personal control, such as substance abuse and anger management programs, are often mandatory for prisoners in both maximum and medium security facilities. While there are a variety of programs available for inmates, including university degree programs, there is a distinct shortage of programs for prisoners who are serving long-term sentences (Fleming, 1995). Canadian prisons are not unique in their inability to respond to the needs of "lifers" and other long-term prisoners.

# Inside the Prison

Prisons emerged as a place of punishment. Prisons are constructed both in terms of their architecture and the culture that develops inside to punish the inmates. From the time of John Howard's famous journeys to observe prison conditions in 18th-century Europe, there has been little to recommend prisons as places other than to be avoided. Prison means the loss of one's freedom, employment, family, and friends. It imposes a stigma on the individual upon returning to society that makes reintegration into the community difficult. Some prison critics have referred to prisons as garbage pails for society (Fitzgerald, 1986).

Prison was seen to have a rehabilitative function, at least in the stated philosophy of prison officials during the last 150 years. Recently, however, penal administrators have begun to admit there is no reality behind the rhetoric. The prison system, for historians like Michel Foucault, is merely a mechanism of circular elimination. By removing unlawful individuals from our society, prisons also effectively removed their plight from public view and attention. While the costs of imprisoning people is very high and continues to rise, we accept the costs as the price to be paid for not having to deal with the problem of crime in our communities. The prison remains a place of punishment and control into which the public rarely has the chance, or the desire, to gaze.

However, some inmates have recounted their prison experiences once outside the prison walls. Roger Caron's book *Go-Boy!* (1978) provides a rare and illuminating insider's account of prison life in Canada during the 1950s, 1960s, and 1970s. Caron was fortunate to recover the manuscript of his book following the 1971 Kingston riot. It is a valuable document, since almost all the information we have about prisoners is strictly controlled by the CSC. Prison mail is routinely censored, and, since most prisoners have little education, few inmates have written books about their experiences on the inside.

Aside from Caron's books, two other accounts have been written by former or current inmates since the inception of the prison system in Canada. Bonnie Walford, a woman serving a sentence for murder, wrote about her own experience and that of other women in her book *Lifers* (1987). Julius Melnitzer, a former lawyer, recorded his experiences as a prisoner in *Maximum, Minimum, Medium* (1995). In the United States, books by prisoners are also rare, but some insightful works have been written by Caryl Chessman (1954), Eldridge Cleaver (1967), and Jack Abbot (1981). Our knowledge of life inside prisons has been greatly enhanced by these personal accounts, by criminological studies (Cayley, 1998; Gosselin, 1977), by journalistic accounts (Marron, 1996), and by a book written by a former prison psychiatrist (Scott, 1982). As well, *The Journal of Prisoners on Prisons* has for the past decade provided an important forum for both prisoners and academics to write about life inside.

# Daily Life in Prison

The strongest characteristic of daily prison life is its highly scheduled, inflexible routine. This routine varies across the four forms of prison in Canada, but the account of Kurt, a life prisoner, is typical:

> "I work in textiles, making clothing to supply other jails across Canada—underwear and shirts—and I enjoy it. Go back, have lunch, come back and work. Three afternoons a week I attend school—SFU [since cancelled]. I look forward to getting back to three o'clock lockup.
>
> We eat around three-thirty.... Then I look forward to gym.
>
> Then we ... pretty well sit around from six till lockup. I want see like, organized things."
>
> John, another lifer, summarizes life inside as repetitive and boring: "It's just over and over and over the same thing. I hate every second I have to be here. You know when you lose your freedom, you've lost everything." (Murphy & Johnson, 1997, pp. 25–26)

## The Inmate Subculture

Upon entry to prison, inmates enter a unique world of norms and rules, termed the **inmate subculture.** Prisoners have even developed their own jargon, called **prison argot** (see Box 9.1). As in wider society, prison subcultures develop their own rules of permissible conduct and penalties. However, inmate codes of conduct are not written down; instead, new inmates learn the codes of conduct by talking to other inmates and by observing interactions among prisoners and between correctional officers and prisoners.

Inmates vary in the degree to which they internalize these rules and norms. Some who feel at ease or empowered in prison subcultures become highly institutionalized. They find it difficult to "shake off" the "joint" mentality—that is, to return to civilian modes of thinking and acting. Despite life skills training, these prisoners find it difficult to succeed in the community.

Most of the rules reinforce the interests of the inmate group against the guards and prison administration. John Irwin (1970), a former prisoner turned criminologist, found that the rules helped to bind inmates together as a group. The rules include not being a "rat" (giving information to the authorities), displaying toughness, and refraining from arguing with other prisoners.

In Canada, research by Marron (1996) has addressed the issue of whether the inmate code exists in Canadian prisons. Given Caron's (1985) account, one would have thought that such an exercise was unnecessary. Marron found that interview

## PRISON ARGOT

Here are some commonly used words that have developed in Canadian prisons to substitute for common words in English. When reading the words, consider how they might have developed.

| | |
|---|---|
| *bingo* | riot |
| *bit* | prison term |
| *bull* | prison guard |
| *cooler* | solitary confinement |
| *diddler* | child molester |
| *double sawbuck* | 20-year sentence |
| *drum* | cell |
| *fish* | newcomer |
| *goof* | jerk |
| *jug-up* | meal time |
| *piped* | hit over the head with a bar |
| *rat* | informer |
| *shank* | homemade knife |
| *short-timer* | sentence near completion |
| *slammer* | prison |
| *wolf pack* | inmate bullies |

Source: Adapted from Caron, 1985.

subjects consistently identified a set of informal rules of conduct. These rules included doing your own time, staying out of the illegal prison economy, not trusting anyone, and showing respect for other inmates. Inmates are advised by other inmates to avoid purchasing products in the illegal prison economy (such as drugs, moonshine, cigarettes, and pornography), since if they fail to repay debts they risk being seriously assaulted or having to repay the debt through sexual acts. Prisoners must also acknowledge the place of other prisoners in the institutional hierarchy. Inmates serving life sentences, so-called lifers, are accorded the highest status in the inmate subculture, as are prisoners who commit serious violent offences. Not only are they serving long sentences, but they are also considered dangerous because of their acts on the outside. New prisoners, called "fish" or "greenhorns," occupy the lowest rung of the hierarchy.

## Violence in Prisons

There is little doubt that prisons are violent places. Violence can take many forms. Inmates may threaten or assault others to gain property. Staff may assault inmates to display their power. In some instances, inmates assault staff. The CSC reported 142 major assaults of this type in the first nine months of 1991–1992. Stabbing constitutes roughly 40 percent of assaults in prison. As a result, cells are regularly searched, or "turned over" by staff, to find illegal weapons and other forms of contraband. Other reported assaults include punching or kicking (33 percent), clubbing (19 percent), sexual assaults (4.7 percent) and burning (2.4 percent). However, given the inmate subculture and the threat of reprisal, there is likely a large dark figure to crimes committed in prison—that is, crimes that are committed but never reported. The majority of assaults occurred in max-imum security prisons (over 50 percent). Drugs accounted for 29 percent of dis-putes, retaliation for 19 percent, attacks on informants for 10 percent, and sexual motivations for 7 percent.

Staff are rarely the targets of serious physical attacks, in keeping with the assertions of both researchers and inmates that the inmates, rather than correc-tional officials, control prison society. Only two to four serious assaults of staff occur each year. Given the low staff-to-inmate ratio, it is surprising that more attacks do not occur. The checks and balances of the inmate code, although of little relevance to life outside the institution, make it possible for staff to run the prison. However, at certain times, inmates may rebel against prison conditions and cause a riot.

## Prison Riots

Prison riots are a rare event in Canadian institutions. The largest riot in Canadian prison history occurred at Kingston in 1971. It has been the subject of both crim-inological analysis and an insider account (Caron, 1978). Riots appear to arise naturally from prison conditions, but this does not mean that they are pre-dictable. Generally, they arise from inmates' concerns about mistreatment or intolerable conditions that prison officials have ignored. Tensions appear to reach a crescendo, and prisoners feel that only direct action will result in change. Taking over the prison provides a forum for them to express demands formally and to receive wider public attention concerning their plight. A minor alterca-tion between staff and prisoner may ignite a wider revolt among prisoners. Most prison riots require planning by the prisoners and thus are not truly spontaneous.

Prisons are what sociologist Erving Goffman (1961) termed *total institutions*, with strict rules of conduct. They are often overcrowded, outdated facilities, with little in the way of rehabilitative programming for long-term prisoners. Double bunking (the practice of assigning two inmates in a cell), which has been declared legal by the Canadian courts, creates significant intrusions on personal privacy. There is little opportunity for either privacy or personal expression. Experts have also viewed prison riots as a method for inmate societies to rid themselves of informers and also to permit new individuals and groups to attain power. Changes in prison administration or the transfer of inmates who are powerful in the subculture can create a gap in the power structure of the prison, making it vulnerable to riots. Finally, as an institution that houses violent people in a violent subculture, prisons might be expected to have riots.

Prison riots, as opposed to strikes, are not generally organized, but they do require some planning among a select group of inmates. The plans remain clandestine but are circulated as a rumour to other inmates. There are several phases that characterize prison riots: explosion, organization, confrontation, termination, reaction, and explanation. As Caron (1978) describes it, the explosion is a period in which inmates engage in a frenzy of drinking, drug use, violence, and sex after overwhelming staff and taking hostages. Pent-up frustrations and a lack of freedom lead to an explosive release. Inmates then organize into smaller groups led by other inmates. Typically, various forms of confrontation with the authorities follow, including threats and small skirmishes. Termination occurs either through a negotiated end to the riot or through the physical retaking of both the buildings and the prisoners. The army may assist correctional authorities in retaking control. Claire Culhane (1985) and others have documented the ramifications of riots for prisoners, during the reaction phase. These consequences may include lengthy periods of solitary confinement or lockdowns, denial of privileges, and physical and psychological attacks by correctional personnel. The final phase is one of "damage control," when correctional authorities issue explanations to inmates and the public to divert public attention from inmate complaints and prison conditions.

---

BOX 9.2

---

## THE KINGSTON PENITENTIARY RIOT

Riots can provide an opportunity for inmates to act violently against other inmates, particularly sex offenders and informers, who are normally segregated in protective custody. Here is Roger Caron's eyewitness account of the riots at Kingston Penitentiary in 1971:

> On the extermination list was a tall, stooped offender dubbed "The Camel" ...
> In his late twenties, the Camel was serving a life sentence for raping two very
> young girls. When the bingo broke out he had somehow been living quietly in
> the prison population ... he had survived several beatings and a stabbing, but
> had stubbornly refused to be locked away for his own protection. That stub-
> bornness was coming back to haunt him now that there were so many convicts
> prowling the tiers thirsting for victims ... the two dragged the rapist struggling
> and screaming from his cell. With great effort the three cons tried mightily to
> throw him over the railing to his death far below. The Camel had developed
> great strength in his hands, which he now used to grip the railing, stubbornly

refusing to let go even when one of the men bit and kicked at his fingers. Finally in exhaustion the three cons gave up and settled for punching and kicking him until he curled up in a ball. Later one of the inmates was asked why they changed their minds, and they replied: "Because he was screaming too much." (Caron, 1985, pp. 126–127).

Curtis and Blanchfield (1985, pp. 126–127) reported that "virtually every moveable item was destroyed" in the rampage. As their anger mounted, the inmates broke into RANGE 1D, which housed the "undesirables"—sex offenders and rats. The rioters pried open the cell doors and dragged the occupants into the Main Dome of the prison in a circle around the bell, hated by inmates, that rang out to mark all events in the prison day. The inmates beat and brutalized the fourteen undesirables during the night, two of whom died as a result of the attacks. Most of the inmates surrendered voluntarily the next day and released their guard prisoners unharmed before being temporarily transferred to Millhaven Penitentiary. Like most riots, the events had provided a way for inmates to vent their pent-up rage and violence but did little to change the conditions under which inmates were living and continued to live once the prison was repaired and reopened.

# The Correctional Officers

Research has identified three types of correctional officers, or guards. First, there are officers who are friendly to inmates. They treat inmates as human beings and talk with them about the community, news, family, prisoner issues, and life. A second group adheres strictly to the rules and generally does not engage inmates in casual conversation. The third group is violent bullies who use prison rules to vent their own anger toward inmates.

In understanding the adaptive styles of correctional officers, it is important that we consider that they are, in fact, committed to the prison environment. With regular and overtime shifts, they will spend more waking time in their lives with prisoners than with significant others in the community. This large amount of time spent within an environment with a significant potential for conflict and violence contributes greatly to the degree of stress officers experience in their work.

# Women in Prison

## The Dark Past of P4W

The Kingston Penitentiary for Women (P4W) was built as a small penitentiary for females. It opened its doors in 1934, at the height of the Great Depression.

Arriving inmates were placed on the "range," the older portion of the prison, which contained two tiers of barred cells. According to Bonny Walford, a prisoner serving a life sentence, the range held approximately 70 inmates. It was hardly a place for the contemplation envisaged by early prison philosophers:

> The range is incredibly noisy; each inmate has her radio, stereo or television on loud enough to drown out everyone else's. It is absolute madness ... this is where most of the fights, trouble, and brew-making go on. There are double the number of guards. (Walford, 1987, p. 2)

P4W was surrounded by 4.5-metre-high walls. A tennis court, gym, bingo room, and baseball diamond were provided, as well as jogging and cycling paths (Walford, 1987). A well-known feature of the prison was the two-bedroom family visiting unit (FVU). An inmate who had maintained good behaviour could apply for three-day family or conjugal visits every six weeks. These visits allowed brief respite from prison life and a chance to visit with family, partners, and children.

As in the men's prison, cells were small and contained only a bed, dresser, toilet, and sink. There were also two wings where "peace and quiet" was the rule. There were no cells in these wings, but rather a series of 25 rooms, each with a bed, desk, dresser, chair, and wardrobe. The dimensions of the rooms were 2 by 3.5 metres, and each had a screened and barred window with an exterior curtain. Toilet and bathing facilities and a washer and dryer were located at the end of the hall. Inmates' visiting between rooms ended at 11 p.m., after which time inmates were allowed to watch television with headphones. Walford states, "The wing is a very cosy and peaceful home to the residents. Pettiness and fights are not tolerated in the wing" (1987, p. 3).

Despite having some comfortable features, P4W was an institution with a violent culture perpetuated by corrections officers. On February 21, 1995, television viewers across Canada watched a video of women prisoners being strip-searched, stripped naked, and left shackled to the walls and pushed with batons. Correctional officers equipped with riot gear pulled the women from their cells. As Marron relates, the video "conjured up images of political atrocities, pornography and extreme sexual abuse" (1996, pp. 124–125).

## BOX 9.3

### THE P4W VIDEO AND VIOLENCE AGAINST PRISONERS

A Native woman who had been stripped while she was apparently half-asleep looked disoriented and totally humiliated, as she was forced to back up against a wall with a transparent plastic riot shield pressed against the front of her naked body. Another naked woman kneeled with hands behind the back of her head, motionless as if in a yoga position, asking in vain for a gown, while a chain was fastened around her waist

> and two guards stood in front of her with their batons raised like erect penises. But perhaps the most disturbing images were of a woman protesting and struggling as two men pinned her, face-down on the floor, and helped a female guard rip her clothes and tear them from her body.

Source: Marron, 1996, p. 124.

The Honourable Louise Arbour conducted the Commission of Inquiry into Certain Events at the Prison for Women in Kingston (1996) and found that the CSC had a profound lack of respect for the underlying principles of justice and fairness in dealing with prisoners. She provided a damning indictment of the events:

> A guilty verdict followed by a custodial sentence is not a grant of authority for the State to disregard the very values that the law, particularly the criminal law, seeks to uphold and vindicate, such as honesty, respect for the physical safety of others, respect for privacy and for human dignity. Corrections officers are held to the same standards of integrity and decency as their partners in the administration of justice. (1996, XI)

Arbour was particularly dismayed to find that while the actions of officers in this case often violated both prison regulations and Canadian law, the CSC did nothing to address the officers' actions and instead blamed the prisoners for the events. It is worthwhile noting that immediately following the release of the report, the then commission of the CSC resigned.

Since 1994, the federal and provincial governments have opened small, "women-centred" regional institutions for women prisoners. On July 6, 2000, P4W was finally officially closed, and women prisoners were transferred to the smaller regional institutions. The majority of these women prisoners are nonviolent offenders, many serving time for drug offences or, as Walford argues, for the crime of being a "party" to an offence. This latter crime is often referred to as "being in the wrong place at the wrong time." More common for women incarcerated at P4W is a history of being victims of sexual, psychological, emotional, and physical abuse. The new regional centres replacing P4W allow for visits by friends and family, more specialized treatment, and work and educational programs, as well as providing better living conditions. Considering that P4W had been condemned in 1977 by a parliamentary committee as "unfit for bears, much less women" (Marron, 1996, p. 127), the building of better facilities was long overdue.

## Women in Prison Today

There are far more men imprisoned in Canada than women. On March 31, 1999, there were 12 532 federally imprisoned men in Canada. In contrast, there were

305 women who were federal prisoners in Canada, 96 of whom occupied cells in maximum security institutions (see Table 9.4). There were 129 women held in medium security and minimum security, and 51 inmates had yet to receive a classification.

TABLE 9.4

PROFILE OF THE FEDERALLY INCARCERATED FEMALE INMATE POPULATION, 1998–1999

| | NUMBER | PERCENT OF FEMALE INMATE POPULATION |
|---|---|---|
| Age 20 to 34 | 170 | 56 |
| Serving a first penitentiary sentence | 210 | 69 |
| Length of sentence | | |
| Under three years | 99 | 32 |
| Three to six years | 103 | 34 |
| Six to ten years | 31 | 10 |
| Ten years or more | 20 | 7 |
| Life or indeterminate | 52 | 17 |
| Offence | | |
| Murder—first degree | 14 | 5 |
| Murder—second degree | 38 | 12 |
| Schedule I (violence) | 153 | 50 |
| Schedule II (drugs) | 71 | 23 |
| Nonscheduled (nonviolent) | 42 | 14 |
| Sexual* | 9 | 3 |
| **Total number of female inmates** | **305** | |

*Sex offences have been presented separately from the violent category to illustrate their proportion in the inmate population.

Source: CSC, 2000.

The crimes of violence that bring women into prison have recently begun to mirror those of their male counterparts. Overall, women have traditionally been sentenced for economic crimes, for crimes of necessity and survival, and for acting as a party or an accomplice to more serious felonies.

Women have been entering the criminal justice system in increasing numbers in the past two decades. Explanations of this increase are often linked to several intriguing theories. First, the disappearance of the justice system's chivalry toward females has had a decided impact. In the past, justice officials tended to view women as helpless and childlike in many cases, and so as less culpable for their actions. Second, the increasing movement of women into full labour force partic-

ipation and demands for equality have translated into the justice system's changed approach to female criminality.

In Canada, two-thirds of women who are sentenced federally are mothers. It is illuminating to consider that 70 percent of that number are single parents. These female inmates report suffering physical abuse in 68 percent of cases, and more than half have reported sexual abuse. More striking, perhaps, is their lack of educational achievement. Over two-thirds of women in prison have primary school education or less and have never held any form of steady employment.

In penitentiaries throughout Canada, women prisoners are required to work or to take various educational or training programs. From Monday to Friday, prisoners work in the kitchen, the school, or the beauty parlour, and some work in cleaning or office jobs in the prison. Women may also take university credits, secretarial courses, woodworking, ceramics, and word processing. Provincial centres for women offer a variety of programs, including core programs in substance abuse, parenting skills, and life skills. Personal development and culturally specific programs focus on Aboriginal lifestyle and religion, and some institutions have programs in music therapy, chaplaincy, and health services. Educational, occupational, and vocational programs, such as canine programs, word processing, and building maintenance, may be offered. There are also specific employment programs that train inmates to be kitchen workers, janitors, maintenance workers, library staff, ceramic artists, and child care assistants. Several other programs focus on spirituality, health/well-being, and creativity. After an appropriate period of imprisonment, women prisoners may be chosen for work outside the institution, where they are paid a small wage for their efforts.

# Prisons and the Future

In the 21st century, prisons are facing a growing number of challenges that will affect the kinds of services they provide and the ability of these institutions to carry out their punitive functions. These changes reflect, to a large extent, the changing nature of our society, and there is little doubt that prisons in the future continue to be forced to adapt to rapidly changing conditions.

## The Spread of HIV/AIDS

HIV/AIDS in prison is one of the greatest challenges confronting Canadian prison administrations. This problem introduces many complexities into the prison environment. First, the number of prisoners who are testing positive for HIV/AIDS has continued to grow significantly in the past decade. Jurgens (1996), writing on behalf of the Canadian HIV/AIDS Legal Network, reported on research conducted both nationally and internationally on this serious problem. He reported a 40 percent increase in the number of known HIV/AIDS cases discovered in Canadian federal correctional institutions in the period from April 1994 to August 1995. As Jurgens reports, one of the major difficulties that this increase presents for prisons is strictly economic. HIV/AIDS prisoners who require expensive medications and intensive care are becoming a substantial financial burden to prisons. More disturbingly, Jurgens found evidence of an increase in high-risk behaviours in prison. HIV/AIDS is spread not only through sexual contact among prisoners but also through shared needles. Jurgens found evidence to support the conclusion that as a result of these behaviours, HIV was being transmitted in prison.

The dilemmas facing prison officials as a result of this modern plague are many. Until recently, the attitude of prison officials was that supplying condoms was inappropriate in a same-sex environment. While sexual liaisons are specifically forbidden by prison regulation, there is little doubt that individuals will find ways to engage in sexual encounters in the closed society of the prison. Approaching the problem by denying condoms and making rules against consensual sex can be argued to promote the spread of HIV/AIDS and other sexually transmitted diseases. Prison officials have difficulty supplying fresh disposable needles to individuals for a similar reason—that is, drug use is strictly prohibited in prison. Yet, prison authorities understand that this behaviour does occur. To deny the inmates needles will lead to needles being shared and to a much greater risk of various diseases spreading. However, to supply needles might be seen as condoning illegal drug use. Needles also can be used as effective weapons in prison. Therefore, the dilemmas that authorities face are not simple, nor are solutions as easy as we might assume.

Parallel to problems with HIV/AIDS in prison are extremely high rates of hepatitis C. Three Canadian studies, reported in Jurgens (1996), discovered that from 28 to 40 percent of all prisoners have been infected. Given that a recent CSC survey of 4285 inmates revealed that a "high proportion" of prisoners engage in high-risk behaviours, there is considerable cause for concern (Jurges, 1996, p. 6). Jurgens rightly points to the Commission of Inquiry into Certain Events at the Prison for Women in Kingston (the Arbour Commission) as a ringing condemnation of the CSC's hypocrisy in comparing its statements regarding respect for rights of the individual versus their actions. The Arbour Commission found a system fraught with shortcomings and characterized by a culture of disrespect for individual's rights. Furthermore, the commission found clear evidence of insularity—that is, an unwillingness to consider external criticisms, whether emanating from the correctional investigator or from another source. This inability or unwillingness to respond had severely hampered efforts to deal effectively with HIV/AIDS and other diseases in the prison environment.

BOX 9.3

## HIV/AIDS: THE PRISON SYSTEM'S LEGAL RESPONSIBILITIES

What are the moral and legal responsibilities of the prison system in dealing with inmates who are suffering with HIV/AIDS? The Canadian courts have ruled that a Toronto detention centre had failed in its duty by not providing appropriate and adequate treatment for prisoners with HIV/AIDS. The administration had also failed in its legal duties by not educating staff. Under the law, employers have a duty to educate staff and to make reasonable accommodations for persons who are disabled. They also have a duty to educate employees about sexual harassment so that in legal cases they cannot claim that their employees were acting in ignorance of the law and of the rights of individuals. Do the prisons have a moral duty, if not a legal one, to protect inmates from unreasonable risks? Failure to do so could lead to a lawsuit being filed by an individual who became infected with HIV because he or she was not provided with condoms or sterile needles. An Australian prisoner has already brought such a case before the courts.

Source: Jurgens, 1996, p. v.

Kevin Marron's interview with prison AIDS activist Gerald Benoit, who was identified as suffering from the disease in 1987, revealed that prisoners with AIDS are now accepted in the general population of the prison. In fact, according to Benoit, "Now the people ostracized are the ones who harass people with AIDS" (Marron, 1996, 102–103). According to Marron's investigation, prison medical facilities are hard pressed to provide the kinds of treatment that AIDS patients require. When prisoners develop full-blown AIDS, they are transferred to hospitals or hospices. Unfortunately, although prison authorities try to transfer inmates who are suffering from a terminal diseases into the community to friends or family, it is not always possible to do so. Marron relates the story of a man who at age 35 was dying of AIDS and who could not find any agency, family, or friends to accept him in the community. Poignantly, the outsider status of prisoners may mean that there is no community outside of prison ready to accept them and meet their needs.

## The Aging of the Prison Population

A further challenge for prisons is the growing number of geriatric prisoners, who, as our general population ages, will begin to overwhelm the capacity of the system to respond. This aging population is one of the reasons that community alternatives to prison will become necessary in future sentencing options. The functions of prisons are not aimed at treating people who are seriously ill. With adult-onset diabetes becoming epidemic and scores of other conditions increasing, including heart problems, stroke, and Alzheimer's disease, society must consider creative alternatives to prison that can meet the goals of criminal justice while balancing the needs of the aging prisoner.

## Inmate Suicide

Suicide is another issue that has received insufficient response within the prison system. Research by Burtch and Ericson (1977), as well as others, has demonstrated a high rate of suicide among prisoners. Suicide is the most frequent cause of death within the Canadian custodial system. During 1997–1998, there were 92 inmate deaths recorded in Canadian institutions. Suicide accounts for 35 percent of all deaths (Canadian Centre for Justice Statistics, 1999). The suicide rate in prison is twice that in the general population.

The reasons for suicide vary among prisoners, but it is apparent that two points in the prison career seem to be more problematic than others: the period immediately following incarceration and the time just prior to release. These periods of danger result from stresses associated with entrance into prison and fear concerning re-entry into the community. Marron reports that in 1993–1994, 20 suicides occurred in federal institutions (this would exclude jails, detention centres, and provincial prisons). P4W was also plagued by suicides but at a lower rate than that in men's prisons. The methods of committing suicide are predominantly hanging and drug overdose. CSC research, according to Marron (1996), has revealed that higher suicide rates are associated with overcrowded prisons. Suicides are also associated typically with longer sentences.

## Privatization of Prisons

Much consideration has recently been given to developing private prisons in Canada. Indeed, several private prisons are already up and running. Ontario opened a boot-camp-style facility for juvenile offenders outside Barrie in 1998 as part of a "get tough" policy with young offenders. The much shorter period of incarceration required with a boot camp sentence is also in keeping with conservative fiscal policies, which predominate in government. A private owner/operator in these institutions may offer a daily rate per prisoner that is seemingly more cost efficient than that available under government schemes. However, studies of private prisons in the United States have failed to find evidence of the rosy predictions of cost savings that governments may have anticipated. While the initial offer to provide prison services may be lower, it is recognized that prisons, unlike other private businesses associated with human service providers, cannot simply close their doors in the face of financial difficulties. Governments must be prepared to provide economic bailouts to private prisons that cannot operate on budget.

Further scrutiny of private prisons also indicates that they are typically staffed by nonunionized employees, whose training may fall short of the level of expertise and experience required to ensure proper management of the institution and to deal with adult inmate populations. A further criticism is that as dealers in human misery, private prison operators have a vested interest in the expansion of the prison industry to provide more "raw product" for their institutions. New and alternative approaches to dealing with crime, including the possible abolition of prisons, run contrary to the private prison operators' interests.

Governments that have been faced with mounting costs for running prisons have chosen to move in two directions to effect cost savings. The first approach is a movement toward privatization, as discussed above. The second approach is the amalgamation of prisons into what are known as "superprisons." Under this latter approach, some institutions are closed and some are expanded and architecturally altered to allow a greatly reduced staff to supervise the inmate population. Maplehurst Correctional Centre in Ontario is "the flagship of the new system and the largest jail in Canada" (*Toronto Star*, 2000, p. A1). Based, it would appear, on the marketing success of one-stop shopping outlets, the idea is to reduce costs from $126 a day per prisoner to roughly $76 per day. While the design has been called "radical," blueprints released by the Ministry of

Correctional Services show clearly that the prison is based on Jeremy Bentham's panopticon. The prison is a series of self-contained units, or "pods," each with its own exercise yard, dining room, and visiting area, constructed in a circular configuration. As reported, all of these areas are "visible from a central control point" (Fleming, 1995). The new "jumbo jails," which would house provincial prisoners, would take in approximately 87 000 inmates each year. The annual cost of running them is $500 million dollars (*The Toronto Star*, 2000). Since there will be little movement within the institutions, the need for correctional officers will have more than halved, from 4000 to 1700 employees. The new Penetanguishene superjail will be privately run after it has been built as an experiment to see if costs savings will be realized. The private contractor would be penalized if recidivism rates among released prisoners exceeded a standard set by the ministry. However, given the current recidivism rate of roughly 66 percent, it is also likely that the standard will be very low.

This new approach to jailing inmates focuses more on economical management and easy control of prisoners than on the human aspects of control. Correctional officers' unions have expressed concern about the loss of the human dimension of service provision—that is, the services that are provided in human interaction. The new institutions provide a sterile, overcontrolled environment, where visiting will be by appointment and conducted by telephone through Plexiglas barriers. Each visit will be subject to a buzzer-controlled, strict 20-minute limit. While the ministry has claimed that the superjails will allow people from small communities better access to services, in reality, they will remove the prisoner not only from contact with relatives and friends, but also from physical human contact while held within the system. How many inmates would prefer living in a clean, electronically gated fishbowl under intense supervision at all times to a drafty, but more human, county jail? However, inmates' experiences and desires have never been a priority with institution planners, many of whom have never spent a day imprisoned in their own facilities.

## Alternatives to Prison

The rising costs of imprisonment have caused governments to consider alternatives to simply putting criminals in the holding pens we call prisons. In 1997–1998, the combined federal and provincial costs of running corrections reached $2.08 billion, representing an 11 percent increase from the same period in 1993–1994 (Canadian Centre for Justice Statistics, 1999). The costs associated with housing a prisoner in 1997–1998 were $140 per day at the federal level and $120 at the provincial level. There are differences in costs across the provinces, from a low in Alberta of $83 per day to a high in the Yukon of $219 per day. Both Nils Christie (1994), a European criminologist and antiprison activist, and Ruth Morris (1997), a Canadian prison abolitionist, have written impassioned books calling for the dismantling of the prison system. Penal abolition is relatively new concept in Canada. The argument proposed is that prisons are not only ineffective at rehabilitating criminals but also a costly luxury that society can no longer afford. Given the massive expenditures directed to prisons, there is little doubt that even a small portion of the corrections budget would support extensive community alternatives to imprisonment. Community corrections have recently gained in popularity, as the limitations of prisons from a rehabilitative perspective have been recognized. If community alternatives are more cost effective and at least as successful, they may be worth considering. In Chapter 10, we consider some of the forms of community alternatives that are being developed in Canada.

# Conclusion

Originally introduced as a method of containing and punishing individuals, the prison has evolved to serve a variety of functions, including rehabilitation. These new functions reflect changes in societal attitudes toward the confinement and treatment of prisoners. Canada's high rate of imprisonment ensures that prisons occupy an important place in discussions of societal values and expenditures in our society. Despite the efforts of prison abolitionists, the prison is unlikely to disappear as a means of dealing with crime. Therefore, dialogues on the structuring of the prison system and its functions are likely to continue to occupy academics, policymakers, politicians, and the public in the 21st century.

## Summary

In this chapter, we have provided an overview of the historical development of the prison system and have analyzed the evolution of various forms of prison systems. We have also focused on the nature of the inmate subculture and on prison violence. Additionally, we have examined prison conditions for both male and female inmates, along with new developments in the justice system's approach to imprisonment. Emerging problems in the prison system have been found to include the aging of the prison population, the increasing incidence of HIV/AIDS, and the growing costs associated with imprisonment.

## Key Terms

Auburn System (p. 182)

incarceration rate (p. 183)

inmate subculture (p. 191)

panopticon (p. 183)

Pennsylvania System (p. 182)

prison argot (p. 191)

protective custody (p. 188)

security classifications (p. 185)

solitary confinement (p. 189)

# Discussion Questions

1. Why did Canada adopt prisons as the main response to dealing with criminals?

2. What are the differences between the Pennsylvania and Auburn approaches to imprisonment?

3. Why does Canada have a higher rate of imprisonment than many other countries?

4. What are some causes of prison riots?

5. What problems will present the greatest challenges to prisons in the future?

# Weblinks

**wysiwyg://fl.83/http://www.homeste...justice01/prisonerstories.ns4.html** This site presents stories about prisoners and the effect of prisons on families, as well as chatrooms with inmates and their families.

**www.csc-scc.gc.ca** This site is loaded with information on corrections and prison studies.

**www.jpp** This is the only journal written by prisoners themselves, with articles, poems, and writing on prison issues.

**www.fcnetwork.org/** FCNetwork, provided by the American Family and Corrections Network, offers information on children of prisoners, parenting programs for prisoners, prison visiting, incarcerated fathers and mothers, hospitality programs, keeping in touch, returning to the community, the impact of the justice system on families, and prison marriage. The site is an excellent resource for policy and research on families of offenders.

**home.istar.ca/~ccja/angl/overc.html** Under the title "Prison Overcrowding and the Reintegration of Offenders," this discussion paper presented by the Canadian Criminal Justice Association addresses the topic of prison conditions.

# CHAPTER 10

# Alternatives to the Prison System

## Objectives

- To explain the meaning of the term *probation* and its conditions.

- To outline the parole process, including hearings and the different forms of prerelease programs.

- To discuss the suspension and revocation processes and problems associated with parole.

- To discuss the concept of the life sentence.

- To describe various community-based alternatives.

## Community Alternatives

Imprisonment has become the dominant method of punishment in the Canadian criminal justice system. The prison offers an established method of dealing with criminals that requires little in the way of community input. However, in both financial and human terms the prison is an extremely costly method of dealing with crime in Canadian society. Alternatives to prison have been slow to develop within our society, reflecting not only the complex issues that surround the punishment of crime in Canada but also the entrenched nature of the existing carceral network. The **carceral network,** a term coined by writer Michel Foucault, is the extensive grouping of institutions, agencies, and staff who are

part of the process of law enforcement, the judicial process, the prison system, and the ancillary programs and agencies that deal with offenders. While there is no means to accurately assess the entire cost of operating this vast network, it can be estimated to exceed several billion dollars. It employs hundreds of thousands of Canadians in direct and related services. Therefore, to say that crime does not pay is actually incorrect—it provides employment and revenues that exceed almost any business enterprise in Canada. It should not be surprising that there is a great deal of reluctance to find meaningful alternatives to prison in Canada, since so many individuals and communities depend on these institutions for their livelihood. Although our society is currently undergoing a technological revolution fuelled by computer technology and the global economy, the prison system remains largely unaffected by these shifts. The most significant threats to the current system of imprisonment are privatization and the development of alternative methods of punishment.

This chapter discusses alternatives to the prison system. Increasingly, the costs associated with prison and the debilitating effects of incarceration on prisoners have lead to the consideration of alternative methods of sentencing in an approach called **community corrections.** This term derives from the nature of these sentencing options, which place offenders in the community. While the economic savings in the variety of community corrections programs will become apparent in the discussion that follows, there are also important philosophical underpinnings to this approach.

Advocates of community corrections view it as a more effective method of punishment, as it allows offenders to maintain or re-establish links with the wider community in which he or she lives. Communities are seen as having the power to assist offenders in reorienting their lives to establish themselves as law-abiding members of society. Offenders benefit not only from being spared the pains of imprisonment but also from being able to maintain a stable life. Families, employment, and relationships, for example, are not fractured as they would be in the case of an offender's entering detention. These sentences are court ordered and do require that the offender remain under supervision and abide by certain rules of behaviour that are expected by the supervising officer. There are a number of programs that can be included under the category of community corrections, including probation, parole, electronic tethering, and new forms of confinement. Additionally, there are a variety of other community-based options, including restitution, community service, mediation, and conditional sentences, which will be considered in this chapter.

# Probation
- - - - - - - - - - - - - - - - - - - -

Probation is a widely used sentencing option that is most often associated with young offenders. This form of sentencing has a long history. Canada did not insti-

tute a system of probation until the early 1950s when the government responded to the Royal Commission to Investigate the Penal System of Canada, which
had pointed out the need for a national body of social workers to assist the prison
system by providing a parole and probation service.

Canadian courts have made widespread use of probation. Currently, it is the
most frequently awarded community sentence. While many community members view probation as a nonsentence, the reality is that probationers must
adhere to a strict regimen of rules and supervision. Violation of the terms of probation can and do result in the offender's serving the remainder of the sentence
in a correctional facility. Probation orders may range from several months to a
maximum of three years; over the past decade, the average period of probation
has been one year. One hundred thousand people served terms of probation in
Canada in the year 2000.

While criminologists have been concerned with the growth of the prison system and increasing rates of incarceration, rates of probation have increased more
rapidly than sentences of imprisonment during the 1990s. The median age of
probationers is 29, the same median age as the homeless population in Canada,
demonstrating that at this age people are most at risk for "falling through the
cracks" (Fleming, 1993).

There are a variety of conditions that may be imposed upon the individual as
part of an order of probation. Three of the conditions are mandatory and com-
monsensical: (1) the probationer may not change residence without informing
the probation officer, (2) the probationer may not accept an order of employment without permission, and (3) the probationer must report to a probation
officer as required. Additionally, probationers are to refrain from associating with
criminals in the community. Under section 737(2) of the Criminal Code, probationers are required to keep the peace, maintain good behaviour, and appear
before the court when required, in addition to reporting to a probation officer.
Further conditions commonly reflect the nature of the offence committed and
the need for personal change by the offender. Conditions could include participation in a substance abuse program, anger management classes, educational
courses, community volunteering, or a course in money management.

Probation officers (POs) provide personal support to probationers, who must
visit them regularly. POs can provide a helping hand to probationers by dispens-
ing advise on problematic areas of social behaviour and guidance to prevent reoffending. However, POs also have a duty to enforce the orders of the court. This
second role may be a barrier to effective rehabilitation of the offender. Since POs
have wide discretionary powers to revoke probation if the probationer violates
the conditions, it is difficult for probationers who are experiencing personal trouble to be forthright with their POs. Some offenders may view probation as a
game of impression management and manipulation of the PO. They offer their
POs an image of themselves that will not provoke incarceration or suspicion of

wrongdoing but that also does not expose problem behaviours. Thus, criminal lifestyles are left relatively unhindered.

Probation is typically imposed following sentencing by a judge. At this point, the sentence is suspended, and a probation order is substituted. Probation may also be imposed as part of a conditional discharge, intermittent sentence, or split sentence, where the sentence combines another penalty, such as a fine or a period of incarceration. By the mid-1990s, approximately 66 percent of offenders in Canada were serving probation orders, representing an increase of almost 50 percent over the number at the beginning of the 1990s.

The courts have enthusiastically embraced probation as an alternative to imprisonment for several reasons. Probation is cost effective when compared with incarceration. As well, rehabilitation is more probable if the offender remains in the community. However, it is worth noting that little research has been conducted in Canada to examine the process of probation, its effects, and its ability to serve offender's needs.

# Parole

**Parole** is a reduction in the sentence of an offender as a reward for good conduct while incarcerated. As a form of condition release, it has a long history in Canada's prisons, beginning in 1868, one year after Confederation. In the latter half of the 1800s, the prison population soared in Canada, resulting in the need for an innovative program to reduce the number of captive inmates. The "ticket-of-leave" program permitted prisoners to get out of prison early, and given the harsh conditions at Kingston, this was no minor incentive for good behaviour. While inmates remained unsupervised until the beginning of the 1900s, by 1910 the government had solicited the assistance of charitable and religious organizations as part of a remission service to manage the parole system.

Parole has been a controversial measure in the last century and a half; some have criticized it as providing prematurely short sentences for dangerous offenders. Prisoners have also criticized the parole process, arguing that subjective rather than objective criteria govern parole decisions. Inmates refer to parole hearings as "kangaroo courts," where rules and due process are distinctly absent. Inmates provide the responses that are expected in order to gain release, rather than honest answers.

Is parole a carrot dangled in front of the inmate to produce compliant, manageable behaviour in prison? Is it perhaps a stick used to psychologically beat the prisoners into submission? Or is it possible that it is nothing more than an illusion? In the sections that follow, we explore the reality of parole in Canada in an attempt to answer these questions.

# The Parole Process

The process of parole begins at the time of sentencing. While judges should not consider the possibility of early release through parole when assessing sentences, there is obviously a tendency to do so. Judges are not elected in Canada, unlike in the United States, but rather are considered political appointees. As lawyers for the status quo and as community members, they cannot reasonably be expected to ignore public concerns regarding sentencing leniency (despite their purported neutrality). For some serious offences, judges may order offenders to serve half of their sentences before parole will be considered.

Since the chance of being granted parole is strongly influenced by an inmate's behaviour while in prison and by correctional authorities assessment of the behaviour, prisoners must develop a realistic release plan. Case management officers aid them in creating this plan. The plan will address issues of possible employment, treatment plans, and residence. Inmates' chances of obtaining parole may be increased by their participation in appropriate programs. However, two substantial criticisms of these programs should be noted. First, many programs are not readily available to inmates without a considerable wait of several months to several years. If successful completion of a treatment program is necessary for mounting a parole application, an inmate's release may be unreasonably delayed. Delays can result in other significant problems for inmates, including depression, heightened stress, and mental illness, which further delay their release. Second, inmates "playing" the parole system may enrol themselves in alcohol and substance abuse programs in order to demonstrate "change" to parole officials when they do not actually need these programs. As one former inmate related, "You just sit there and talk seriously and they give you certificates to wave at the parole boys. They're proof you've really changed."

The parole file contains information from the presentence report, institutional records, and various forms of criminal, medical, and psychiatric records. These documents may help the parole board members come to an informed decision.

Parole boards have been consistently criticized by legal authorities, criminologists, and former inmates. Some have viewed parole board decisions as arbitrary, with no objective criteria being employed to render decisions. Parole boards have consistently been unable to develop prediction instruments that can assess the suitability of particular inmates for parole; thus, decisions are often subjective. The Canadian Sentencing Commission (1987) commented that parole boards have more power than judges in determining the length of sentences. One of the more disturbing trends that researchers have observed is the decision to grant parole more readily to inmates serving long sentences of imprisonment. Therefore, although one individual may receive a much shorter sentence then another at court, they may both serve roughly the equivalent amount of jail time. This means that more serious crimes are punished as though they are less serious crimes.

Another criticism is that inmates remain disadvantaged in parole hearings, since there are few guidelines to inform them of the criteria they must meet to gain their freedom. Another factor, rarely noted by researchers, is the limited ability of many prisoners to prepare a parole application, given their level of academic achievement. Prisoners who depend on institutional assistance are often unable to make a convincing case before parole authorities.

## The Parole Hearing

Parole board hearings are conducted on a rotating basis at all penal institutions. Members are essentially political appointees, called *order-in-council appointees*. They serve a term fixed by various levels of provincial and federal government. Parole officials often have no experience of corrections, but instead mirror the current thinking of the government in power concerning approaches to crime. Recent appointments in Ontario, for example, have stressed a law and order approach to crime, thus limiting the granting of parole. Members serve on a part-time basis.

Inmates are required to apply for a parole hearing. However, as correctional investigator Ron Stewart found, many who are eligible do not bother to enter an application (Fleming, 1995). Most readers could not imagine forgoing any opportunity to gain release; however, this is a view from the outside. If the inside is "turned out" (Ericson, 1973), failure to apply is more readily understandable. Reasons given include lack of access to a necessary program or treatment, difficulty in finding employment outside the institution, lack of familial supports, and problems in locating a place of residence.

Inmates are informed of their date for parole eligibility and can make an appointment to present their case to the parole board members. There are two types of parole that can be granted. *Day parole* is a more limited form of parole that provides some safeguards for the community through supervision of parolees. Parolees are required to live in a halfway house until ready for full parole. *Full parole* is granted to those who are ready for release to the community with their own living arrangements. Many parolees live with friends or relatives or on their own. However, since parolees are often short of funds when released from prison, they frequently must live in homeless shelters. In Toronto, Seaton House, the largest men's shelter in North America, is home to many ex-prisoners who need a place to live following incarceration.

# The Parole Experience

Parole officers assist and monitor the parolee after he or she is released from the institution. The task of parole officers is to monitor the behaviour of inmates in the areas of employment, criminal activity, housing, and relationships to prevent a relapse into crime, which would lead to further incarceration. Parole officers, like probation officers, also serve an important function in providing counsel and a sounding board for parolees. Moving out of prison life proves to be a difficult transition for almost all individuals. The John Howard Society promoted a campaign in the 1990s that described the difficulties parolees experience reintegrating into the community: "Now the sentence is over, the hard part begins!"

Inmates on parole are required to live up to their parole conditions, including regularly visiting the parole officer and residing in a particular area. They may not leave the area they live in without the permission of the parole officer. Conditions that are regularly imposed include refraining from associating with known criminals, abstaining from alcohol consumption, and taking treatment for specific problems. These conditions act as controls on the types of behaviour and associations that have prompted criminality in the past.

Fleming's (1982) study on the reintegration of offenders demonstrated the difficulties that confront prisoners upon release. His study, conducted in England with long-term prisoners, showed the considerable difficulties that ex-prisoners must face. In some cases the people had been institutionalized so long that the monetary system of the country had changed. Many found it difficult to

use a telephone or to cross a road, things that we take for granted in negotiating the everyday world. Returning to society is particularly difficult for men and women who have no familial supports awaiting them, as noted in numerous studies conducted of prison life and release (Morris, 1965; Morris & Morris, 1963).

Parole board hearings predominate in the federal corrections system; however, almost 50 percent of parolees are released from provincial institutions. Some two-thirds of applicants for parole are successful in obtaining parole.

## Prerelease Programs

Prisoners are entitled to apply for a number of **prerelease programs,** including escorted and unescorted temporary absences, day parole, and work release. Escorted temporary passes are issued for a variety of reasons. The philosophy underlying them is that a means should be found to make it easier for the individual to re-enter society. By being permitted increasing, temporary freedom outside of prison walls, the individual can make a better adjustment to full freedom when it is eventually awarded. The inmate is assessed in terms of potential threat posed to the community if he or she were to escape on a temporary absence. Therefore, inmates must present a minimal risk to society before being awarded these forms of absence. Of over 40 000 passes granted each year (CSC, 1999), only a handful result in attempted or actual escape. Escorted passes generally apply for a day or two, with a maximum of five days if a person is seeking medical treatment. Most often, passes are granted to allow offenders to obtain further education or to visit relatives in the community.

Following a period of significant incarceration, inmates may apply for unescorted absences. Typically, these passes are for short periods of time, from several days to one week in duration (with some exceptional cases involving longer periods). In considering readiness for this form of freer release, authorities will examine various facets of the individual's life while in custody, such as the person's behaviour while incarcerated, as well as the planning that has gone into the proposed absence and the inmate's potential threat to the community.

Upon granting these absences, correctional authorities must notify the police. They also must give notice to victims who have made formal requests to be alerted when inmates will be released. Individuals who are serving time in a maximum security institution and dangerous offenders are not permitted unescorted absences.

As inmates approach the end of their institutional sentence, they are permitted to apply for day parole. This program permits the inmate to spend the entire day in the community before returning to the prison at night. For some, day parole allows time for job searches or for seeking accommodation. Inmates at this stage in the carceral network will typically reside in a halfway house. These are facilities in the community that provide treatment for offenders to prepare them for bridging the gap between the institution and society.

Work release programs facilitate the transition back to society by permitting inmates to work in a full-time job, or in some instances in a voluntary position, while returning to the institution or halfway house at night. Alan Eagleson, the former NHL players' agent and attorney, was permitted to work in a Toronto-area factory on such a program.

Full parole may be granted to persons who have served one-third of the sentence awarded by the court. Life prisoners are required to serve a sentence of 25 years. However, under section 745 of the Criminal Code (the so-called faint hope clause), offenders may seek an early eligibility date after serving 15 years. The most infamous inmate to seek early eligibility under this clause is serial murderer Clifford Olson. Time served before trial is not relevant in determining the time that must be served before an offender is eligible for parole.

**Statutory release** (formerly called *mandatory supervision*) begins after a prisoner has served two-thirds of a sentence. At this time, the offender may be eligible for release into the community. This is the most common form of release from federal facilities. Since those released must be supervised by a parole officer, many inmates prefer to wait until the end of their sentence before release. There is little debate that supervised release is preferable to an inmate's re-entering society completely on his or her own. Supervision forms part of the carceral network envisioned by Michel Foucault (1977), who argued that the reinforcement of control messages throughout society was necessary to maintain adherence to societal norms. The question that arises for parole authorities is whether there is a danger that an inmate will hurt someone after release. In England until the mid-1970s, for example, supervision following release was not provided for criminally insane offenders. This lack of supervision led to several tragic murders by released individuals who, through regular contact and supervision, could possibly have been identified as being in danger of reoffending. This dilemma is discussed by Kevin Marron in his book *The Slammer*. An offender, Darren, was serving seven years for sexual and physical assault, and having served two-thirds of his sentence was applying for statutory release:

> The parole board would have no trouble deciding that Darren was dangerous. But would keeping him in jail for another two years lessen or increase the risk to the public? Would he benefit from more treatment in jail or would he become even more anti-social? Would it be safer to let him out now and insist that he attend treatment programs in the community?... Members of the parole board are frequently faced with impossible dilemmas, as they are asked to weigh imponderable risks. (A parole board member asked) "Do you think hitting her on the head was a failure to control violent impulses?" Darren responded, "The reason I did that was to stun her so she would stop screaming." The board members ordered that Darren be detained until the end of his sentence. (1996, p. 244)

# Revocation of Parole

Inmates risk **suspension** of parole if they commit a technical violation of their parole. This violation involves breaching one of the conditions of their parole, most notably when it involves one or more of the behaviours involved in previous crimes. Committing another offence will automatically lead to suspension. Parole officers conduct unannounced visits to their parolees, including "curfew checks" (Marron, 1996). These checks are conducted by pairs of parole officers because many parolees are forced to accept accommodation in dangerous locales owing to their poor financial circumstances.

Most parole officers have a caseload of 25 to 35 offenders. Parolees are required to visit the parole officer approximately once a week to discuss their progress and problems. Marron's research reveals that the groups supervised by each officer are mixed: "About half of all offenders supervised by parole officers have been convicted of non-violent crimes, another quarter have been serving time for robbery, while the remaining quarter committed violent crimes or sex offences" (1996, p. 268–269).

When parole is suspended, the parolee is placed in custody. The parole board is then required to meet with the offender in the next 45 days to determine whether it will take the more serious step of revoking parole or whether it will release the person to continue parole. If the individual has committed a breach that is not of a serious nature and is not considered a serious risk to society, the parolee can be returned to the community. More conditions may be added at this time if it is felt they are necessary to ensure the success of the offender.

**Revocation** is initiated when the board considers the offender to present a significant chance of reoffending. The breaches that the parolee commits may signal a deterioration of his or her condition and so are taken seriously. For example, if an offender who has a long history of committing crimes while under the influence breaches parole in a tavern, considerable risk is demonstrated. Similarly, if an individual who has a history of committing sexual offences against children is found loitering near a school, the implications can be serious for the community. However, one of the difficulties in this approach is understanding which behaviours constitute merely a minor violation with no significant consequences, and which are serious and require intervention. According to Zamble, "We have no specificity of what is a serious violation and what is trivial lack of conformity" (2000, p. 3). For Zamble, parole officers are put in the position of acting like fortune tellers, since they have no specific tools for predicting an offender's behaviour. The research of Zamble and his colleagues points to the possibility of developing a model for predicting recidivism. Since he argues that offenders "appear to have had little or no perception of their movement toward recidivism" (p. 3), his model, which is based on the offender's choices of response to precipitating environmental situations, points to the individual's inadequate coping resources. The ineffective responding of the offender results in negative thoughts and emotions, which are "identifiable, distinctive and characteristic of offenders in similar circumstances" (Zamble, 2000, p. 5). Thus, officers could use this model to provide effective interventions when the behaviour is serious, rather than employing draconian measures when the behaviour is not serious. This model is not considered foolproof, however, since the complex nature of offending and the environment that either encourages or reinforces criminal behaviour must also be considered.

One of the questions most often addressed in complaints concerning the laxity of the parole system is whether it is an effective tool of rehabilitation. Three researchers (Nouwens, Motiuk, & Boe, 1993) studied a large sample of offenders released on parole over a 10-year period, from 1975 to 1985. In examining the cases of 42 000 parolees, they found that the majority were successful in completing parole. Roughly 20 percent had difficulties that involved committing a crime on parole, and 25 percent had their parole revoked either for a crime or for a technical violation, with the reasons being equally divided between each group.

---

BOX 10.1

## PROBLEMATIC SITUATIONS FOR PAROLE SUPERVISION

A supervising officer must decide whether to suspend release when an offender commits each of the following breaches of parole:

1. Is seen drinking in a local pub
2. Is chronically late for appointments
3. Leaves the district without permission to visit a girlfriend
4. Appears somewhat depressed
5. Breaks up with his wife
6. Tests positive for cocaine through urinalysis
7. Fails to appear for his monthly appointment and does not answer his phone

Which behaviour do you think constitutes a serious breach of parole?

Source: Edward Zamble. 2000. "Community Supervision: Current Practice and Future Directions." CSC Canada Web site. Available: www.csc-scc.gc.ca.

# Life Sentences in Canada

In 1976, bowing to world pressure and enlightened research, Canada revoked the death penalty for capital offences. No one had been executed in Canada since 1962, as during this period there had been a moratorium on the death penalty. In Canada, at least two cases played a significant part in ending the use of the death penalty. The execution of Wilfred Coffin was a clear case of the hanging of an innocent man (Belliveau, 1956). Coffin, a sometimes trapper, guide, and woodsman in the Gaspé region of Quebec, was convicted of the murders of three American game hunters. The evidence against Coffin was circumstantial: he had been one of the last people to see the victims alive, he was in possession of a pocket knife owned by one of the victims (which he claimed was a gift), and he had American money in his pocket (in an era when Canadian and American money was at par and freely circulated as such). Coffin claimed to have seen a distinctive jeep bearing American plates and two men dressed in army fatigues in the area just before the murders occurred. During the trial Coffin's lawyer offered no defence, calling no witnesses on his behalf, and refusing to let Coffin take the stand. After his conviction, several eyewitnesses came forward and confirmed his story regarding the jeep carrying the two Americans who had acted suspiciously; two of the eyewitnesses were doctors at a Toronto hospital, and another was the owner of a local gas station located just a few miles from the cutoff road for the woods where the victims were found. This evidence, though strong, was not heard by the court since the rules of evidence at the time did not permit an appeal on new evidence. Coffin went to his death an innocent man. One of the junior lawyers assisting on his case, Pierre Trudeau, later became the prime minister who repealed the death penalty.

The second case, that of Steven Truscott, has recently resurfaced as a matter of public debate, some 40 years after the original crime. In 1959, Truscott was convicted of the rape-strangulation murder of an 11-year-old girl, Lynn Harper. Both were residents of a military base in the small town of Clinton, Ontario. At the time, there was no other recorded case in common law involving a juvenile offender committing such a heinous crime. Truscott was convicted on circumstantial evidence. There were indications that the police and the military suppressed evidence in his favour, and that other suspects were not fully pursued (LeBourdais, 1966; Trent, 1971). Particularly suspicious was the military's transfer of Steven's family to Ottawa before the commencement of his trial for murder. As a young offender facing the death penalty, this separation from his family would have been particularly hard. Truscott was convicted and sentenced to death. His sentence was commuted by the Cabinet of Lester B. Pearson to one of life imprisonment. Throughout his incarceration, and during his exemplary civilian life since release, Steven Truscott has told the same story and maintained his innocence.

Before the death sentence was repealed, murderers whose sentence was commuted served approximately 10 years before release. Following the repeal of the death penalty, the time served before release was increased to 25 years. Thus, an individual sentenced six months before the changes would serve less than half of the sentence of a person convicted six months later. The 25-year sentence was arbitrarily decided, rather than based on criminological studies and penological experience. Little consideration was given to the costs involved in housing prisoners, the difficulties they would have adjusting to society upon release, and the effects of long-term imprisonment (Fleming, 1995).

The authors of the **Life-25** policy also instigated what is commonly known as the faint-hope clause. Under section 745 of the Criminal Code, inmates may apply for early parole after serving 15 years of their sentence. Those hearing the application can reduce the sentence remaining before parole eligibility or even order immediate release. A hearing is held before a judge and jury in the community where the original crime was committed. The original conviction is not revisited in court; instead, the behaviour and plans of the inmate while in prison are considered. Consideration is given to the nature of the original offence and the likely risk the inmate still poses to society. Over 2000 inmates will have been eligible for this review in the first few years of this new century.

Early analysis of applications has shown a provincial difference in the granting of early eligibility. Quebec applicants have enjoyed a much higher success rate than their contemporaries in Ontario or Alberta. Some criminologists have questioned the criteria employed to assess eligibility, pointing out the apparent inequities in the present system. The case of Rene Vaillancourt, who as an 18-year-old killed a Toronto police constable during a bank hold-up, is interesting to compare with that of Larry Sheldon. Vaillancourt was denied early eligibility, despite an essentially model prison career. Sheldon, who was reported to be a model inmate, had been sentenced for abducting, raping, and dissecting a child near Gimli, Manitoba. Sheldon was successful in his section 745 application (Fleming, 1995).

Despite exceptions such as this, applicants who have committed horrendous crimes are unlikely to be successful in obtaining either early release or eventual release. Under legislation passed since the public outcry over Clifford Olson's application, multiple murderers have been excluded from applying for judicial review. Paul Bernardo, a multiple murderer and serial rapist, can legally be detained in prison for the remainder of his natural life if parole is denied him. Since Bernardo poses such a continuing threat to the community, it is difficult to imagine any parole board releasing him into society unless he were so physically incapacitated that he no longer constituted a threat of any kind.

Dangerous offenders are a special category under the Criminal Code. These individuals are declared a danger to society because of the violent, repetitive nature of their crimes. While there is some controversy surrounding the designation of persons as dangerous, particularly women, the long criminal careers and extremely violent nature of their offences make them poor candidates for parole.

# Problems with Parole

It has already been argued that most inmates view parole as a form of kangaroo court. But it is also interesting to note that many experts hold this same view. Their criticisms of the decision-making process in parole concern two areas: (1) the composition of parole boards and the relative competence of their members to render decisions and (2) a lack of clear criteria that can inform decisions. Regarding the first issue, the political nature of appointments to the parole board means that such positions are often given to individuals as a reward for party support, rather than as a reflection of their understanding of criminal behaviour. These positions command a pay scale approaching $100 000 per annum. Since few members of the board have any previous training in criminal justice or in human behaviour, it is difficult to establish working criteria that are understood by board members and that reflect objective assessment of issues. Often, the kinds of issues that have to be debated are complex and may be incomprehensible to members who lack the appropriate background.

Birnie (1990), a former member of the board who began her duties with minimal training, voices these criticisms. She critiques the arbitrary nature of decisions and argues that decisions reflect the inadequacy of training of members and board composition, rather than objective criteria. Therefore, the criteria by which individuals are judged suitable for parole in one jurisdiction may vary widely with those used in another location. Given that parole board members are informed of the success or failure of their decisions in terms of recidivism only in high-profile cases, they fail to receive the kinds of information that would allow them to reconsider or alter misguided decision-making processes.

Parole board members, thus, are empowered to make decisions concerning the release or continuing incarceration of individuals even though they are ill trained, fail to use objective criteria, and are unaware of the outcome of their decisions. Consequently, it is little wonder that parole board members may lean toward the conservative or seemingly safe decision of continuing incarceration. After all, a parole board that releases very few inmates has less chance of being blamed for the failure of their releasees. However, the safety of this approach can be questioned. If offenders are unjustly held in prison for no apparent reason after making serious efforts to reform their behaviour, they may come out embittered by the justice system and with a grudge against society. Thus, holding a prisoner can result in more serious criminal exploits, although these are merely delayed by continuing incarceration. Conversely, release at an earlier date may forge a stronger bond between a merciful society and the inmate.

The foregoing discussion of parole has considered both its benefits and drawbacks. For society and correctional officials, parole is both a carrot and a stick. It is a carrot to induce good behaviour and thus more efficient management of institutionalized persons, as well as a stick to punish those who do not conform.

Outside the institution, parole can be used to continue the connection of the released prisoner with the institution, as disobeying a condition of parole may mean returning to finish out a sentence. Parole, under conservative governments, has become a way of further punishing criminals by denying it in all but the most "safe" cases, rather using it as a tool for rehabilitation. If parole boards reject the dual role of balancing rehabilitation of the individual with the protection of society, and instead opt for concentrating on the latter consideration, then the intended purpose of parole is defeated. Some criminologists have called for determinate sentences of reasonable duration, followed by supervision in the community in the form of support rather than law enforcement. For inmates, parole is more of an illusion. Applying for parole is seen as a "crapshoot," reflecting the lack of due process safeguards in the parole process, the lack of training for board members, the arbitrary standards, and the limited skills inmates possess to represent themselves at parole hearings.

Alan Manson, speaking on sentencing at a symposium held at the University of Windsor (1989), has addressed the importance of early release mechanisms. As one of the few attorneys who regularly represents inmates in various hearings, he has a unique perspective on the prison system. Given the high rate of imprisonment in Canada and the long sentences that are imposed, he argues that the possibility of early release is necessary to instill hope in inmates and to preserve and nurture the very skills necessary to constructive participation in a democratic society.

The increasing call for accountability in parole hearings, emanating on the one hand from governments that wish to impress society with their "hard line" regarding law and order and on the other hand from inmates who feel the process is questionable, seems to indicate the need for a more open process of parole. If society wishes to instill in inmates the recognition of the need for fair play and reasonableness in dealing with others, then it is incumbent upon society to construct a parole process that is marked by due process and by objective criteria, against which inmates can measure their progress toward release and make necessary adjustments to ensure success. It is only then that parole will be transformed into more than an illusion for Canadian prisoners.

---

BOX 10.2

### DID YOU KNOW?

The success rate for day parole is 95 percent. Full parole (regular) is successful 89 percent of the time and statutory release 88 percent of the time. The success rate for escorted and unescorted temporary absences is 99 percent.

Source: CSC, 1998.

# Community-Based Alternatives

Increasingly, fiscal crises (O'Connor, 1970) have forced governments to consider less-costly alternatives to imprisonment. Researchers have identified other factors in the European context that could be transferable to Canada. Joutsen has identified trends in Canada that reflect the need for alternatives to incarceration:

1. Increasing fear of crime
2. Disillusionment with the effectiveness of treatment programs
3. Lack of confidence in the ability of the system to rehabilitate or produce law-abiding citizens
4. Increasing use of prisons as an administrative measure
5. Increasing attractiveness of a "just deserts" philosophy of punishment (CSC, 2000, p. 1)

As Joutsen argues, it is difficult to muster the political will to move to alternative measures when public fear of crime is heightened. Interestingly, fear of crime is typically unrelated to actual crimes committed in a community or to crime statistics. In an era of declining rates of serious crime, it is curious that fears of crime have escalated. A large measure of this fear seems to be intergenerational—that is, the aging population fears young offenders. Although we understand by reviewing statistics on young offenders that the overwhelming majority of their crimes are directed against other young people, fear of crime is fed not by hard facts, but by a media that seeks to exploit violent crime for readership. As well, governments have realized the value of fanning the flames of fear in the electorate. Put simply, if crime is "out of control," governments will argue, then people have reason to fear, and they can trust in government to crack down on criminals. The Ontario government, in the fall sitting of Parliament for 1999, identified the elimination of squeegee kids in Ontario as its number-one legislative priority. In passing the so-called Safe Streets Bill, it played to a the moral panic that it had created about the criminal intent of "aggressive panhandlers." Extrapolating from the European experience, it can be argued that it is in the interests of politicians to "use harsher measures to draw attention away from the failures of society" (CSC, 2000).

For some observers, such as prison abolitionists Ruth Morris (1997) and Nils Christie (1994), prisons are an unacceptable form of punishment for the majority of offenders. In order to convince the public of the acceptability of alternative approaches, it is necessary to convince them both of the appropriateness of community sanctions and of their effectiveness when compared with institutional sentences. While rhetoric by law and order emphasizes the need to get tough with offenders, the grim reality of prison expenditure means that governments must consider alternatives. It would be hypocritical for governments to suggest that health, education, welfare, and social services should be cut, whereas prison budgets should be permitted to expand exponentially. To that end, in April 1997 Parliament passed a series of sentencing and corrections reforms that allowed for the development or expansion of new community-based alternatives.

The movement of governments to cut costs is not new. During the 1970s and 1980s, governments deinstitutionalized mentally ill patients as a cost-saving measure. It was argued that living in the community was better for the mental health of individuals, who could benefit from outpatient clinic services and from social support and interaction with the community. However, some analysts, including Scull (1983) and Fleming (1982), have argued that such programs reflected the goal of saving costs, rather than a real transfer of resources to the community to assist the mentally ill. Unsupervised and living in substandard housing, the "walking wounded" posed a considerable problem for policing, hospitals, and the court systems in their community, which had few resources and little training to deal with mental health crises.

The philosophy underlying noncustodial sentences is that nonviolent offenders who have committed crimes that are minor in nature are more effectively dealt with in the community (CSC, 2000). Public safety is not an issue with these offenders, so confinement serves no purpose other than retribution, which has been rejected as a valid goal by eminent legal scholars.

One alternative with significant potential to assist the justice system in its efforts to divert offenders from secure custody is **community service orders.** These orders, issued by a judge, compel a convicted offender to complete a requisite number of hours of work in the community. The CSC believes that community service orders can be "far more meaningful, effective and less costly to taxpayers than a jail sentence. And better yet, it can help to instill good work habits, a sense of responsibility, and may even lead to stable employment" (CSC, 2000, p. 1). There is little doubt that individuals may benefit from remaining in their communities, as it may be unnecessary to remove the person from gainful employment, from familial relations and obligations, or from educational training. For those offenders who do not enjoy such bonds in their community, this experience teaches that the ends of justice can be met in the community, rather than in a prison cell. By leaving an offender in the community, we potentially extend to them the opportunity to atone for their crimes without suffering all of the pains associated with imprisonment.

A second developing area of community corrections is **mediation services.** This option is offered in cooperation with the office of the Crown attorney. The express aim of this option is to put the offender together with the victim(s) to provide victim–offender mediation. In this approach, victims are given the opportunity to confront the author of the crime committed against them. For offenders, it is a unique opportunity to gain insight into the consequences of their actions. Few criminals actually witness the impact the crimes they commit have on their victims. In a neutral mediated session, the victims are able to express pent-up feelings of anger about the criminal, the crime, and its negative effects on their life. For offenders, it represents a chance to learn and to apologize to the victim. Another component of mediation services is restitution. The offender, faced with the direct consequences of his or her actions, is asked to consider a means of making recompense to the victim. This restitution could take the form of financial compensation, work performed for the victim, community service in lieu of assistance to a victim who may feel uncomfortable with further contact, or another mutually agreeable option. The option must answer the needs not only of the victim but also of the offender, as well as the need for rehabilitation.

Sentencing circles and elder panels are further methods of dealing with the offender outside of prison walls. These options, which emerged in Canada from Aboriginal forms of justice, have recently received a great deal of public attention. In Aboriginal communities there has always been a greater emphasis on reclaiming the individual while maintaining the person in the community. In Aboriginal society, the community is seen as the centre of healing for offenders, and removal from society is rarely viewed as a positive option (unless it is a sentence that forces the individual to be isolated in a wilderness area to get back in touch with core values). The Aboriginal experience with the Canadian criminal justice system has never been positive. The location of prison facilities has typically meant that in Prairie provinces, Aboriginal offenders are removed from their reserve or home communities and are transported hundreds of kilometres away to serve their sentences. This process further disenfranchises offenders in terms of their own communities and unique sets of cultural values.

**Elder panels** are composed of respected members of the community who have knowledge of and respect for Aboriginal approaches to justice. This approach represents a meeting of the Canadian and Aboriginal justice systems, as elders sit with judges to assist them in constructing appropriate sentences for offenders. The advice, according to the CSC, can be offered either in open court or in chambers—that is, behind closed doors in the judge's chambers.

The **sentencing circle** reflects Aboriginal beliefs in the connectedness of all life. The offender is not apart from the community but is part of it. Under this approach, the offender is involved with members of the community and with elders in establishing how the case should be dealt with. The judge will make the final decision in the case but will take into account the recommendations of the sentencing circle or the elder panel. This approach allows the community that is most affected by the activities of the offender to have a direct input into sentencing options. The CSC has found that "the offender is more likely to heed the

concerns and suggestions of the community rather than those of a judge acting alone" (2000, p. 1).

**Electronic monitoring,** or tethering, is another form of alternative community punishment that has been in existence since 1987 (CSC, 1998) and is administered by four provinces, including Ontario, British Columbia, Newfoundland, and Saskatchewan. Recent improvements in technology have allowed the development of sophisticated electronic monitors, which permit offenders to serve sentences in their own homes. Offenders in this program do not simply remain in the household, since few would be able to sustain themselves throughout an extended sentence. Instead, most are employed, attend school, or are engaged in other programs that the judge approves as a condition of monitoring. The appeal of electronic monitoring is dual—it is an inexpensive alternative to custodial sentences, and it also permits offenders to benefit from remaining in the community with minimal disruption of their lives. However, certain conditions are attached to monitoring, including strict curfews and restrictions of movement. The tether, which is worn on the leg, is "read" by a telephone dial-in system to ensure that the offender is at the appropriate place at required times. A nonresponse at the home after curfew, for example, would send police to investigate the unauthorized absence.

Another program, **fine options,** is a response to previous inequities in the criminal justice system that disadvantaged poor offenders. Aboriginal Canadians have historically been overrepresented in the prison system, particularly in the Prairie provinces. They often have served prison sentences in provincial jails owing to an inability to pay fines ordered by the court. The CSC reported that in 1998 over one-quarter of all people serving time in provincial jails were doing so because of their inability to pay fines. Enlightened reform indicates that alternatives, such as community service or probation, may be more equitable in serving both the offender and the community.

Another new development that has much promise is **restitution.** This is a new approach that permits judges to rule that the offender must compensate victims of property crime or for personal injuries sustained during the commission of a crime. While the pain the victim suffered may include emotional and psychological effects, there are personal costs as well, including loss of property, loss of employment income, and medical expenses, which can severely affect them. Crimes often have a complex impact on the victim that is difficult to measure. Understanding these costs requires the court to listen to victims and receive evidence regarding these costs. Restitution has recently experienced a renaissance, particularly in Ontario, where the provincial government introduced legislation to require the parents of young offenders to compensate the victims of crime. The restitution order is filed as a civil judgment. Enforcement of these orders, as might be expected, is often difficult, if not impossible, if the offender has few or no financial resources. If an individual is able to pay a fine but fails to do so, the province can refuse to renew licences until the fines are paid.

All of the above programs can be viewed as part of a movement toward what is called *restorative justice* (see Chapter 8). This approach focuses on a consultative process that brings together the offender, the victim, and the community in order to permit healing and repair (CSC, 2000). Derived from the writings of criminologist Richard Quinney, this form of "peacemaking criminology" focuses not on punishment but rather on "making things right" through a process of communication and problem solving between the parties. Two further programs that spring from this approach are family group conferencing and community sentencing panels. In the former, the victim, the offender, and family and supporters meet to resolve financial and emotional issues, as well as to examine means of providing restitution to the victim. The latter is a program that involves volunteers from the community. The panel can look at the issues that lie at the heart of offending through considering reparations, restitution, conciliation, and victim involvement. The panel is also empowered to make recommendations concerning the environmental factors in the community that may be conducive to crime or facilitate criminal activities.

# Conclusion

Probation and parole have long been important components of Canada's criminal justice system. These approaches have been successful as alternatives to prison by providing both cost savings and opportunities for convicted criminals to benefit from serving their sentences in the community. A variety of community service options have become part of the correctional arsenal in the past two decades. These sentencing options allow the long-term reintegration of offenders into the community. Community alternatives, while relatively new in Canada, hold the promise of creating a more humane and effective criminal justice system.

## Summary

This chapter has focused on alternatives to prison, specifically parole and probation, as well as community service models. We have explored both the strengths and weaknesses of probation as the most widely employed form of alternative sentencing in Canada. Parole, although effective as an early-release mechanism, has proved to present many problems, in terms of its administration and the ability of inmates to have fair and impartial hearings that ascribe to the dictates of due process and justice. We have explored a variety of prerelease programs, which allow inmates to more effectively re-enter civilian life. Finally, we have discussed the controversial "faint-hope clause," section 745 of the Criminal Code, in terms of its fairness and value as a rehabilitative tool.

## Key Terms

carceral network (p. 207)

community corrections (p. 208)

community service orders (p. 223)

elder panels (p. 224)

electronic monitoring (p. 225)

fine opinions (p. 225)

Life-25 (p. 219)

mediation services (p. 223)

parole (p. 210)

prerelease programs (p. 214)

restitution (p. 226)

revocation (p. 216)

sentencing circles (p. 224)

statutory release (p. 215)

suspension (p. 216)

# Discussion Questions

1. Why have the courts have made such wide-scale use of probation?

2. Do you think parole is a carrot, a stick, or an illusion? Explain why.

3. What are the prisoner's responsibilities to ensure a positive parole outcome?

4. Why do inmates refer to parole hearings as a kangaroo court?

5. How do the various prerelease programs differ in their purpose? Why do they enjoy a high success rate?

6. Is the process of parole supervision and revocation fair and effective, in your estimation?

7. Is Life-25 an effective sentence?

8. Why are community-based alternatives becoming increasingly popular with governments?

# Weblinks

**www.npb-cnlc.gc.ca/** The National Parole Board, as part of the criminal justice system, makes independent, quality conditional release and pardon decisions and clemency recommendations. Their Web site provides information on the NPB and its role, as well as offering links to relevant legislation.

**www.parole.obp.gov.on.ca/** The Ontario Parole Board site offers a wealth of information on parole statistics, fiscal reviews, parole criteria, the hearing process, review, and victim participation.

**www.johnhoward.ca/** The John Howard Society of Canada works in an advocacy, research, community education, and crime prevention capacity with people who have come into conflict with the law.

**www.lcc.gc.ca/en/forum/rj/index.html** The Transformative Justice Project site is the work of the Law Commission of Canada and explores restorative justice issues in Canada and around the world. The site also provides an excellent resource for Canadian justice and law links.

**www.sgc.gc.ca/epub/Abocor/e199805b/e199805b.htm** Published by the Solicitor General's Aboriginal Corrections Policy Unit, this study deals with community corrections and healing projects in aboriginal communities.

# CHAPTER 11

# Victims of Crime

## Objectives

- To define victimization and victimology.
- To describe the services and programs offered to victims.
- To note the patterns of victimization in Canada.
- To address some of the issues surrounding the emergence of victims' needs in justice administration.
- To describe the place of the victim in the criminal justice process.

## The Place of Victims in the Crime Picture

Unless you or someone close to you has been directly affected by a crime, you have probably spent little time concerning yourself with victimization. Most people spend more time thinking about those who commit crime than about those who have been victimized by crime. Yet the victims themselves have alerted us to victimization and have urged lawmakers and officials of the criminal justice system to pay them more heed. Much of the focus on the interests of victims in crime policy is a result of the efforts of reformers whose energies have been sparked by their own victimization. In this way, crime policy and, to a lesser extent, criminal procedure reflect times past, when victims deployed voluntary and state resources to avenge or recoup their losses.

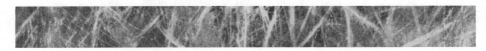

Until recently, it had been assumed that victims were being duly represented in the criminal justice system. After all, wasn't the state devoting considerable resources to prosecuting and punishing crime on the victim's behalf? In practice, however, victims were rarely consulted about their wishes, and pretrial and trial procedure gave them little or no opportunity to raise concerns about the plea or the sentence. Therefore, many observers and participants came to see the criminal procedure as officially furthering the victim's alienation and mistreatment through what is generally referred to as *secondary victimization.*

The recent surge of interest in victims—of placing victims more centrally or at least less peripherally in the criminal justice process and in policy development—is partly the result of politics. In this chapter, we will review some of the features of these politics. In addition, we will explore what is meant by **victim-ology,** a new branch of criminology that deals with the psychological, cultural, social, and political processes that contribute to victimization and the societal processes that contribute to the conferral of the victim status. Finally, we will offer a statistical and normative portrait of victims and victimization by drawing on victimization surveys and self-report studies.

# Victimology

## Who or What Is a Victim?

Under criminal law, a *victim* is person against whom a criminal act has been perpetrated. According to Quinney (1972) and others, under the law there is no crime without a victim (a person, a corporation, or some other entity) and a finding of guilt. Schneider (1982) defines a victim as a person, an organization, or a moral aspect of society that is harmed or jeopardized by a crime. Nagel (1974) argues that a victim is one who is acted against criminally.

However, when the legal system clears a defendant of responsibility for a criminal act—for example, when the defendant has committed only a technical violation of the law—it may clear the only person who has any factual causative responsibility for the act. This is also the case when the accused is found not criminally responsible owing to mental disorder. Unless a new suit is launched, this act of the court amounts to a technical declaration that there is, under law, no act that can definitively be said to have been criminal. And if there is no criminal act, then there is, under the strict legal definition, no victim. Therefore, a strict legal definition of victim and victimization is unsatisfactory, as it will negate instances of victimization and make validation of victimization dependent on legal authority alone.

A strict legal definition is unlikely to validate the experience of many victims. Even victimization surveys may fail to reveal the full extent of criminal victimization because some respondents may be unwilling to acknowledge that an act committed against them was criminal. Many other acts that may engender loss or cause great harm, such as industrial polluting, may not be outlawed or considered criminal.

For these and other reasons, early victimologists went beyond the definition of victimization as loss from criminal wrongdoing to carve out the scope of victimology. One proponent of an inclusive view of the victim was Benjamin Mendelsohn (1976), who argued that people could even be victims of natural phenomena and of industrialization. Others, such as Merlene Young-Rifai (1982) and Robert Elias (1986), sought to use human rights violations as the template against which to define victims.

For many, however, the inclusivity of the term *victim* also can be unmanageable. Charles Sykes (1992) complained in his book on U.S. culture, *A Nation of Victims*, that too many people have come to define themselves as victims and that the whole exercise has become culturally and economically untenable. While there is much in the book to question, the argument hit a chord in the early 1990s. The 1990s saw a backlash against the inclusivity of victim status: many people felt that too many people were claiming to be victims and that the multitude of claims was becoming a burden on society.

While we may not insist on illegality of acts as a condition of victimization, we also cannot rely entirely on subjective experience. Our definition of victimization should require recognition by a third party or external authority. Under this condition, only after a person is accorded the status of victim will a third party intervene on his or her behalf. There are limits on the capacities of social, political, and economic bodies to mobilize in the service of aggrieved parties, and thus there will be limits to who is accorded the victim status, or to who is validated. There are even more limits on compensation. Here, it is important to recognize that there are a variety of contexts or stages on which a person may seek validation of victimization, and denial or invalidation in one context does not presume invalidation in another. For example, the mass media may define a person subjected to an illegitimate violation as a victim, even if the violation may not mobilize criminal or civil remedies.

## "What Is Victimization?"

**Victimization** can be defined as "an illegitimate violation of a person by another, resulting in an experience of loss as recognized by a moral authority." Take, as an example, the execution of the individual by the state. In some societies, this practice is permitted both according to law and by popular consent. Gary

Gilmore was executed in Nevada in 1977. His person was violated when the bullets pierced his heart. He was infringed, his body broken, his life taken. But if we accept the legitimacy of the state in performing the execution—and some of us may not—the violation is neither unwarranted nor illegitimate, and therefore he was not a victim.

The phrase "experience of loss" in the definition above is important. The victim must experience a loss. When we say "experience," we refer to a *subjective* phenomenon. You *feel* the loss of your stolen bicycle. Why? Because it breached your personal circumference or your privacy wall. You expect to have a relationship with the social world in which your privacy, person, and property are protected. Because this expectation is part of the norms of society, you experience a general feeling of insecurity when your belongings are stolen. More specifically, you feel the loss because something you enjoyed is no longer there for you, leaving you with one less resource with which to take pleasure from your existence.

The clause "which is recognized by a moral authority" is also significant in the definition above. This qualification is very important to the designation of victim status. Marlene Young-Rifai (1982) has argued that what is important in our definition of victimology is both whether there is an imbalance of power between the victim and the other and whether the action of victimization is seen as an injustice. When we think of events in terms of who has the power and what serves justice, we are not restricting ourselves necessarily to the acts forbidden under the law. Political scientists, psychologists, sociologists, and other expert authorities will differ in their perceptions of who rightfully belongs in the category of victims, but we depend on them, in addition to our legal authorities, to define this category. You may tell a police officer or a social scientist that you are a victim or have experienced a violation or loss, but until your definition of that experience matches legal, social scientific, and, to some extent, cultural designations, you will not be recognized as a victim.

The authority, once certifying that the loss is illegitimate according to its standard, takes some form of intervention. At a minimum, such intervention is merely the recognition that the violation suffered is illegitimate. Recognition is not to be underestimated, because it is prefatory to further intervention, such as compensation. The authority must then recognize the violation as being sufficient to meet some standard of third-party intervention. Violations that are seen as not requiring such intervention are eventually recast as normative actions.

## The Context of Victimization

There are three considerations of context in assessing victimization: the balance of power, the rules of interaction, and the legitimacy of the authority granting the victim status. The balance of power is an essential consideration of any discussion of victims. Another way of conceptualizing victimization is as a person's exploitation of weakness in furthering an advantage. Victimization can be seen as the taking of power or autonomy from another; this, in many cases, is the essential loss that the victim experiences. The designation of victim status will in part be a consideration of the distribution of power between two or more parties. The question is, Which of the parties to an interaction is in a position of advantage?

Take the idea of "playing the victim." What is meant by this accusation? Only when we consider the victim in the balance of power does it make sense. The person claiming the role of the victim does not deserve the status of the role because, it is implied, the aspirant has failed to present the case that she or he has been in a position of relative *disadvantage*. People may seek to gain the advantages of victim status by presenting the context or circumstances in which they have suffered a loss as overwhelmingly sided against them, in order to benefit from third-party recognition of their victimization. We would hardly see the United States as a victim in the context of international relations, unless we were given some very strong evidence of the country's powerlessness in a given arena. Similarly, we need to understand the victim within the context of relationships of power.

A second essential feature of context in assessing victimization is the *normal rules of interaction* governing conduct at the site at which the victimization is alleged to have taken place. Have both parties conducted themselves within the norms of communication and conduct that pertain to the site of their interaction? For example, in a queue at the cafeteria, a person who tackles the last in line violates the norms of interaction that apply to the situation. Even within the play of a football game, such action is well circumscribed. But the ball carrier who is hit by such a tackle during play has little claim to victim status, even if the play-by-play announcer claims that a mugging has occurred.

A third feature of context concerns the *legitimacy of the authority* who grants victim status. What is the degree of neutrality of the arbiter? What is used to measure violations? Are subjective or objective measures used? Does the interpretive framework itself adequately encompass the diversity of individual experience? Is the interpretive framework structurally biased in some way?

All of these questions go beyond the rules at the particular site and begin to apply to more universal evaluations, such as general principles of justice or human rights. For example, a totalitarian regime may imprison journalists who question the policy of the government. Such imprisonment may be sanctioned not only by the executive branch but also by the legislative branch and the judiciary. These parties will see the denial of rights and freedoms to the journalists not as an illegitimate violation but rather as an essential measure in promoting the internal security of the "just state." However, observers may argue that the legitimacy of the authority is questionable, and critical victimologists would likewise argue that a wider frame of reference than that offered by an individual

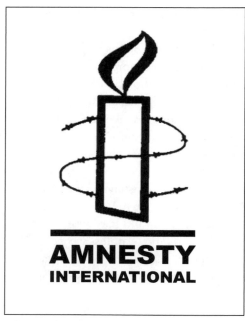

Copyright © Amnesty International.

nation's justice system is needed in determining injustice and illegitimate violations. Using a wider frame of reference, the attribution of victimization is made not by local or state authorities, but by the international community or by another moral authority, such as a religious or human rights group.

We may use human rights criteria or standards (although they are not free of cultural bias) to assign victimization within the prescriptions of cultural practices. Amnesty International and Human Rights Watch are organizations that "discover" victims who are not recognized by indigenous authorities. The practice of female circumcision in certain Muslim societies and other communities, for example, may be a part of the normative rites of passage, falling within parameters of legitimate violation and loss. As well, certain states may sanction the incarceration of preadolescents or the execution of youths below the age of majority. Human rights agencies apply universal codes of conduct to review such practices. These acts may then be seen as crimes against humanity or as unjust and therefore falling within an expanded, international definition of crime. With the larger, international definition of illegitimate violation, there is also an expanded discovery of victims, as is the case in Amnesty International's "death watch" of executed prisoners in the United States.

Recognition of victimization is often sought to achieve political empowerment, whether at the level of personal or state politics. Because victim status can be politically useful, parties or people often will seek recognition, even when the ultimate purpose is not to progress from the status of victim to the status of survivor. At bottom, this politicization of the victim draws on the fact that victim recognition is necessary before scarce resources will be allocated on the victims' behalf. Because victimization is dependent on recognition, it is not long before someone's real experience of loss becomes someone else's opportunity to advance a political agenda. This occurred in California when Governor Pete Wilson posed with Marc Klass, whose 14-year-old daughter, Polly, was murdered by a person with a long criminal record, in order to promote "three strikes" legislation.

# The Victim's Role in the Victimization Process

Only recently has it become a research question to think about the role of the victim, as opposed to the motivation of the offender, in conceptualizing crime theories. This change resulted from three developments in the 1970s:

1. The victim's rights movement and an attendant interest in a crime prevention policy based on sound empirical data
2. The proliferation of victimization surveys, which were first used in the mid-1960s and detailed the circumstances of crime, including victim characteristics
3. The disenchantment with traditional offender-centred theorizing about crime, since it had failed to yield improved understanding of changes to rates of victimization (Sacco & Kennedy, 1998)

In short, there was a movement in the direction of seeing the victim as a key part to understanding rates of victimization and therefore to formulating crime prevention policy.

The earliest scholars of victimology, including Hans Von Hentig and Marvin Wolfgang, argued that it is wrong to neglect to understand interpersonal crime as an interaction between victim and offender. Studies of the dynamics of the victim–offender exchange have revealed that many victims play a role in precipitating their own victimization. Wolfgang (1958) studied homicides in Philadelphia in the 1950s and found that in a quarter of the cases, the eventual victim was the first to brandish the weapon or threaten lethal violence. He defined these cases as **victim-precipitated crimes.** Also in Philadelphia, Menachem Amir (1971) studied rape cases and found, using highly generous criteria for precipitation, that one in five rape cases fit the characterization of victim-precipitated crimes. Donald Black (1983) argued that many victimizations are actually forms of conflict management or punishment; he called this type of victimization *self-help*—the eventual offender takes his or her own decision to correct an intolerable situation, such as when a woman kills her husband after years of abuse.

## The Situated Transaction

The emphasis on dynamics, or on what goes on between the participants in a criminal event, rather than on what one person does to another, is referred to by Edwin Luckenbill as the **situated transaction.** This concept allows us to bring into the mix the behaviour of third parties, such as bystanders. It also allows us to use an ethnomethodological approach, by seeing the situated transaction as a script with set scenes and plot lines. Luckenbill (1977) looked at 70 homicides and concluded that they could be seen as character contests in which the disputants tried to save face by responding to insults, for example, with deadly attacks. Luckenbill described the homicide as a "transactional product" resulting from a chain of events, beginning usually with an action of the eventual victim that led the eventual offender to attempt to save face. The offender confronted the victim, and bystanders may have also urged a confrontation, leading the offender to feel trapped into using violence.

The idea that we all try to follow scripts in our social actions or decision making can be extended to theorizing about crime. The series of events leading up to a criminal act can be seen as the outcome of a person's attempts to play one role (in which he or she is not the loser) in preference over another (in which he or she is). In this way, scripts are used in the attempt to maximize the chances of a certain outcome. This perspective emphasizes the duality of the transaction and the cultural context of conflict.

Drawing from previous research and theorizing, Meithe and Meier (1990) argue that the major factors in victimization include proximity to crime, exposure to crime, target attractiveness, and capable guardianship. Thus, the smaller the physical distance between potential targets and potential offenders, the more likely that victimization rates will be higher. In addition, the more a person is exposed, accessible, and visible by being in a risky or vulnerable situation, such as by spending time in bars, the higher the chances of victimization. Target attractiveness and guardianship are also important. The potential offender will subjectively evaluate the characteristics of individual targets, such as according to their portability or likelihood of offering resistance. Whether targets are guarded by others or by security systems or informal, official, or voluntary social control agents also determines the likelihood of victimization.

## Criminal Responsibility

Although sociologists are committed to understanding the full social context of criminal (and noncriminal) victimization and also to selecting certain forms of victimization to be remedied by criminal sanction, the criminal process, as we have seen, takes a much narrower view of an event. While criminal law allows for the defences of duress and provocation, it also assumes that people are responsible for the actions they have chosen to commit. Under criminal law, much of the context of the criminal action is stripped away so that responsibility may be more cleanly assigned to a single party.

It is important, therefore, to distinguish between sociological causation and criminal responsibility. Criminal law would be rendered meaningless if each act were analyzed according to the role of each of the many factors sociologists find useful in assigning crime causation, including family background, socioeconomic status, and age. Theoretically, the event could be explained as being determined by the sum of these factors. Instead, a sociological finding of victim pre-cipitation in the case of an assault is distinguished from a legal finding of respon-sibility, and the findings referred to above do not absolve offenders of legal responsibility.

# Patterns of Victimization in Canada

As noted in Chapter 2, in addition to the UCR, victimization surveys are used to reveal the extent of crime in society. These surveys are used under the idea that victims may be more willing to acknowledge their victimization anonymously and that many complaints to the police may go unrecorded.

There have been a number of victimization surveys in Canada, beginning with the Canadian Urban Victimization Survey (CUVS), which surveyed 61 000 people by telephone in St. John's, Halifax-Dartmouth, Montreal, Toronto, Winnipeg, Edmonton, and Vancouver in 1982. One of the many interesting find-ings of the survey was that, of the total offences reported to the survey, only 42 percent had been reported to the police.

In addition to the CUVS, Statistics Canada has carried out the General Social Survey (GSS) since the mid-1980s, and two cycles of the survey—in 1988 and 1993—included questions about risk and victimization by crime. This sample interviewed 10 000 residents 15 years or older by telephone. The 1993 survey found the following:

- In both the 1988 and 1993 samples, 24 percent of Canadians were victim-ized in a crime or attempted crime during the preceding year.
- The rate of personal victimization is 11 percent higher for women than for men.
- Violent victimization rates are higher in low-income families.
- Of sexual assaults, 90 percent were not reported to the police.
- Young people are more likely to be victims and are less likely to report victimization.
- In total, 27 percent of Canadians and 42 percent of women feel unsafe walking alone in their neighbourhoods after dark.

Victimization surveys have also confirmed a decrease in crime found in the UCR. In the United States, the National Crime Victimization Survey has report-ed a dramatic decline in crimes of violence, including rape, robbery, and assault, between 1994 and 1998. In 1994, the rate stood at 51.8, and in 1998, the rate had fallen to 36.6. This was the lowest rate recorded since the survey's inception in 1973.

The GSS and U.S. victimization surveys have been able to tell us some other facts about the typical profile of a crime victim. As we've already seen in

The White Ribbon Campaign is a men's organization working to end violence against women.

Chapter 2, victims are more likely to be young, to be have lower incomes, and to live in an urban environment.

In terms of age patterns, the United States Bureau of Justice Statistics found in 1997 (Perkins, 1997) that the victimization rate increases through the teenage years and crests around age 20, decreasing in the remaining years. The GSS found that total personal victimization between the ages of 15 and 24 was 318/1000, decreasing to 156/1000 for the 24 to 44 age group, and dwindling to 74/1000 in the 45 to 64 age group (CCJS, 1995a).

What we have also found is that victimization rates are higher in the west and north of Canada than in the east, particularly the Maritimes. Among ethnic groups, Aboriginal peoples have the highest rates of personal victimization. In the United States, the risks of violent victimization are noted in Bureau of Justice Statistics UCR data that compare the chances of becoming a homicide victim for black and white Americans: in 1988, black males had a 1 in 30 chance of becoming a homicide victim in their lifetime, while a white male had a 1 in 179 chance (Bureau of Justice Statistics, 1989).

While the GSS found that women's personal victimization rates were higher than men's, other surveys have found the opposite. The 1998 National Crime Victimization Survey found that in rates of violent crime, the male rate was 43.1/1000 and the female rate was 30.4/1000. Only in personal thefts and rape or sexual assault did women's victimization exceed that of men's.

However, when seen over the course of a lifetime, rather than over the course of a year, violence against women is revealed to be a major social problem. In 1993, the Violence Against Women (VAW) survey of Statistics Canada inquired into various kinds of abuse experienced by Canadian women. It found that 29 percent of women experienced at least one sexual assault since turning 16, and that 29 percent of women who have lived with a spouse (married or common law) have experienced at least one episode of spousal violence (CCJS, 1995b).

Surveys like the VAW also reveal that while we most fear being victimized by strangers, we are most likely to be victimized by someone we know. Of the women in the VAW who reported being sexually assaulted, 79 percent said that they were assaulted by men known to them.

Other survey findings relate to routine activities. Surveys have found that people who go out more are also more likely to be victimized, and victimization occurs disproportionately in the evenings, on weekends, and in the summer months. Attached persons are less likely to be victims than unattached persons.

# The Emergence of Victims in Criminal Justice

Before the advent of our modern system of criminal prosecution, victims played a major role in the administration of justice. In 16th- and 17th-century England, prosecution relied on the complainant's initiative in bringing about an arrest, in making a charge, and in securing a penalty or compensation.

Gradually, with the arrival of the centralized state and the emergence of lawyers in the court, and later public police, criminal prosecutions came to be public and to be administered by professionals, with the state taking over the case of the victim in an adversarial contest with the accused. Both public police and public prosecutors came to represent the claims of the victim in the name of the state. With this representation, the victim's claims for compensation and reparation came to be secondary or even tertiary considerations, following the interests of the state in its own legitimacy and the interests in the appearance of due process for the accused. The distinction between a civilian model and a state-based model of justice administration is the relative weight given to appearance of justice for the sake of society as a whole, versus the special interest in the individual victim's experience of justice.

Throughout the 19th and most of the 20th century, the administration of justice in nations based on the adversarial model developed into highly rationalized structures, in which only well-educated specialists could find their way about. Because the interest of the victim was subsumed under the interest of the state in a just process, the victim of crime came to be excommunicated from justice delivery, and indeed, to be often treated as an afterthought or a nuisance.

There are differing accounts of the sequence of events that have led to the situation today, in which victim's rights have again become a fulcrum of justice policy. In criminology in the late 1950s, several important papers and symposia on victimology appeared (Elias, 1986). An groundbreaking study by Wolfgang (1958) on victim precipitation in criminal homicide in Philadelphia also alerted scholarly attention to the dynamics of victim–offender interaction. In addition, attention to victims was supported by the first national survey on victimization in the United States in 1966 (1958). Victimology took off as a distinct field of inquiry, with several important papers published in the late 1960s and early 1970s.

In public policy, following the work of Sara Margary Fry in the 1950s, compensation schemes for victims of crime emerged first in New Zealand in 1963, and then in Great Britain and California in 1964. (Elias, 1986). Together with the proliferation of victimization surveys and a political and cultural backlash against the civil rights gains of the 1960s and 1970s, these schemes, known as Criminal Injuries Compensation Boards (CICBs), helped to focus attention on the rights of victims as a major political value.

# Programs for Victims

In general, we can distinguish between two types of innovations when it comes to changing the relationship of the victim with the criminal justice system: victim-centred measures and restorative justice measures. CICBs are today one of several initiatives that have brought victims back into the picture of crime (Mathews & Young, 1992). In the remaining part of this chapter, we will focus on victim-centred measures.

Initiatives such as victim–offender reconciliation programs, community justice forums, family group conferences, and justice circles are also part of the panoply of interventions that are aimed at giving the victim of crime a voice in the administration of justice. While some programs are intended exclusively to aid victims or to compensate them or offer retribution to others in their name, Cavadion and Dignan (1997) have pointed out that there is another group of strategies known as *restorative justice measures*. Restorative justice is an alternative approach in which the victim's voice is to be a major component of lasting redress and peacekeeping.

## Victim-Centred Measures

### Victim Impact Statement

A **victim impact statement (VIS)** is a testimony of loss suffered by the victim owing to the harm caused by the crime. It allows the victim or family of the victim to inform the court of the emotional and financial consequences of the act of victimization. In Canada, the Criminal Code requires the court to consider a VIS at the time of sentencing if the victim of the offence has prepared such a statement. The provinces or territories will stipulate the form of the statement. Under section 662 of the Criminal Code, a VIS takes the form of a written submission attached to the probation officers' presentence report. A VIS may also be read aloud at the discretion of the judge. In general, the victim will get a VIS form from the police and may even get help in filling it out. The form will often have spaces for physical injury, financial and property loss, and so on, and can be withdrawn at any time at the victim's discretion.

The VIS is intended to help in victim rehabilitation by reducing the victim's feelings of helplessness and alienation from the community. Research has found that many victims fail to use this opportunity to speak because they are unaware of it, have become disenchanted with the system, or fear some form of retaliation (Erez & Tontodonato, 1992). Some research has found that when victims are made aware of their eligibility to use the VIS, they may feel less alienation from the process. But some recent research has found that the use of the VIS has little impact on victim satisfaction or on the harshness of sentences (Davis & Smith, 1994, 1995).

Critics argue that these statements have no place in the courtroom, as the emotional quality of the documents may interfere with the neutrality and objectivity of the sentencing decision. Some also argue that they may create sentence disparity because statements are not always provided, and some statements are more rhetorically powerful than others. Legal professionals have also argued that allowing time for these statements adds to the length of the process. However, disparity is already built into the system in the discretionary purviews of officials, including police officers, defence attorneys, prosecutors, and judges. Furthermore, research has failed to find that their use contributes to making court proceedings any less speedy (Davis, Henley, & Smith, 1990).

## Court-Ordered Restitution Orders

*Restitution* refers to a court-ordered sanction involving the offender's payment to the victim for injuries suffered as a result of the criminal act. Federal law allows criminal courts to impose a sentence of restitution in addition to any other penalty for convicted offenders. Courts may impose a restitution order on their own motion or following an application by the prosecutor. Restitution may be ordered when the court is satisfied that the victim has suffered a property loss or has incurred medical expenses or other pecuniary costs owing to the offender's actions. The restitution order will specify a time period for payment, and if the order is not carried out, the victim may file the order in any civil court, where it will have the effect of a judgment of damages made in civil court. The sheriff can then seize bank accounts or place liens on property.

## Compensation

*Compensation* refers to direct payment to the victim to cover financial loss resulting from injuries or death suffered as a result of a criminal act. Compensation is delivered through CICBs, which exist in every province except Prince Edward Island (Riedel, 1989). The CICBs are quasi-judicial tribunals that hear applications where credible evidence is provided and where the criminal conviction of the offender is seen as conclusive evidence. Application is made by the aggrieved party or his or her lawyer and is evaluated by the board. In Ontario, the CICB will reward a financial compensation to victims of violent crimes, providing they make the application within a year of the event. Compensation is awarded for expenses, lost income, and pain and suffering as a result of injury or death. Compensation is also awarded for the maintenance of a child born as a result of sexual assault. The board also takes into consideration the extent of the injury and whether the victim has been awarded insurance or compensation at civil law. As well, the CICB will consider whether the victim's behaviour contributed to the injuries or death and whether the victim has received compensation from other sources, such as private insurance or worker's compensation schemes. It also weighs against the applicant any uncooperativeness with the police.

## Victim Services

### The Police

Many provincial police acts now mandate that the police provide victim services. Throughout Canada, assisting victims of crime is part of the core mission of police services. In Ontario, the Police Services Act, as amended in 1998, stipulates that police must offer services to victims. Following the passing of An Act Respecting Victims of Crime in 1996, police officers are specifically mandated to provide victims of crime with information on services and to treat them with courtesy and respect.

Consequently, Victim Services Units provide support initiatives for victims of crime and disaster, as well as awareness programs for police and correctional officers. These units offer counselling and referral services around the clock to victims. Through the Victim Crisis Assistance and Referral Service (VCARS), each community in Ontario is serviced by volunteers who are available 24 hours a day and who provide on-site assistance to victims.

### The Courts

The courts serve the interests of victims in a number of ways, including, fundamentally, by providing the court of law itself. However, in the past and even now, victims have often been an afterthought of procedure. Victims become witnesses who may be compelled to testify and who have often spent hours waiting outside the courtroom, only to be told that their case has been continued or to come face to face with the accused as he or she enters the courtroom. The courts have responded to criticisms that prosecutors are indifferent to the plight of victims by instituting court worker programs and Victim Witness Assistance Programs (VWAPs). The latter were created under the assumption that offering better services to victims would increase the likelihood of their being effective witnesses, as well as under the mandate of governments through legislation to recognize victims' concerns.

VWAPs offer a variety of services, including providing agency personnel to transport the victim/witness to and from court, crisis counselling, translators, and information pamphlets detailing what can be expected in the courtroom, which other witness protection services are available, and how to apply for compensation. Some VWAPs also offer mediation services for victims who might want to reconcile differences with an offender.

## Voluntary Organizations

The voluntary sector has been the main proponent of the need of the criminal justice system to incorporate victims' interests to a much greater degree. As previously noted, new initiatives often have their source in an individual instance of victimization, which has then been converted into a "moral crusade." These crusades have brought victims and others together under a lobby banner alerting attention to some deficiency in our social policy.

For example, CAVEAT, which stands for Canadians Against Violence Everywhere Advocating for its Termination, is an organization that began when Nina de Villiers was abducted and murdered while jogging in Burlington, Ontario. The murderer was Jonathan Yeo, a man with a long history of violence who was out on $3000 bail. A coroner's inquest was struck to examine Jonathan Yeo's 11-year history of attacks on women and the justice and mental health systems' apparent inability to prevent his continually slipping through the cracks. CAVEAT came into being as a vehicle to lobby the 137 recommendations of the inquest and to convert the outpouring of support for the de Villiers family into a reform agenda. A petition was signed by 2.5 million Canadians and delivered to Alan Rock, then minister of justice, in 1994. In general, CAVEAT seeks greater protection of communities from dangerous offenders through crime prevention, public education, changes to the justice system, and ensuring the rights of victims.

# Current Legislation

Current legislation in aid of victims in Canada is found in the Criminal Code, the Corrections and Conditional Release Act, and the Youth Criminal Justice Act, as well as in provincial and territorial legislation. Federal, provincial, and territorial legislation is guided by the Canadian Statement of Basic Principles of Justice for Victims of Crime.

In July of 1988, Bill C-89 added amendments to the Criminal Code that established new legal rights for victims of crime, including a right to restitution and a right to make a victim impact statement.

Another provision of the Criminal Code is the Victim Fine Surcharge (VFS). This is an additional payment that every offender convicted of a Criminal Code offence or of an offence under the Controlled Drugs and Substances Act is required to pay in addition to any other punishment, so that revenue can be collected to provide assistance to victims. Each province may then use this money to support the victim's services programs as the lieutenant governor in council directs, and the majority of provincial and territorial victim services are financed by this revenue. The maximum VFS is 15 percent of any fine imposed, or $35.

The administration of justice is the jurisdiction of the province, and all provinces now have legislation aimed at helping victims of crime to recover losses. In Ontario, such legislation includes the Victim's Bill of Rights (S.O. 1995 c. 6), Compensation for Victims of Crime Act (S.O. 1990 c. 24), and Victims Rights to Proceeds of Crime Act (S.O. 1994 c. 39).

Ontario's Victim's Bill of Rights established a set of principles according to which justice system officials are to treat victims of crime. These principles include the requirements that victims be treated with courtesy and compassion; that their privacy be respected; that timely access to information be afforded to them, including notification of the conditional release of offenders or their parole; and that their property be returned to them in a timely fashion.

The bill also states that a person convicted of a crime is liable for damages awarded in civil court. The offender's criminal sentence is not to be weighed against the victim's claim of civil damages; rather, a victim of domestic assault or sexual assault is presumed to have suffered emotional distress that may be cited as evidence at civil trial. Also under the bill, money collected under the VFS is expressly dedicated to a victim's justice fund solely dedicated to providing services for victims.

The Ontario government also operates, funds, or otherwise assists several victims' initiatives. It provides funding for 33 community-based sexual assault crises centres (SACS), which provide 24-hour crisis lines; counselling services; public education and referral; and court, police, and hospital accompaniment and support. The Ontario government also operates an automated victim support line (VSL) to keep victims informed of changes in the status of adult offenders who are provincially incarcerated and to provide information on victims' services and other general information on what to expect from the court process. Through the VSL, victims can register for automated updates on the status of an offender through a victim notification system, including information on escape from custody, parole hearing dates, changes in scheduled release dates, transfers or readmissions, and the name and phone number of the supervising probation officer.

In addition, the Ontario government helps to fund the Victim Crisis Assistance and Referral Services (VCARS), which is a community program providing round-the-clock help to victims of crime or disaster. VCARS volunteers are alerted by the police on the victim's request and provide short-term, on-site counselling services. As mentioned in the government's Web site, these local victim services programs allow police to meet their legislated mandate of responding to victims' needs.

# Restorative Justice

Much emphasis on the traditional retributive model has been on validating the victim's experience by punishing the offender. In general, studies have found that victims' satisfaction with the justice process, even when an offender has been sentenced to punishment, has been weak.

This finding has led to calls for alternative models of justice delivery that place the victim back in the centre of the justice process. Christie (1977) was among the earliest proponents of a radical change in administration, in which communities would have greater participation in conflict resolution. In New Zealand and Australia, experiments with family group conferences (Briathwaite & Mugford, 1994), and here in Canada with **victim–offender reconciliation programs (VORPs)**, have reportedly been successful in bringing the wishes of the victim into the inner circle of justice delivery. In both such schemes, the interests of the community and of the state in certifying that justice is not totally civilianized have been secured with steps that also secure state and community representation.

The VORP allows an offender the opportunity to acknowledge his or her guilt and, under the authority of the judge, to make restitution according to an agreement hashed out in a meeting between victim and offender, which is mediated by a social worker, a probation officer, or some other official. Similarly, the family group conference has been used in Auckland and Wagga Wagga, New Zealand, primarily among teenage offenders. This program involves a meeting among victim and support parties, offender and support parties, and a facilitator, who may be a police officer or a social worker. In these meetings, guilt is acknowledged, the act is condemned, the actor is distinguished from his or her act, and a package of reparation is put together and overseen by the offender's designate.

# Conclusion

In the past 25 years, much activity has taken place to bring victims back into the circle of justice. Victims are now part of a powerful lobby for criminal justice reform and are now recognized as primary partners in justice delivery. What we need to watch for, as we continue to move away from retributive justice, is just how the public interest will be represented. A number of critics have argued that the wishes of the victim have no business informing criminal sentences because it is the public interest in condemning a criminal act that is of utmost importance. As this century progresses, we risk seeing a gradual erosion of the concern in justice policy for both the victim and the public interest. However, the failure of private forms of justice is precisely their inability to incorporate notions of fairness and equal treatment under the law.

It is important to recognize that during most of the past century, justice administration was often hostile to victims' long-term interests. The adversarial process from the side of the prosecution, in the main, looks upon justice in the terms of conviction. In their quest for convictions, prosecutors view victims as witnesses who are more or less likely to add to the chances of winning the case. When victims are perceived as instruments in this way, it is no wonder that their interests as suffering individuals tend to fall by the wayside. Today, this institutional indifference is being overturned, and it is now possible to ask whether a resolution serves the victim's interest. The pendulum has been swinging back.

## Summary

This chapter has explored the concept of victimization and the services to victims offered in Canada. It has also addressed some issues surrounding the emergence of the victim's needs in justice administration, and it has detailed some of the specific strategies and programs that are available. The chapter has stressed that an understanding of victimization must include attention to the notion of the victim's loss. It was also noted that there is a politicization of the victim status and that the relationship between victim and offender can be a complicated one, in which the official designation of victim status may be preceded by victim precipitation.

## Key Terms

situated transaction (p. 235)
victim impact statement (p. 240)
victimization (p. 231)
victim–offender reconciliation programs (VORPs) (p. 245)
victimology (p. 230)
victim-precipitated crimes (p. 235)

# Discussion Questions

1. Why is it important in conceptualizing victimization that we pay attention to the subjective experience of victimization?

2. Describe some of the factors that contribute to a person's likelihood of being victimized.

3. List the advantage and disadvantages of allowing victim impact statements to be read in court.

4. Describe the process involved in victim–offender reconciliation programs.

5. Define victim-precipitated crime.

# Weblinks

**www.caveat.org** CAVEAT, an organization dedicated to the rights of victims, argues that the protection of the public must be the overriding goal of the justice system, and that the offender's rights should not be greater than those of the victim. Their Web site offers information, event listings, educational material, publications, and relevant links.

**canada.justice.gc.ca/en/ps/voc/** The Department of Justice's Policy Centre for Victims' Issues Web site has the text of the Canadian Statement of Basic Principles of Justice for Victims of Crime, as well as information on legislation, funding, and news. The site also provides information on government programs and services, such as aboriginal justice and child custody.

**www.gov.ab.ca/justicesummit/process/dwb/delwork32.htm** The report by the Alberta Summit on Justice, titled "Victims—Their Rights and Their Involvement in the System," provides a detailed look at the treatment of crime victims in Alberta.

**www.crcvc.ca** The Canadian Resource Centre for Victims of Crime is sponsored by the Police Association of Canada and acts as a non-profit victim advocacy group in Ottawa. Their site offers information on their resources, publications, news releases, and links to provincial resources.

**www.state.gov/www/global/human_rights/hrp_reports_mainhp.html** The Country Reports on Human Rights Practices are submitted annually by the US Department of State to the US Congress. The reports cover internationally recognized individual, civil, political, and worker rights, as set forth in the Universal Declaration of Human Rights.

# CHAPTER 12

# The Future of Crime Control

## Objectives

- To outline the concept of decriminalization and problems associated with its implementation.

- To discuss the issues associated with the decriminalization of marijuana use, as well as prostitution and associated acts.

- To describe community policing models and their limitations.

## Questions about Crime

In this final chapter, we consider the means of preventing, eliminating, and reducing the amount of crime that is committed in our communities each year. Having read the previous chapters on crime and punishment, readers are well equipped to understand both the nature and the extent of criminal activity in Canada. For most of us, the question of whether crime rates are rising or falling is a central issue. This question leads us to consider whether we are more or less likely to become the victim of particular crimes. But there are perhaps even more important questions concerning the nature of what we call crime and our attempts to police and punish these acts.

A Canadian criminologist, Peter McNaughtan Smith, posed an interesting question over a quarter of a century ago. He asked, "What is crime and why do

we fight it?" This is a more significant question than it at first appears. The acts that society identifies as crimes have overwhelming significance for every member of that society, whether as victims, offenders, workers in the justice system or allied fields, or taxpayers who support the administration of justice. It is a simple fact that the more crimes we have "on the books," the more crimes we will record in society, and the more it will cost us as a society in both human and economic terms to uphold these laws. The current edition of the Criminal Code contains over 1000 pages of prohibited acts and their prescribed penalties. The number of laws that circumscribe our lives is not diminishing, but rather has grown with each passing decade of the 20th century. Spending on law enforcement and corrections is exponential in character. So, the question of what constitutes crime is worth considering in more detail, since its impact reverberates strongly in our society and shapes the lives of many members of our communities.

# Decriminalization

Given the increasing number of laws governing our lives, we need to seriously consider the issue of **decriminalization.** This is a term used to describe behaviours that have been outlawed in our society but that have assumed the status of social norms. In other words, the behaviours or acts in question are now accepted as "normal" or perhaps "tolerable" by members of society (Stebbins, 1996). If this process has occurred, then criminologists and advocacy groups will raise the question of whether the penalties associated with these crimes should be reduced or whether the acts should be legalized. However, once an act has become defined as criminal through the legislative process (*mala prohibita* crimes), it is a long and difficult process to have it removed from the Criminal Code. Two forms of behaviour that are currently criminalized are worth considering in this context: marijuana use and acts associated with prostitution.

## Marijuana Use

Marijuana has been widely used in Canada since the late 1960s, when the hippy revolution popularized the drug. Pot smoking was previously confined to the small number of people who were involved with the "jazz scene" in Canada and to the "beat generation," a group of beatniks, poets, and folk musicians. Marijuana quickly became the drug of choice during the musical revolution of the 1960s, as well-known rock stars extolled its virtues in song and in public statements. Millions of young Canadians experimented with alternative forms of consciousness that could be obtained through smoking marijuana or derivatives such as hashish. Marijuana was an easily transportable drug that was both cheap and in ready supply. It was relatively easy to grow, so both imported and domestic crops of the plant were available to users.

While young people praised the virtues of marijuana, parents, educators, police, and politicans panicked at its widespread appeal and its link with anti-establishment attitudes. The mantra of the hippie era was Timothy Leary's "Turn on, tune in, drop out," by which he meant that getting high led to a higher consciousness and to rejection of traditional societal values. For those in power, who had exercised strict control over young people for generations, the linking of pot to protest and to the rejection of the culture they had built made it a target for criminalization. Some of the rhetoric surrounding the criminalization of marijuana use and the mounting of a long and expensive campaign of policing focused on the medical threats to users. Marijuana smokers were said to be threatening their health and sanity by smoking the "vile weed." A second avenue of attack focused on the effects of marijuana on users' image and work habits. Pot became linked with "dirty hippies," who were considered lazy, unreliable, and useless. Pot led smokers to become irresponsible in a world that demanded responsibility.

Using these rationale, the groups cited above joined forces as moral crusaders to criminalize marijuana and punish its users. By 1980, several hundred thousand young Canadians had a record for simple possession of marijuana (Erickson, 1980) at a cost of hundreds of millions in enforcement and justice system expenditures. The sheer number of arrests should have indicated to authorities that marijuana smoking had become a social norm among young people. Laws criminalizing marijuana reflected a generation gap that punished the young for rejecting the chemicals of an earlier generation: alcohol, prescription medications, and cigarettes, all of which were supported by big businesses with a vested interest in hooking another generation.

The criminalization of marijuana use was ineffective in preventing people from smoking pot. Rather, it had the same effect as the prohibition against liquor consumption in the 1920s. Like the war on marijuana, advocates of liquor prohibition were convinced that the consumption of liquor led to social evil. Prohibition was advocated by women's religious groups in New York, particularly the Women's Christian Temperance Movement, and by other Protestant churches that believed that violence, family woes, and illness sprang from alcohol use. However, Prohibition's effect was to drive the production and distribution of liquor underground, paving the way for a huge black market. Criminals such as Al Capone were able to control vast illegal liquor and crime empires, since the government would not sanction the legal use of liquor. Despite Prohibition, people were still able to obtain liquor, and the threat of criminal sanction did little to stop prospective drinkers or sellers of alcohol.

Marijuana use also continued despite the efforts of police organizations across Canada, particularly the RCMP's drug squad. If a large cross-section of

Canadians wishes to smoke marijuana, the question of why it is a criminal act is important. The vast majority of adult Canadians (and many teenagers) drink alcohol. Alcohol is associated with early death, absenteeism from work, fatal traffic accidents, family violence, criminal activity, and a variety of medical conditions. Cirrhosis of the liver is the third leading cause of death in Canada. Smoking is also associated with death, serious illnesses, and a variety of medical maladies. Are either of these drugs any more dangerous than marijuana? Given the widespread use of alcohol and tobacco, should the government have the right to criminalize marijuana use?

Recently, people suffering from various debilitating diseases have initiated legal challenges to the right of the government to criminalize marijuana use. Marijuana use has been found to be beneficial to persons suffering from HIV/AIDS, multiple sclerosis, and various forms of cancer by relieving pain or symptoms. The court has ruled that medical use of marijuana is legal. The next legal challenge is to laws prohibiting the cultivation of marijuana, since people with medical conditions want to be able to grow and control the quality of the drug they are using. If the use of marijuana for medical purposes is legal, but the supply must be obtained illegally, then the possibility that an individual will receive tainted drugs rises substantially.

In many U.S. jurisdictions, marijuana possession for individual use is now treated as a misdemeanour. Offenders are given a ticket and asked to pay a fine. In Amsterdam, marijuana smoking is legal, and smokers may visit "pot cafés," where they can sample various types and blends of the drug. Which direction will Canada move toward on this issue in the future?

Neil Boyd, in his book *High Society* (1991), has suggested that legalization of marijuana is the logical path for governments to follow. Making pot legal allows governments to control the quality of the drug and to eliminate the influence and profit for individuals who currently market the drug. Furthermore, legalization allows for the taxation of marijuana. Given the popularity of alcohol and tobacco and the enormous revenues they generate for governments through taxation, taxes on marijuana would provide for greater incomes for government, as well as generating funds for treatment of various forms of drug addiction. While governments until recently took a high moral line on gambling, it has now become a staple of fiscal planning for cash-strapped governments, as it represents a way of taxing leisure activities. Given the difficulty of establishing a proven link between marijuana use and further drug involvement and the comparatively minor side effects of pot use when compared with cigarettes and alcohol, decriminalization appears to be evolving as a more accurate reflection of societal norms. For most people, marijuana use remains a tolerable form of deviance, one that if practised in private represents an individual choice. Should a person who drinks a dozen beers every weekend not be subject to criminalization, while a person who smokes a joint (marijuana cigarette) is? This is a question that should soon be answered as marijuana smokers use the courts to challenge the power of the state to regulate pot use.

## Prostitution and Associated Acts

A great number of Canadians think that prostitution is a crime. In reality, the act of prostitution is, in itself, not a crime in Canada. Canada moved to liberalize its laws regarding prostitution following the report of several commissions that examined the state of prostitution in Canada. The Fraser Commission (1985) and the Badgely Report (1987) gathered information from prostitutes, their customers, politicans, interest groups, and academics in Canada. An earlier report in England, the Wolfendon Report, looked at the problems associated with prostitution and its control within an evolving capitalist society.

Canada moved to liberalize its prostitution laws for several reasons. In the wake of the feminist revolution, it increasingly became apparent that female and male prostitutes considered their services to be a job. The individual, rather than the state, had ownership of his or her body and the right to decide how it would be used (or abused). Yet state intervention had long been based on moral considerations of the undesirability of prostitution. Concerns about public health and the morality of communities also propelled a draconian approach to dealing with prostitutes. However, most policing authorities recognized long ago the futility of policing prostitution, and people arrested for prostitution were generally dealt with by fines and quick release. Attempting to police prostitution often placed officers in compromising situations that the courts considered entrapment; that is, the police induced people to commit a crime that they would not otherwise have committed or brought the law into disrepute by acting as customers. Most community members viewed prostitution as a "necessary evil" that could be tolerated as long as it was not visible.

The form of prostitution that has caused the most concern for communities is referred to as *street walking*. Prostitutes walk in areas, called *strolls* or *tracks*, that are well known to johns (customers). Most customers approach prostitutes in their automobiles. They "cruise" the hookers, find one who is appealing, and then stop to discuss business. The hooker normally puts her head in through the window of the car and then discusses acts and prices. If a deal is struck, the prostitute and customer retreat to a dark parking lot or in some cases to a cheap motel room for sex. The greatest percentage of streetwalkers' sex exchanges involve oral sex or masturbation.

Streetwalkers have a number of negative effects on the locales they choose as a stroll. They can be loud and disturb the public peace, which is particularly annoying for residential neighbours. As well, since some sex acts take place in public places, they and their customers may leave behind used condoms and needles employed in drug use. This refuse is both dangerous and disturbing for residents of the area. Cruising johns also cause traffic problems in the neighbourhood. Residents may feel that they are being prevented from quietly enjoying their homes, and they may be accosted coming and going from their homes when prostitutes are on the street. Prostitution also brings other criminal, quasi-criminal, and illegal behaviours in its wake, including violence. All of these problems can have a serious negative impact on a neighbourhood's quality of life and property values.

Consequently, Canadian laws were altered to reflect the overwhelming concern with streetwalkers and their customers. Currently, Canadian law targets several behaviours associated with prostitution. First, communication for the purposes of engaging in prostitution is illegal. Under this law, discussion of sex acts and their costs is reason for arrest. Second, solicitation is a crime. Solicitation involves a prostitute's asking the customer to engage in sex acts in exchange for money, or a customer's requesting sexual services in exchange for money. Since customers are often unable to distinguish prostitutes from other females walking on the street, these laws are intended to shunt prostitution off the streets. Police in Toronto, Vancouver, and other large urban areas regularly engage in operations to remove customers from the street. Female police officers pose as prostitutes in an undercover sting intended to catch johns. Once arrested, most customers are sentenced at court to a fine and to mandatory attendance at "john school." This educational institution is run by the police in cooperation with ex-prostitutes and is meant to educate johns about the substantial health risks associated with using street prostitutes. Finally, living on the avails of prostitution, or pimping, is another crime associated with prostitution.

Street prostitutes have significant rates of use and addiction to a variety of drugs, primarily crack cocaine. Prostitutes who are high on drugs or alcohol (or both) are far less likely to practise safe sex. Prostitutes who are homeless and desperate for food, drugs, alcohol, or a place to sleep may not be in a position to insist on safe sex, particularly when customers offer substantial financial inducements to forgo the use of a condom. Therefore, street prostitutes are also more likely to contract and transmit venereal diseases and HIV than are prostitutes who work in more protected settings.

The difference in legal interest between streetwalkers and other kinds of prostitutes is evident in the different enforcement patterns that characterize relationships between the police and hookers. In all major Canadian cities there are pages of listings in the business telephone directory for escort/massage services. Similarly, local entertainment newspapers, such as *NOW* in Toronto and the *Georgia Straight* in Vancouver, contain many pages of listings for escort and massage services and individual prostitutes' advertisements for either in-call or out-call services. Prostitutes working for escort and massage agencies provide sexual services in massage parlours or in hotel rooms or private homes. Individual prostitutes offer sex in their own homes ("incalls") or in the client's hotel room or home ("outcalls"). Police rarely, if ever, arrest people who are engaged in these two forms of prostitution, except if there are public complaints.

Which factors underscore these different enforcement patterns? Essentially, it is the public character of streetwalking that dooms participants to be the target of law enforcement. Historically, Canadians have had low tolerance for public displays of deviance. Consider, for example, Canadians' reaction to public drunkenness as opposed to inebriation that occurs in a private setting. The former can provoke police action, whereas the latter is of no concern for police. The public nature of streetwalking condemns those who engage in it to police action, while the private nature of other forms of prostitution provides virtual indemnity against charges. It is also important to consider the impossibility of the police filing charges related to prostitution against those who engage in sex trade work in private. To do so, the police would have to engage literally in "under the covers" work. Prostitutes are generally astute enough to discern undercover police officers. They have also developed a working pattern that rules out effective prosecution. Prostitutes in massage parlours and saunas do not discuss sex acts and their costs until the customer is naked with a towel around his waist and lying on a massage table. Quite often the prostitute discusses price while touching the customer's genitals. It is easy to imagine the difficulty an officer would have in convincing the court that communication or solicitation took place while he was not a willing participant. Furthermore, a reasonable defence can be raised that sex was given freely to the customer because he was "so attractive" and that money changed hands merely to cover the "date."

What is the future of legal intervention in prostitution? John Lowman, a criminological researcher, has spent a great deal of time talking with and researching the lives and work of prostitutes. He and other researchers have recognized the need to focus on street prostitution as commerce and as part of the sex trade. Street prostitutes are perhaps unfairly targeted for police action, since their personal circumstances prevent them from having the capital to work out of their own apartments. In many cases they are unsuitable candidates for working in massage parlours. Age, physical appearance, drug and/or alcohol problems, day jobs that they would lose if their alternative source of income were discovered all prevent them from enjoying the relative safety of other forms of prostitution. But should their acts be criminalized simply because they cannot afford to move off the streets?

It is apparent that current Canadian laws on prostitution seek to criminalize the acts of a specific form of prostitute and customer, while leaving others to engage in the same sexual acts without legal repercussions. Some criminologists have argued that prostitution is a victimless crime, as it involves two consenting adults engaging in conduct that some observers in the community consider immoral. In these forms of activities, who is harmed? The prosecution of street prostitutes through the criminal law is both costly and ineffective. Our concern with street prostitutes has more to do with our sensibilities regarding supposedly public spaces than with protection of the community. Do prostitutes' customers really need to be told of all the diseases they could get from a street hooker? Are customers really that uninformed? The answer is no. John schools support the notion that the criminal law can be used to enforce public morality and to force people to confront their own weaknesses. Is it really necessary to arrest customers in order to get this message across, or could the police simply caution them, give them a pamphlet, and issue a verbal warning? Furthermore, is the task of law enforcement to be public health officers?

Men will always seek sexual thrills in anonymous interactions with prostitutes. For some customers, the act of public solicitation itself is more sexually charged than paying for sex in a clean and controlled massage parlour. While the threat of further prosecution is an inducement for customers to stop frequenting street prostitutes, john schools function like the stocks of old, forcing sinners to be put on public display (if only in front of other johns) and humiliated for their desire and supposed ignorance. These schools also educate johns about risks associated with street prostition, including STDs, violence, and robbery.

Prostitution and acts associated with it will likely be removed from the public purview in the future. The costs associated with enforcement are high, and enforcement has little effect in reducing the amount of prostitution in any city. One alternative to criminalization is establishing a clearly demarcated red-light district, where prostitutes and other sex trade workers can offer services. This approach has met with great success in Amsterdam, but it is less popular in some U.S. jurisdictions. The natural tendency of prostitution to attract other forms of criminal activity has meant that red-light districts have the potential to deteriorate unless there is strict urban regulation through appropriate bylaws.

Another possible solution is retraining prostitutes so that they will find alternative employment. For individuals who wish to move away from the sex trade, this may represent a positive investment in their lives. Street prostitution can be invested with extreme violence, as demonstrated by the murders of prostitutes in Vancouver, Toronto, and other major urban centres. The fact that prostitutes work in a profession that requires accompanying complete strangers to out-of-the-way locations for sex poses a serious threat to their physical well-being.

If street prostitution were decriminalized, would it follow that a free market in street sex should be permitted? Most observers who support the notion of the sex trade as commerce argue that, as with any legitimate business, prostitution must be regulated. This regulation would involve licensing, health and safety regulation (through testing for sexually transmitted diseases), the maintenance of business records, and the payment of taxes. Given the mobility of street prostitutes, such regulation would likely be difficult if not impossible to achieve.

Furthermore, even if prostitution were decriminalized, cities would undoubtedly pass bylaws restricting the activities of streetwalkers.

# Crime Prevention

One of the most promising developments in Canadian criminal justice is crime prevention. On the surface, crime prevention seems to be a priority for most agencies that deal with crime control in Canada. However, crime prevention strategies have grown significantly in both depth and scope over the past decade as innovative approaches have been developed. Crime prevention techniques have focused on several key areas, which are worthy of brief discussion.

## Crime Prevention Techniques

Many clinicians and criminological studies have pointed to the centrality of the family and parent–child relationships in controlling deviant and antisocial behaviour. Parental attitudes and skill levels can have a great impact in reducing delinquency and dealing with aggressive and inappropriate behaviour. Troubled youth often direct their inappropriate behaviour toward parents through lying and aggression. Studies of gang behaviours have found that minors are able to lie to their parents about school attendance and performance particularly when a language barrier exits between the school and the family.

Whatever the context and aggravating factors, it is certain that parents who improve their parenting skills are more able to control delinquent or unacceptable behaviour. As well, they can help their children to establish the kinds of inner and outer controls that will allow them to succeed in civil society. The focus on the importance of effective parenting is one of the most promising areas of crime prevention research and techniques.

Crime prevention also involves programs that protect neighbourhoods and their residents. One school of research has argued that crime prevention is best achieved through environmental design. Most of us are aware of some of the everyday methods for preventing victimization by criminals, such as stopping newspapers when on holiday, leaving lights on when out of the home during the evening, installing alarm systems, placing bars on basement windows (a common entry point for break and entry), and allowing for a clear view of entrance points to the home. Environmental design goes one step further by actually engineering streets and homes that will make criminal activities difficult. Lighting, access points to housing, distance from the road, placement of windows and garages, and door and window types all can greatly affect the potential for victimization.

# The Factors behind Crime Prevention

Criminologists have identified certain key components for effective crime prevention models. Most important, there is a need for efforts to be proactive rather than reactive. It is important to take measures that will prevent individuals from having the opportunity to commit crimes. Gwynn Nettler (1984), a pioneering criminologist, argued that crimes are often the result of the intersection of opportunity with desire. If we remove opportunities, then desires can be thwarted. Thus, designing safe communities, streets, and houses is one approach to reducing crime.

Effective crime prevention is not a short-term process but rather involves planning; consultation among residents, police authorities, and planning experts; and investment in projects. While the desired effect may not be achieved immediately, there is some evidence that investment pays off for crime prevention projects in the long run. One example of an effective program is the **neighbourhood watch** system. This program is aimed at reducing residential theft, interpersonal crime, and property damage. Residents cooperate with the police by first marking all of their valuables for identification, which under an ancillary program, operation identification, assists police in identifying stolen goods. Community members post stickers at the entrances to their homes and on windows to indicate that they are part of neighbourhood watch. This process is called *target hardening*—it makes the home less desirable to the prospective

thief since the items he or she steals will be less saleable and more identifiable. Under the neighbourhood watch program, community members are vigilant in noting people or automobiles in their area that do not belong to the neighbourhood and report suspicious behaviour to the police. Through a telephone message system, the police update watch captains in the neighbourhood on crimes committed locally so that neighbours can be informed and take precautions. Prevention is most important, since recovery rates for stolen property in Canada are very low (Fleming & Jorgenson, 1982).

Crime prevention programs require active participation by the community and its members in attacking the opportunity for criminal activities (Hastings, 1997). Therefore, citizens must be supportive of law enforcement efforts and be willing to assist rather than to think of the task of crime prevention as belonging solely to the police. The Regents' Park neighbourhood of Toronto, for example, has had significant problems with drug dealing and drug use in housing projects. Consequently, residents engaged in a variety of activities that were intended to prevent the commission of crime and to reclaim their neighbourhood, rendering it safe for walking and family outings. The residents began to videotape drug deals, form groups to harass the dealers, install lighting in appropriate places, and hold family block parties in the middle of the dealers' territories. This proactive form of crime prevention proved successful in moving the drug dealers out of the neighbourhood. However, although the dealers retreated from this area, there is a need for constant vigilance by residents to ensure that criminals do not begin to infiltrate the streets again.

Crime prevention programs also require the infusion of government funds. Crime prevention is an interactive process that involves changing the nature of policing to be more effective and accountable to citizens, particularly in sharing information on local crime patterns. Many crime prevention programs reflect the basics of solid communities in which an investment is made in the lives of young people to provide alternatives to gang involvement, relieve the effects of poverty, and provide mentoring and effective role models. Gang recruitment, for example, targets youths who are disaffiliated with society and disenchanted with their lives. These gang recruits are without the benefit of positive role models or mentors who can forge a link between the young person and society. Mentors can encourage youths to develop self-esteem, improve their school performance, and make career plans. When there are few opportunities for young people to interact in after-school programs, community-organized activities, or mentoring programs, the chance of involvement in delinquent activities rises rapidly. They are youths with too much time on their hands.

Schools have an important role to play in crime prevention initiatives. Children and adolescents spend a large majority of their day in these institutions, and so the potential for positive intervention is enormous. School programs can focus on providing children with the skills to succeed in everyday life and in promising careers by promoting high academic achievement in concert with innovative skills. Schools also need to establish clearly articulated norms of behaviour, which are enforced daily.

On a limited basis in Canada, police organizations have begun to take up the challenge of innovative community policing. Under the initiative of Mayor Mel Lastman, Toronto instituted a program of intensified policing in 1999. This blitz of policing was directed at problem areas in the city that have consistently shown a higher rate and incidence of crime. Toronto police departments track crime occurrence rates through geographic crime profiling and thus are able to identify areas in need of intensified policing. Some critics have argued that this form of policing campaign has targeted the poorest and the least politically powerful in the city. For example, in the downtown area policing has been directed toward squeegee kids, the homeless, drug dealers, and street prostitutes. However, there is strong evidence that local residents see the increased presence of police as comforting reassurance and applaud the removal of homeless people and others from their neighbourhoods. Yet, critics have noted that if the homeless are removed from one neighbourhood, surely they must show up in another neighbourhood. Critics have also pointed out that policing blitzes in the name of crime prevention seem to target minorities. Following the Lewis Report on racism and discrimination in the Ontario criminal justice system, there is little dispute that unacceptable attitudes and behaviour do occur in police relations with minorities. However, police response to crime hot spots is based not on minority residence but rather on crime incidence. Law-abiding residents have little to fear and much to gain from cooperating with police and police agencies in removing criminals from their midst and "cooling out" crime.

In Windsor, Ontario, the police service has responded to community concerns by establishing police mini-stations. The Sandwich district facility provides the local neighbourhood with a visible police presence and with quicker response times. The local station is also more finely attuned to the needs of the persons it serves and more aware of local trouble spots. The use of surveys has assisted police, as well, in meeting community requests for changes in policing priorities.

# Community Policing

Community policing is not a new concept. As discussed in the previous section, community policing often involves collaboration between an accessible and accountable police force and community members. Many of the underlying precepts of community policing hearken back to an earlier era of policing in Canada and as far back as Victorian England, when police "walked the beat" and were known and highly visible to community residents. Essentially, in community policing the police are involved in the community as law officers, who monitor the neighbourhood through foot patrols (and bicycle patrols), and as participants in other activities to create a community presence. All of these factors require that police be removed from faceless mobile response units and become people interacting within the community. The shift of a fraction of police resources from automobile-based policing to more accessible forms is ideal for urban communities with established neighbourhoods in which residents share elements of a common identity. Central to this approach is the notion that police officers may do more good by simply being visible in the communities they serve. This approach inspires confidence in policing measures and bolsters community cooperation. The focus on safe communities and safe streets helps to preserve the community and its quality of life.

**Foot patrols** are essential to community policing in urban centres. Foot patrols allow law enforcement officials to hear community issues and concerns that they would otherwise hear only in rare community meetings between the police and residents. In this approach, the police officers are able to directly monitor and intervene in the types of activities associated with the decline of neighbourhoods. Street violence, graffiti spraying, vandalism, littering, property damage, and drug dealing are all much more controllable when officers are on

the ground level in communities. Residents can assist officers in identifying culprits and pointing out areas where petty criminals congregate after dark. Under this cooperative model, citizens help to preserve their neighbourhoods while allowing police an opportunity to respond to community issues. Criminological research and police experience confirm that police officers who are on foot are easily approachable and become privy to valuable information from an enforcement perspective when talking with community members. Rapid technological advances have meant that foot and bicycle patrols can be in constant communication with police command and often are able to respond to crime scenes more quickly when traffic jams are a problem.

However, critics of community-based policing have argued that this approach is ineffective. Police are viewed as having little impact on crime control and as functioning merely as peacekeepers in the community. Some also criticize the police for their view of what constitutes the "community." Rather than responding to communities' needs, police serve the community according to their traditional administrative approach. Furthermore, instead of defining neighbourhoods in terms of the shared norms, values, or boundaries of the community, police divide the community in terms of policing priorities and needs. Police have begun to develop a greater sensitivity to ecological areas, rather than administrative areas. Since neighbourhoods often have very different views of the police and their role in the community, it takes a great deal of effort and research on the part of police to sensitize themselves to community boundaries, views, and priorities.

Another problem is how to integrate a variety of police services, from foot patrols to bicycle patrols to mobile units. While communication is not a significant problem today, there is still substantial debate over how to use these services and whether they should act independently or in conjunction with one another. Most police forces combine the strengths of all the approaches, providing the most comprehensive response possible.

Community policing also makes certain assumptions about the desirability of a police presence in neighbourhoods. Some neighbourhoods both fear and loath the police owing to a number of important factors. Recent immigrants from countries in which the police are viewed as violent intervenors with the potential to torture, jail, or even kill people have little reason to want more police in their streets. Given reported racism within police forces in Canada, there are neighbourhoods in which the police are not welcome. The presence of more police in a neighbourhood, some analysts suggest, is a signal of neighbourhood decline and thus could have a negative impact on both quality of life and real estate values. As well, Vincent (1990) has identified troubling aspects of police culture and inadequacies in training. Given the subculture of policing, with its emphasis on secrecy, isolation, and suspicion of the public, it is difficult to argue that police can adequately perform these new cooperative roles without training to prepare them for their new duties. It is obvious that concerns about racism and sensitivity to diversity warrant a directional change in policing that may appear quite radical to policing organizations. Police, in future, will likely be called upon to perform multiple roles that have not traditionally been part of the police mandate. To prepare the fully functioning police officer of tomorrow, police forces must take new directions in training, including accepting postsecondary education and training in dealing with diversity and sensitivity to community members.

# Conclusion

Prostitution remains a difficult subject in Canada, with little consensus on solutions to the problem. While the harm of prostitution may not be as apparent as that associated with other deviant or criminal activities, there is real community concern over the acts associated with this area of the sex trade. Policymakers need to consider both the needs of the community and the position in which prostitutes find themselves on a daily basis. Similarly, the criminalization of marijuana use has been a much-discussed issue in Canada over the past three decades. While the issue remains controversial, there are signs that both public and law enforcement attitudes toward the criminalization of marijuana use are shifting dramatically. Recently, Chief Julian Fantino of the Metropolitan Toronto Police called for the decriminalization of marijuana use. His attitude reflects the widespread popularity of the drug, the difficulties and costs associated with enforcement, and the relatively minor status of this criminal offence. It is likely that marijuana use will be decriminalized in the near future, both as a response to societal attitudes and as a method of generating revenue, with the potential to overshadow gambling, alcohol, and tobacco tax revenues in Canada.

Community policing is in its infancy in Canada, yet pilot programs are increasingly emerging from police initiatives. It is a tool that reflects an earlier era in policing and one with the potential to allow greater accommodation between the police and communities and increased accountability of police forces.

## Summary

In this chapter, we have explored the issue of crime control in Canadian society. We have discussed decriminalization, focusing on both prostitution and marijuana use as controversial offences that may be candidates for decriminalization. Both of these crimes are seen as complex issues involving questions of community standards and societal protection. We have also examined the rise of community policing in Canada and have described some of the innovative programs that move police officers from the patrol car to the street, allowing greater involvement in the communities they police.

## Key Terms

decriminalization (p. 249)

foot patrols (p. 260)

neighbourhood watch (p. 257)

## Discussion Questions

1. Which crimes do you think should be decriminalized in the future?

2. What are some of the problems associated with decriminalizing a criminal act?

3. Discuss arguments both in favour and against the idea of legalizing prostitution.

4. Should marijuana use be legalized? Why or why not?

5. Why do advocates of community policing consider foot patrols important?

6. Discuss the strengths and weaknesses of community policing.

## Weblinks

**www.crime-prevention.org/english/main.html** The National Crime Prevention Centre Web site offers information about crime prevention projects in Canada, the National Strategy on Community Safety and Crime Prevention, the National Crime Prevention Centre, and its programs and services.

**www.blockparent.ca** The Web site of the Block Parent Program of Canada, the neighbourhood program which emphasizes children's safety issues.

**www.web.net/~bccsc/** The BC Coalition for Safer Communities aims to reduce crime and violence through community initiatives. Working together with various members from the community, including organizations supporting children and youth, health care providers, women's organizations, government, police, and business, the BCCSC emphasizes the importance of addressing the root causes of crime.

**www.lcc.gc.ca/en/index.html** The Law Commission of Canada is an independent law-reform agency, responsible to the Parliament of Canada. Its Web site includes information on its current and past projects.

**www.crime-prevention-intl.org** The International Center for the Prevention of Crime is a Canadian initiative, with the purpose of assisting cities and countries to reduce delinquency, violence, and insecurity. Their Web site is a great resource for information on crime prevention programs around the world.

# Appendix

CANADA ACT 1982

including the

CONSTITUTION ACT, 1982

1982, c. 11 (U.K.)

*[29th March 1982]*

[Note: The English version of the Canada Act 1982 is contained in the body of the Act; its French version is found in Schedule A. Schedule B contains the English and French versions of the *Constitution Act, 1982.*]

An Act to give effect to a request by the Senate and House of Commons of Canada

Whereas Canada has requested and consented to the enactment of an Act of the Parliament of the United Kingdom to give effect to the provisions hereinafter set forth and the Senate and the House of Commons of Canada in Parliament assembled have submitted an address to Her Majesty requesting that Her Majesty may graciously be pleased to cause a Bill to be laid before the Parliament of the United Kingdom for that purpose.

Be it therefore enacted by the Queen's Most Excellent Majesty, by and with the advice and consent of the Lords Spiritual and Temporal, and Commons, in this present Parliament assembled, and by the authority of the same, as follows:

*Constitution Act, 1982 enacted*

**1.** *The Constitution Act, 1982* set out in Schedule B to this Act is hereby enacted for and shall have the force of law in Canada and shall come into force as provided in that Act.

*Termination of power to legislate for Canada*

**2.** No Act of the Parliament of the United Kingdom passed after the *Constitution Act, 1982* comes into force shall extend to Canada as part of its law.

*French version*

**3.** So far as it is not contained in Schedule B, the French version of this Act is set out in Schedule A to this Act and has the same authority in Canada as the English version thereof.

*Short title*

**4.** This Act may be cited as the Canada Act, 1982.

# SCHEDULE B

## CONSTITUTION ACT, 1982

### PART I

## CANADIAN CHARTER OF RIGHTS AND FREEDOMS

Whereas Canada is founded upon principles that recognize the supremacy of God and the rule of law:

### Guarantee of Rights and Freedoms

**1.** The Canadian Charter of Rights and Freedoms guarantees the rights and freedoms set out in it subject only to such reasonable limits prescribed by law as can be demonstrably justified in a free and democratic society.

*Rights and freedoms in Canada*

### Fundamental Freedoms

**2.** Everyone has the following fundamental freedoms:

*Fundamental freedoms*

- *(a)* freedom of conscience and religion;
- *(b)* freedom of thought, belief, opinion and expression, including freedom of the press and other media of communication;
- *(c)* freedom of peaceful assembly; and
- *(d)* freedom of association.

### Democratic Rights

**3.** Every citizen of Canada has the right to vote in an election of members of the House of Commons or of a legislative assembly and to be qualified for membership therein.

*Democratic rights of citizens*

**4.** (1) No House of Commons and no legislative assembly shall continue for longer than five years from the date fixed for the return of the writs at a general election of its members.

*Maximum duration of legislative bodies*

(2) In time of real or apprehended war, invasion or insurrection, a House of Commons may be continued by Parliament and a legislative assembly may be continued by the legislature beyond five years if such continuation is not opposed by the votes of more than one-third of the members of the House of Commons or the legislative assembly, as the case may be.

*Continuation in special circumstances*

**5.** There shall be a sitting of Parliament and of each legislature at least once every twelve months.

*Annual sitting of legislative bodies*

### Mobility Rights

**6.** (1) Every citizen of Canada has the right to enter, remain in and leave Canada.

*Mobility of citizens*

(2) Every citizen of Canada and every person who has the status of a permanent resident of Canada has the right

*Rights to move and gain livelihood*

(a) to move to and take up residence in any province; and

(b) to pursue the gaining of a livelihood in any province.

**Limitation**

(3) The rights specified in subsection (2) are subject to

(a) any laws or practices of general application in force in a province other than those that discriminate among persons primarily on the basis of province of present or previous residence; and

(b) any laws providing for reasonable residency requirements as a qualification for the receipt of publicly provided social services.

**Affirmative action programs**

(4) Subsections (2) and (3) do not preclude any law, program or activity that has as its object the amelioration in a province of conditions of individuals in that province who are socially or economically disadvantaged if the rate of employment in that provide is below the rate of employment in Canada.

## Legal Rights

**Life, liberty and security of person**

**7.** Everyone has the right to life, liberty and security of the person and the right not to be deprived thereof except in accordance with the principles of fundamental justice.

**Search and seizure**

**8.** Everyone has the right to be secure against unreasonable search or seizure.

**Detention or imprisonment**

**9.** Everyone has the right not to be arbitrarily detained or imprisoned.

**Arrest or detention**

**10.** Everyone has the right on arrest or detention

(*a*) to be informed promptly of the reasons therefor;

(*b*) to retain and instruct counsel without delay and to be informed of that right; and

(*c*) to have the validity of the detention determined by way of habeas corpus and to be released if the detention is not lawful.

**Proceedings in criminal and penal matters**

**11.** Any person charged with an offence has the right

(*a*) to be informed without unreasonable delay of the specific offence;

(*b*) to be tried within a reasonable time;

(*c*) not to be compelled to be a witness in proceedings against that person in respect of the offence;

(*d*) to be presumed innocent until proven guilty according to law in a fair and public hearing by an independent and impartial tribunal;

(*e*) not to be denied reasonable bail without just cause;

(*f*) except in the case of an offence under military law tried before a military tribunal, to the benefit of trial by jury where the maximum punishment for the offence is imprisonment for five years or a more severe punishment;

(*g*) not to be found guilty on account of any act or omission unless, at the time of the act or omission, it constituted an offence under Canadian or international law or was criminal according to the general principles of law recognized by the community of nations;

(h) if finally acquitted of the offence, not to be tried for it again and, if finally found guilty and punished for the offence, not to be tried or punished for it again; and

(i) if found guilty of the offence and if the punishment for the offence has been varied between the time of commission and the time of sentencing, to the benefit of the lesser punishment.

**12.** Everyone has the right not to be subjected to any cruel and unusual treatment or punishment.

*Treatment or punishment*

**13.** A witness who testifies in any proceedings has the right not to have any incriminating evidence so given used to incriminate that witness in any other proceedings, except in a prosecution for perjury or for the giving of contradictory evidence.

*Self-crimination*

**14.** A party or witness in any proceedings who does not understand or speak the language in which the proceedings are conducted or who is deaf has the right to the assistance of an interpreter.

*Interpreter*

### Equality Rights

**15.** (1) Every individual is equal before and under the law and has the right to the equal protection and equal benefit of the law without discrimination and, in particular, without discrimination based on race, national or ethnic origin, colour, religion, sex, age or mental or physical disability.

*Equality before and under law and equal protection and benefit of law*

(2) Subsection (1) does not preclude any law, program or activity that has as its object the amelioration of conditions of disadvantaged individuals or groups including those that are disadvantaged because of race, national or ethnic origin, colour, religion, sex, age or mental or physical disability.
[Note: This section became effective on April 17, 1985. See subsection 32(2) and the note thereto.]

*Affirmative action programs*

### Official Languages of Canada

**16.** (1) English and French are the official languages of Canada and have equality of status and equal rights and privileges as to their use in all institutions of the Parliament and government of Canada.

*Official languages of Canada*

(2) English and French are the official languages of New Brunswick and have equality of status and equal rights and privileges as to their use in all institutions of the legislature and government of New Brunswick.

*Official languages of New Brunswick*

(3) Nothing in this Charter limits the authority of Parliament or a legislature to advance the equality of status or use of English and French.

*Advancement of status and use*

**17.** (1) Everyone has the right to use English or French in any debates and other proceedings of Parliament.

*Proceedings of Parliament*

(2) Everyone has the right to use English or French in any debates and other proceedings of the legislature of New Brunswick.

**18.** (1) The statutes, records and journals of Parliament shall be printed and published in English and French and both language versions are equally authoritative.

(2) The statutes, records and journals of the legislature of New Brunswick shall be printed and published in English and French and both language versions are equally authoritative.

**19.** (1) Either English or French may be used by any person in, or in any pleading in or process issuing from, any court established by Parliament.

(2) Either English or French may be used by any person in, or in any pleading in or process issuing from, any court of New Brunswick.

**20.** (1) Any member of the public in Canada has the right to communicate with, and to receive available services from, any head or central office of an institution of the Parliament or government of Canada in English or French, and has the same right with respect to any other office of any such institution where
 (a) there is a significant demand for communications with and services from that office in such language; or
 (b) due to the nature of the office, it is reasonable that communications with and services from that office be available in both English and French.

(2) Any member of the public in New Brunswick has the right to communicate with, and to receive available services from, any office of an institution of the legislature or government of New Brunswick in English or French.

**21.** Nothing in sections 16 to 20 abrogates or derogates from any right, privilege or obligation with respect to the English and French languages, or either of them, that exists or is continued by virtue of any other provision of the Constitution of Canada.

**22.** Nothing in sections 16 to 20 abrogates or derogates from any legal or customary right or privilege acquired or enjoyed either before or after the coming into force of this Charter with respect to any language that is not English or French.

*Minority Language Educational Rights*

**23.** (1) Citizens of Canada
 (a) whose first language learned and still understood is that of the English or French linguistic minority population of the province in which they reside, or

(b) who have received their primary school instruction in Canada in English or French and reside in a province where the language in which they received that instruction is the language of the English or French linguistic minority population of the province,

have the right to have their children receive primary and secondary school instruction in that language in that province.

[Note: See also section 59 and the note thereto.]

(2) Citizens of Canada of whom any child has received or is receiving primary or secondary school instruction in English or French in Canada, have the right to have all their children receive primary and secondary school instruction in the same language.

Continuity of language instruction

(3) The right of citizens of Canada under subsections (1) and (2) to have their children receive primary and secondary school instruction in the language of the English or French linguistic minority population of a province.

Application where numbers warrant

(a) applies wherever in the province the number of children of citizens who have such a right is sufficient to warrant the provision to them out of public funds of minority language instruction; and

(b) includes, where the number of those children so warrants, the right to have them receive that instruction in minority language educational facilities provided out of public funds.

### Enforcement

**24.** (1) Anyone whose rights or freedoms, as guaranteed by this Charter, have been infringed or denied may apply to a court of competent jurisdiction to obtain such remedy as the court considers appropriate and just in the circumstances.

Enforcement of guaranteed rights and freedoms

(2) Where, in proceedings under subsection (1), a court concludes that evidence was obtained in a manner that infringed or denied any rights or freedoms guaranteed by this Charter, the evidence shall be excluded if it is established that, having regard to all the circumstances, the admission of it in the proceedings would bring the administration of justice into disrepute.

Exclusion of evidence bringing administration of justice into disrepute

### General

**25.** The guarantee in this Charter of certain rights and freedoms shall not be construed so as to abrogate or derogate from any aboriginal, treaty or other rights or freedoms that pertain to the aboriginal peoples of Canada including

Aboriginal rights and freedoms not affected by Charter

(a) any rights or freedoms that have been recognized by the Royal Proclamation of October 7, 1763; and

(b) *any rights or freedoms that may be acquired by the aboriginal peoples of Canada by way of land claims settlement.*

(b) any rights or freedoms that now exist by way of land claims agreements or may be so acquired.

[Note: Paragraph 25(b) (in italics) was repealed and the new paragraph substituted by the *Constitution Amendment Proclamation, 1983* (No. 46 *infra*).]

**Other rights and freedoms not affected by Charter**

**26.** The guarantee in this Charter of certain rights and freedoms shall not be construed as denying the existence of any other rights or freedoms that exist in Canada.

**Multicultural heritage**

**27.** This Charter shall be interpreted in a manner consistent with the preservation and enhancement of the multicultural heritage of Canadians.

**Rights guaranteed equally to both sexes**

**28.** Notwithstanding anything in this Charter, the rights and freedoms referred to in it are guaranteed equally to male and female persons.

**Rights respecting certain schools preserved**

**29.** Nothing in this Charter abrogates or derogates from any rights or privileges guaranteed by or under the Constitution of Canada in respect of denominational, separate or dissentient schools.

**Application to territories and territorial authorities**

**30.** A reference in this Charter to a province or to the legislative assembly or legislature of a province shall be deemed to include a reference to the Yukon Territory and the Northwest Territories, or to the appropriate legislative authority thereof, as the case may be.

**Legislative powers not extended**

**31.** Nothing in this Charter extends the legislative powers of any body or authority.

*Application of Charter*

**Application of Charter**

**32.** (1) This Charter applies
(*a*) to the Parliament and government of Canada in respect of all matters within the authority of Parliament including all matters relating to the Yukon Territory and Northwest Territories; and
(*b*) to the legislature and government of each province in respect of all matters within the authority of the legislature of each province.

**Exception**

(2) Notwithstanding subsection (1), section 15 shall not have effect until three years after this section comes into force.
[Note: This section came into force on April 17, 1982. See the proclamation of that date (No. 45 *infra*).]

**Exception where express declaration**

**33.** (1) Parliament or the legislature of a province may expressly declare in an Act of Parliament or of the legislature, as the case may be, that the Act or a provision thereof shall operate notwithstanding a provision included in section 2 or sections 7 to 15 of this Charter.

**Operation of exception**

(2) An Act or a provision of an Act in respect of which a declaration made under this section is in effect shall have such operation as it would have but for the provision of this Charter referred to in the declaration.

**Five year limitation**

(3) A declaration made under subsection (1) shall cease to have effect five years after it comes into force or on such earlier date as may be specified in the declaration.

(4) Parliament or the legislature of a province may re-enact a declaration made under subsection (1).

Re-enactment

(5) Subsection (3) applies in respect of a re-enactment made under subsection (4).

Five year limitation

### *Citation*

**34.** This Part may be cited as the Canadian Charter of Rights and Freedoms.

Citation

# Glossary

**Actus Neus** The criminal act (literally, "the guilty act"), which leads to criminal liability when *mens rea* is also present.

**Arrest** The detaining of a suspect in legal custody. Involves suspension of the individual's rights and freedoms.

**Auburn System** An approach to imprisonment in the 19th century based on the idea that hard labour was the path to reform of the convict. It has also been referred to as the *silent system,* since prisoners were forbidden to speak to one another.

**Canadian Charter of Rights and Freedoms (the Charter)** A document, established in the Constitution Act of 1982, that formally states the rights and freedoms of all Canadians.

**Carceral Network** The institutions, agencies, and staff that are part of law enforcement, the judicial process, the prison system, and the ancillary programs and agencies that deal with offenders.

**Case Law** Laws based on precedence in both criminal and civil cases.

**Choice-Structuring Properties** The situational elements that lead individuals to choose to commit particular crimes.

**Circumstantial Evidence** Evidence that is ambiguous and that will have to be evaluated by the judge and jury to determine its veracity (e.g., testimony given by a witness who saw the accused running from the crime scene or who previously heard the accused threatening the victim).

**Civil Law** Laws dealing with noncriminal relationships involving persons, businesses and other organizations, or government agencies. Civil lawsuits seek compensation, rather than punishment, for alleged wrongs.

**Classical Criminology** A school of criminology based on the Enlightenment thinking that morality was influenced by social institutions, rather than God, and thus these institutions needed to be reformed. Classical criminologists asserted that criminal law should operate primarily to deter crime and that this function could best be achieved through principles of rationality, transparency, proportionality, and humaneness.

**Community Corrections** Methods of sentencing as alternatives to prison that involve placing offenders within the community.

**Community Policing** Policing by officers who are knowledgeable about or part of the communities they patrol.

**Community Service Orders** Orders, issued by a judge, that compel a convicted offender to complete a requisite number of hours of unpaid work in the community.

**Concurrent Sentence** A form of sentencing that requires a person sentenced on several charges to serve only the longest term imposed (e.g., an offender sentenced to three years for one charge and ten years for another would serve a total of ten years).

**Conflict Criminology** A perspective in criminology that aims to explain not what causes criminal behaviour but rather the process by which certain behaviours and individuals are designated as criminal. The conflict perspective holds that there is an ongoing contest for power in society, and that the criminal law and agencies of law enforcement act, both directly and indirectly, in the interests of the powerful.

**Consecutive Sentence** A form of sentencing that requires a person convicted on several charges to serve the sentence imposed for each charge in sequence (e.g., an offender sentenced to three years for one charge and ten years for another would serve a total of thirteen years).

**Corporate Crime** Crime committed by businesses (e.g., polluting the environment, forming illegal monopolies, fixing prices of goods and services, or manipulating the stock market).

**Corpus Delicti** The essential facts and features that are evidence of a crime (literally, "the body of the crime").

**Corrections** The system of treatment of criminal offenders through incarceration, parole, community sentencing, etc.

**Court System** In Canada, the area of the justice system that hears and submits rulings on cases at law and comprises the provincial courts, the superior courts, and the appeal courts.

**Courts of Appeal** Superior courts that hear cases that have been decided in a lower court but sent for appeal against the court's judgment. The court of appeal usually consists of a panel of judges who examine the evidence and the findings of the original judge and extensively question the defence and prosecution lawyers. The judges review the transcript of the lower court to ensure that the hearing was fair and in accordance with statutory and case law.

**Crime Rate** The number of offences that occur per population, calculated by totalling all the offences occurring in a given population and dividing that number by the population.

**Crime** Acts that violate the law and that are punishable upon conviction.

**Criminal Code** The federal statute comprising the criminal laws of Canada and requirements for criminal procedures and sentencing.

**Criminal Insanity Defence** A defence based on the premise that a person cannot be held legally accountable for crimes committed at a time when he or she could not comprehend the illegality or moral reprehensibility of the act.

**Criminal Justice System** The police, the courts, and corrections.

**Criminal Law** A body of rules for prosecuting crime set out by political authority and applying uniformly to all members of society.

**Criminal Sanctions** Penalties intended to enforce obedience to the law.

**Criminology** The study of criminal justice and criminal behaviour.

**Crown Attorney** The prosecutor who acts on behalf of the government in prosecuting indictable charges.

**Dark Figure of Crime** The amount of actual crime in society, a figure that is unknown because not all crimes are reported.

**Decriminalization** A term used to describe behaviours that had been outlawed in our society but have assumed the status of social norms and thus have been legalized.

**Defence Counsel** The legal counsel for the accused.

**Demographics** Statistics that reveal patterns or distributions in a population.

**Deterrence** The attempt to prevent crime by imposing penalties that are constructed to convince potential offenders that they will lose, rather than benefit, from committing criminal acts.

**Deterrence Theory** The theory that people can be discouraged from committing crime through punishment and prevention. *General deterrence* refers to the use of punishment to inhibit crime rates or the behaviour of specific populations, rather than individuals. *Specific deterrence* refers to discouraging the activity of a particular individual through such steps as incarceration, electronic monitoring, or shaming.

**Deviance** Behaviour that does not conform with societal standards.

**Direct Evidence** Factual evidence, such as wiretaps, videos, photographs, or eyewitness testimony.

**Diversion Programs** Programs for young offenders that intend to reconcile the offender and victim, to compensate the victim, and to divert young offenders from the youth court system.

**Due Process** In law, the system of following established rules in order to obtain fair justice for all accused and to protect the legal and human rights of those charged with criminal offences.

**Duress** A legal defence claiming that a defendant should be excused from criminal liability because he or she was forced to commit the criminal act under threat of death or bodily harm for failing to do so.

**Elder Panels** A community sentencing option in which elders in Aboriginal communities assist judges in constructing appropriate sentences for offenders. Elder panels may offer their advice either in open court or behind closed doors in the judge's chambers.

**Electronic Monitoring** The use of electronic devices, such as wristbands, to supervise sentenced offenders, who are allowed to remain in the community provided they adhere to certain conditions, including curfews and restrictions to their movements.

**Espionage** The gathering of secret information related to national defence by spying.

**Federal Court of Canada** A court that is not involved in criminal cases, but instead deals exclusively with legal actions brought against the federal government and federal agencies. The court is divided into a trial and an appellate division.

**Felony** The most serious crime carrying the most severe punishment, usually imprisonment for more than one year. Examples include first or second degree murder, manslaughter, armed robbery, drug possession, aggravated assault, sexual assault, burglary, and arson.

**Fine Options** Alternatives to fines, such as community service or probation, especially for poor offenders who might be imprisoned if unable to pay fines ordered by the court.

**Foot Patrols** Police officers' patrolling of neighbourhoods on foot. Foot patrols are essential to community policing, as they allow officers to hear community issues and concerns and to monitor and intervene in the types of activities associated with the decline of neighbourhoods.

**Hedonistic Calculus** Jeremy Bentham's theory of the weighing of pleasure and pain: the individual seeks to maximize his or her own happiness and to minimize pain, and thus the pain from crime must be greater than the pleasure derived from it.

**Incapacitation** A sentencing approach that, in Canada, involves imprisonment of offenders.

**Incarceration Rate** The number of people jailed per 100 000 population.

**Incidence of Crime** The average number of offences per offender, measured by dividing the number of offences by the number of offenders.

**Indictable Offences** More serious crimes prosecutable under the Criminal Code, such as murder, robbery, sexual assault, kidnapping, or fraud. People charged with these offences are tried before a judge and jury, and if convicted can be sentenced to prison terms or placed on probation.

**Inmate Subculture** The norms and rules within prisons. New inmates learn codes of conduct by talking to other inmates and by observing interactions among prisoners and between correctional officers and prisoners.

**Interest Group** A group of people with a common interest or goal.

**Intoxication Defence** A legal defence stating that a defendant is not responsible for a crime because at the time of the act the person was intoxicated and could not comprehend his or her actions as criminal.

**Just Deserts** A sentencing approach that focuses on the act or events that led the individual to be convicted; the underlying philosophy is that the criminal has benefited from the crime and now must pay society back for his or her misdeeds.

**Labelling Theories** The theory that societal reactions help to shape the individual's identity. For example, when a judge tells a youth that he is a thief, the youth is more likely to act according to this label.

**Law Enforcement** A duty of the police to both reactively and proactively enforce the law by preventing crime from occurring and by apprehending violators of the law.

**Life-25** A sentence of 25 years, which murderers must serve in full.

**Mediation Services** A community sentencing option that involves bringing the offender and victim together to encourage victim–offender mediation and to allow the offender to make restitution to the victim.

**Mens Rea** The intent to commit a criminal act (literally, "the guilty mind").

**Misdemeanour** Minor crimes, such as petty theft, disorderly conduct, or possession of marijuana. Punishment is usually a fine for first-time offenders and probation or a short prison sentence for repeat offenders.

**Mistake of Fact** A legal defence stating that the defendant committed the actus reus of the offence but had no reason to believe that he or she was committing a crime.

**Mistake of Law** A legal defence stating that the defendant committed an act in the belief that it was not criminal because he or she misinterpreted the law.

**Moral Behaviour** Behaviour reflecting societal standards of right and wrong.

**Necessity** A legal defence based on the contention that although the defendant committed a crime, he or she should not be convicted because breaking the law was the only option and thus was necessary.

**Neighbourhood Watch** A crime prevention program that involves residents of a community marking their valuables for identification by police and noting suspicious activity in their neighbourhood.

**Official Statistics** Crime statistics recorded by the police, the courts, and corrections agencies.

**Order Maintenance** A more passive role of the police in deterring crime, such as ensuring that public demonstrations are peaceful. The presence of police acts as a sufficient general deterrent.

**Panopticon** A circular, multi-tiered institution designed by Jeremy Bentham in the 17th century. Few guards were required to maintain control because tiers permitted them to "lock down" segments of the prison, whole tiers, or individual cells.

**Parole** Release of a prisoner before serving the entire the sentence as a reward for good behaviour while incarcerated. Parolees granted day parole are required to live in a halfway house. Full parole is granted to those who are ready for release into the community and to their own living arrangements.

**Peacekeeping** A role of police that involves taking an active role in settling disputes and preventing them from escalating.

**Pennsylvania System** An approach to incarceration in the 19th century that was strongly connected to religious and moral ideals. Prisoners were confined to small cells, where they were to read the Bible, contemplate their acts, and repent, and were allowed less than one hour of exercise in a small yard per day.

**Plea Bargaining** An arrangement whereby the Crown and the defence together decide on a common plea and sentence that they present to the judge. The defendant pleads guilty to a lesser charge in order to obtain a more lenient sentence.

**Police Accountability** The requirement that police account for actions taken or not taken through various mechanisms, such as internal investigations, external review by monitoring agencies, and civil lawsuits.

**Police Discretion** The freedom of police officers to choose between two available courses of action.

**Police Powers** The authority of the police to enforce warrants of the court, pursue arrests, preserve the peace, search premises with a search warrant, and use force when justified.

**Positivist Criminology** An approach that focuses on the idea that the human condition is determined but changeable, and therefore crime can be prevented or remedied through social engineering.

**Preliminary Inquiry** A stage of the criminal court process where a provincial court judge determines whether the Crown has sufficient admissible evidence in a case to send it to a superior court for trial.

**Prerelease Programs** Programs that allow temporary release from prison, including escorted and unescorted temporary absences, day parole, and work release, to allow the offender to reintegrate in the community.

**Prevalence of Crime** The number of people participating in crime at a given time, measured by dividing the number of offenders by the size of the population.

**Prison Argot** The jargon developed by prisoners.

**Probation** A community sentence, ranging from several months to a maximum of three years, whereby an offender's sentence of incarceration is suspended providing that the offender adheres to strict rules under supervision.

**Protective Custody** The separating of prisoners, often rapists, pedophiles, and informers, from the general inmate population for their own protection.

**Provincial Courts** Courts that hear less serious civil and criminal cases. The provincial court system has separate divisions, including small claims, family, youth, traffic, and criminal courts. The provincial governments appoint provincial court judges and pay their salaries.

**Rational Choice Theory** The belief that some offenders are rational decision makers who seek to benefit themselves through their criminal behaviour. According to this theory, potential offenders can be deterred when the choice-structuring properties of an offence are altered.

**Rehabilitation** A sentencing option that provides training, education, and treatment programs in order to allow offenders to change themselves and thus avoid future involvement in crime.

**Restitution** A sentencing approach that involves the offender's compensating victims for loss of property owing to the crime or for personal injuries sustained during the commission of a crime.

**Restorative Justice** A sentencing approach that brings together the offender, the victim, and the community to deal with the harm caused to the victim. The focus is not on punishing the offender, but rather on restoring peace and permitting healing through communication and problem solving.

**Revocation** The ending of parole and reincarceration of the offender for breaching conditions of parole.

**Routine Activities Theory** A theory that attempts to explain changes in crime rates over time by considering social and economic conditions that determine the chances of a crime being committed. According to this theory, people will, in the absence of deterrence, exploit illegal chances that come their way. Routine activities theory argues that we can understand changes in crime rates if we look at changes in three variables: suitable targets, capable guardians, and motivated offenders.

**Security Classifications** The classifications given to inmates based on the risks they present. Incoming prisoners are assessed for classification according to the risk they pose for escaping, for being a danger to other inmates or correctional officers, and for breaking the rules of the prison. In Canada, prisoners are classified as minimum security, medium security, maximum security, and multilevel.

**Self-Defence** A criminal defence arguing that a criminal act was justified because it was necessary to avoid personal harm.

**Self-Report Survey** A survey that asks people to report on their own delinquency or criminal past.

**Sentencing Circles** An approach to corrections in Aboriginal communities in which members of the community and elders meet with the offender to establish how the case should be dealt with. The judge will make the final decision in the case but will take into account the sentencing circle's recommendations.

**Situated Transaction** Edwin Luckenbill's term for the emphasis on the dynamics between the participants in a criminal event, rather than on what one person does to another.

**Social Control** The way in which societies encourage conformity.

**Social Process Theories** Criminological theories that are based on the idea that criminal behaviour is normal, learned behaviour and that examine how people come to have beliefs and knowledge that predispose them to criminality.

**Social Reaction Theories** Criminological theories that purport that criminal behaviour is learned, but the interaction between social control agents, such as the courts, the police, and schools, also contributes to criminality. Situations that are favourable to the commission of crime are followed by societal reaction to the criminal act.

**Solitary Confinement** The isolation of incarcerated offenders in order to punish them for failing to obey institutional rules or for committing violence against others.

**Statutory Law** Laws passed by legislation and known as the Criminal Code.

**Statutory Release** Release of an offender into the community after he or she has served two-thirds of a sentence of incarceration.

**Strain Theory** Robert K. Merton's theory that societies promote certain goals but that the legitimate means to achieve these goals are unequally distributed.

**Summary Conviction Offences** Less serious types of crimes under the Criminal Code, such as trespassing, vagrancy, and petty theft. People charged with these offences are usually tried in provincial courts without a jury and punished by a fine, or for repeat offenders, by not more than six months in prison.

**Superior Courts** The highest provincial courts, with federally appointed judges. Superior courts hear serious cases, such as first degree murder cases.

**Supreme Court of Canada** The highest court of appeal in Canada. The Supreme Court hears cases from the Federal Court of Canada and provincial courts of appeal involving some aspect of case or statute law or an issue of national importance.

**Suspended Sentence** A sentence that is handed down but is unenforced provided the offender commits no further crimes.

**Suspension** The cessation of parole by the parole officer because the parolee has breached the conditions of parole or committed a new crime. At this point, the parole board holds a hearing to determine whether the parole should be continued or revoked.

**Tipping Level** The point at which the probability of being arrested is high enough to act as a deterrent.

**Treason** The crime of helping a foreign government to overthrow or make war against one's own government.

**Unofficial Statistics** Crime statistics that are estimated based on self-report and victimization surveys.

**Victim Impact Statement (VIS)** A testimony of loss suffered by the victim owing to the harm caused by the crime. It allows the victim or the family of the victim to inform the court of the emotional and financial consequences of the criminal act.

**Victim Precipitated Crimes** Crimes brought about by some action of the victim, such as brandishing a weapon.

**Victimization** An illegitimate violation of a person by another, resulting in an experience of loss as recognized by a moral authority.

**Victimization Surveys** Questionnaires that ask people to provide information about their experience as victims of crimes.

**Victimless Crimes** Crimes, such as drug use, prostitution, and pornography, that are considered to have no victims because the participants are willing.

**Victim–Offender Reconciliation Program (VORP)** A program that allows an offender the opportunity to acknowledge his or her guilt and, under the authority of the judge, to make restitution according to an agreement reached in a meeting between victim and offender, mediated by a social worker, a probation officer, or another official.

**Victimology** A branch of criminology that deals with the psychological, cultural, social, and political processes that contribute to victimization and the societal processes that contribute to the conferral of the victim status.

**Young Offenders Act (YOA)** An Act passed by Parliament in 1984 that defined young offenders as being between 12 and 17 years of age, defined criteria and procedures for diversion from court, mandated the use of legal counsel, and permitted the youth courts to issue only determinate sentences.

**Youth Court** The courts that deal specifically with cases involving young offenders—those from 12 to 17 years of age.

# References

Abbot, J. 1981. *In the Belly of the Beast.* New York: Random House.

Adler, F. 1975. *Sisters in Crime: The Rise of the New Female Criminal.* New York: Basic Books.

Akers, R. 1985. *Deviant Behaviour: A Social Learning Approach* (3rd ed.). Belmont, CA: Wadsworth.

Amir, M. 1971. *Patterns of Forcible Rape.* Chicago: University of Chicago Press.

Arbour, the Honourable Louise, Commissioner. 1996. *Commission of Inquiry into Certain Events at the Prison for Women in Kingston.* Ottawa: Public Works and Government Services Canada.

Badgley, R. 1987. *The Badgley Report on Prostitution.* Ottawa: Government Printing Office.

Barkhan, S. 1997. *Criminology. A Sociological Understanding.* Englewood Cliffs, NJ: Prentice-Hall.

Barsh, R. L., & C. Marlor. 1999. "Alternative Paradigms: Law as Power, Law as Process" in N. Larsen & B. Burtch (Eds.), *Law in Society. Canadian Readings.* Toronto: Harcourt Brace, pp. 132–151.

Beccaria, C. 1963. *On Crimes and Punishment.* Trans. Henry Paolucci. Indianapolis: Bobbs-Merrill. (Original work published 1764.)

Becker, H. S. 1963. *Outsiders: Studies in the Sociology of Deviance.* Glencoe, IL: Free Press.

Beddoes, D. 1989. *Pal Hal.* Toronto: Macmillan.

Belliveau, J. E. 1956. *The Coffin Murder Case.* Toronto: Kingswood House.

Bentham, J. 1988. *An Introduction to the Principles of Morals and Legislation.* Buffalo, NY: Prometheus Press. (Original work published 1789.)

Bernard, T. 1987. "Testing Structural Strain Theories." *Journal of Research in Crime and Delinquency,* 24: 262–280.

Birnie, 1990. *A Rock and a Hard Place: Inside Canada's Parole Board.* Toronto: Macmillan.

Black, D. 1983. "Crime as Social Control." *American Sociological Review,* 48: 34–45.

Blau, J., & P. M. Blau. 1982. "The Cost of Inequality: Metropolitan Structure and Violent Crime." *American Sociological Review,* 47: 114–129.

Bonger, W. 1916. *Criminality and Economic Conditions.* Boston: Little, Brown.

Bonta, J., & R. B. Cormier, 1999. "Corrections Research in Canada." *The Canadian Journal of Criminology,* 41: 235–247.

Booth, A., & D. W. Osgood. 1993. "The Influence of Testosterone on Deviance in Adulthood: Assessing and Explaining the Relationship." *Criminology,* 31: 93–117.

Boyd, N. 1989. *The Last Dance: Murder in Canada.* Toronto: Prentice Hall.

_____. 1991. *High Society.* Toronto: Key Porter.

_____. 1998. *Canadian Law. An Introduction* (2nd ed.). Toronto: Harcourt Brace.

Brady, P. 1990. *Sentencing Environmental Offenders: Individuals versus Corporations.* Master's thesis, University of Windsor, Ontario.

Braithwaite, J. 1997. "John Braithwaite's 'Control Balance' and 'Criminological Theory.'" *Theoretical Criminology,* 1(1): 77–98.

Braithwaite, J., & S. Mugford. 1994. "Conditions of Successful Reintegration Ceremonies." *British Journal of Criminology,* 34(2): 139–170.

Brantingham, P. J., S. Mu, & A. Verma. 1995. "Patterns in Crime" in M. A. Jackson & C. T. Griffiths (Eds.), *Canadian Criminology: Perspectives in Crime and Criminality* (2nd ed.). Toronto: Harcourt Brace, Chapter 6.

Brockman, J., & V. G. Rose. 1996. *An Introduction to Canadian Criminal Procedure and Evidence.* Scarborough, ON: Nelson Canada.

Brown, S. E., F. A. Esbensen, & G. Geis. 1998. *Criminology: Explaining Crime and Its Context* (3rd ed.). Cincinnati, OH: Anderson.

Bugliosi, V. 1996. *Outrage: The Five Reasons Why O.J. Simpson Got Away with Murder.* New York: Island Books.

*Bureau of Justice Statistics Data Report.* 1989. Online. Available: www.vix.com/pub/men/abuse/studies/murder.rate.html

Burnside, S., & A. Cairns. 1995. *Deadly Innocence.* New York: Time Warner.

Burtch, B. 1992. *Sociology of Law.* Toronto: Harcourt Brace.

Burtch, B., & R. V. Ericson. 1977. *The Silent System.* Toronto: Centre of Criminology.

Canadian Centre for Justice Statistics (CCJS). 1994. "Trends in Criminal Victimization: 1988–1993." *Juristat,* 13(3).

_____. 1995a. "Factfinder on Crime and the Administration of Justice in Canada." *Juristat,* 15(10).

_____. 1995b. "Victims' Use of Police and Social Services." *Juristat,* 15(6).

_____. 1997. "Canadian Crime Statistics, 1996." *Juristat,* 17(8).

_____. 1999a. "Justice Spending in Canada." *Juristat,* 19(4): 4.

_____. 1999b. *Police Resources in Canada* (Cat. no. 85-225-XIE). Statistics Canada: Minister of Supply and Services Canada.

Canadian Sentencing Commission. 1987. *Report of the Canadian Sentencing Commission.* Ottawa: Supply and Services Canada.

*Canadian Urban Victimization Survey.* 1982. Ottawa: Solicitor General of Canada, Program Branch, Research and Statistic Group.

Caputo, T., Kennedy, M., Reasons, C., & Brannigan, A. 1989. *Law and Society: A Critical Perspective.* Toronto: Harcourt Brace.

Carlen, P., D. Christina, J. Hicks, J. O'Swyer, & C. Tchaikowsky. 1985. *Criminal Women.* Oxford: Polity Press.

Caron, R. 1978. *Go-Boy!* Toronto: McGraw-Hill Ryerson.

_____. 1985. *Bingo!* Toronto: Methuen.

Cavadion, M., & J. Dignan. 1997. *The Penal System: An Introduction* (2nd ed.). London: Sage.

Cayley, D. 1998. *The Expanding Prison.* Toronto: House of Anansi.

Chambliss, W. (Ed.). 1975. *Crime and the Legal Process.* New York: McGraw-Hill.

_____. 1967. "Types of Deviance and the Effectiveness of Legal Sanctions." *Wisconsin Law Review,* 3: 703–719.

Chamelin, M. 1991. "A Longitudinal Analysis of Arrest-Crime Relationship: A Further Explanation of the Tipping Effect." *Justice Quarterly,* 8: 187–199.

Chesney-Lind, M. 1977. "Judicial Paternalism and the Female Status Offender: Training Women to Know Their Place." *Crime and Delinquency,* 23: 121–130.

Chessman, C. 1954. *Cell 2455 Death Row.* Englewood Cliffs, NJ: Prentice-Hall.

Christie, N. 1977. "Conflicts as Property." *British Journal of Criminology,* 17(1): 1–15.

_____. 1994. *Crime Control at Industry: Towards Gulags Western Style* (2nd ed.). New York: Routledge.

Clairmont, D. H., & D. W. Magill. 1987. *Africville: The Life and Death of a Canadian Black Community.* Toronto: Canadian Scholars' Press.

Clarke, R. 1995. "Situational Crime Prevention" in M. Tonry & D. Farrington (Eds.), *Crime and Justice: A Review of the Research* (vol. 19). Chicago: University of Chicago Press, pp. 91–150.

Clarke, R. V., & R. Homel. 1997. "A Revised Classification of Situational Crime Prevention Techniques" in S. P. Lab (Ed.), *Crime Prevention at a Crossroads.* Cincinnati, OH: Anderson.

Cleaver, E. 1967. *Soul on Ice.* New York: McGraw-Hill.

Cloward, R., & L. Ohlin. 1960. *Delinquency and Opportunity.* Glencoe, IL: Free Press.

Cohen, A. K. 1955. *Delinquent Boys*. Glencoe, IL: Free Press.

Cohen, S., & L. Taylor. 1976. *Prison Secrets*. London: Radical Alternatives to Prison.

*Constitution Act, 1982* [en. by the Canada Act 1982 (U.K.), c. 11, s. 1], pt. I (Canadian Charter of Rights and Freedoms).

Cornish, D. B., & R. V. G. Clarke. 1987. "Understanding Criminal Displacement: An Application of Rational Choice Theory." *Criminology*, 25(4): 933–947.

Correctional Services of Canada (CSC). 2000. Web site. Available: www.csc-scc.gc.ca.

Culhane, C. 1985. *Barred from Prison*. Montreal: Black Rose.

_____. 1987. *No Longer Barred from Prison*. Montreal: Black Rose.

Cunningham, A. H., & C. T. Griffiths. 1997. *Canadian Criminal Justice. A Primer*. Toronto: Harcourt Brace.

Currie, E. 1998. "Market, Crime and Community: Toward a Midrange Theory of Post-Industrial Violence." *Theoretical Criminology*, 1(2): 247–272.

Curtis, D., & C. Blanchfield. 1985. *Kingston Penitentiary: The First One Hundred Years, 1835–1985*. Ottawa: CSC.

Davis, R. C., & B. Smith. 1994. "Victim Impact Statements and Victim Satisfaction: An Unfulfilled Promise?" *Journal of Criminal Justice*, 22: 1–12.

_____. 1995. "Domestic Violence Reforms: Empty Promises or Fulfilled Expectations." *Crime and Delinquency*, 41: 541–552.

Davis, R. C., M. Henley, & B. Smith. 1990. *Victim Impact Statements: Their Effects on Court Outcomes and Victim Satisfaction*. Washington, DC: National Institute of Justice.

Denno, D. 1988. "Human Biology and Criminal Responsibility: Free Will or Free Ride?" *University of Pennsylvania Law Review*, 137(2): 217–671.

Desroches, F. J. 1995. *Force and Fear: Robbery in Canada*. Scarborough, ON: Nelson Canada.

Doob, A., & V. Marionos. 1995. *Youth Crime and the Youth Justice System in Canada: A Research Perspective*. Ottawa: Department of Justice Canada, Research, Statistics and Evaluation.

Durkheim, E. 1951. *Suicide: A Study of Sociology*. New York: Free Press. (Original work published 1897)

Ekstedt, J., & C. T. Griffiths. 1988. *Corrections in Canada: Policy and Practice*. Toronto: Butterworths.

Elias, R. 1986. *The Politics of Victimization: Victims, Victimology and Human Rights*. New York: Oxford University Press.

Erez, E., & P. Tontodonato. 1992. "The Effect of Victim Participation in Sentencing on Sentence Outcome." *Criminology*, 28: 451–474.

Erickson, P. 1980. *Cannabis Criminals*. Toronto: Addiction Research Foundation.

Ericson, R. V. 1974. "Turning the Inside Out: On Limiting the Use of Imprisonment." *Community Education Series*, 1(3), John Howard Society of Ontario.

Ericson, R.; P. Baranek, & J. Chan. 1987. *Visualizing Deviance*. Toronto: University of Toronto Press.

_____. 1989. *Negotiating Control*. Toronto: University of Toronto Press.

Felson, M., & L. E. Cohen. 1979. "Social Change and Crime Rate Trends: A Routine Activities Approach." *American Sociological Review*, 44: 588–609.

Fischer, D. G., & R. Jeune. 1987. "Juvenile Diversion: A Process Analysis." *Canadian Psychology*, 28: 60–70.

Fishbein, D. 1996. "Selected Studies on the Biology of Antisocial Behaviour" in J. Conklin (Ed.), *New Perspectives in Criminology*. Needham Heights, MA: Allyn and Bacon.

Fitzgerald, M. 1986. *Prisons in Revolt*. London: RAP.

Fleming, T. 1974. *The Chronic Drunkeness Offender and the Courts*. Unpublished honours B.A. thesis, University of Toronto, Ontario.

_____. 1982. *The Release of Mentally Disordered, Dangerous and Psychopathic Offender-Patients from a Special Hospital.* London: Unpublished Ph.D. thesis.

_____. 1993. *Down and Out in Canada: Homeless Canadians.* Toronto: Canadian Scholars' Press.

_____. 1995. "The Dark Factory" in L. Visano & K. McCormick (Eds.), *Canadian Penology: Advanced Perspectives.* Toronto: Canadian Scholars' Press, pp. 291–317.

_____. 2000. *The Science of Criminology.* Toronto: Academic Press.

Fleming, T., & B. Jorgenson. 1982. *Stolen Property.* Toronto: Solicitor General.

Foot, D. 1996. *Boom, Bust, and Echo.* Toronto: Macfarlane Walter and Ross.

Foran, T., & M. Reed. 1996. "The Correctional System" in L. Kennedy & V. Sacco (Eds.), *Crime Counts: A Criminal Event Analysis.* Scarborough, ON: Nelson Canada, pp. 293–311.

Forcese, D. 1999. *Policing Canadian Society* (2nd ed.). Scarborough, ON: Prentice Hall.

Foucault, M. 1977. *Discipline and Punish: The Birth of the Prison.* London: Vintage.

_____. 1995. *Discipline and Punish.* New York: Vintage.

*The Fraser Commission on Pornography and Prostitution.* 1985. Ottawa: Government Printing Office.

Friedenberg, E. J. 1985. "Law in a Cynical Society" in D. Gibson & J. Baldwin (Eds.), *Law in a Cynical Society: Opinion and Law in the 1980s.* Vancouver: Carswell.

Gall, G. 1995. *The Canadian Legal System* (4th ed.). Toronto: Carswell.

Gittens, M., D. Cole, T. Williams, S. Skanda-Rajah, M. Tam, & E. Ratnshny. 1995, December. *Final Report of the Commission on Systemic Racism in the Ontario Criminal Justice System.* Toronto: Queen's Printer.

Goff, C. 1997. *Criminal Justice in Canada: An Introduction.* Scarborough, ON: ITP Nelson.

Goffman, E. 1961. *Asylums.* Garden City, NY: Anchor Books.

Gomme, I. 1998. *The Shadow Line.* Toronto: Harcourt Brace.

Gosselin, L. 1977. *Prisons in Canada.* Montreal: Black Rose.

Grana, S., & J. Ollenburger. 1999. *The Social Context of Law.* Upper Saddle River, NJ: Prentice-Hall.

Greenspan, E., & G. Jonas. 1987. *Greenspan: The Case for the Defence.* Toronto: Macmillan.

Griffiths, C., & S. Verdun-Jones. 1994. *Canadian Criminal Justice* (2nd ed.). Toronto: Harcourt Brace.

Hagan, J. (Ed.). 1989. *Structural Criminology.* New Brunswick, NJ: Rutgers University Press.

_____. 1974. "Extra-legal Attributes and Criminal Sentencing: An Assessment of a Sociological Viewpoint." *Law and Society Review,* 8(3): 357–383.

_____. 1985. "The Class Structure of Gender and Delinquency." *American Journal of Sociology,* 90: 1151–1178.

Hagan, J., R. Gillis, & R. Simpson. 1985. "The Class Structure of Gender and Delinquency: Toward a Power-Control Theory of Common Delinquent Behavior." *American Journal of Sociology,* 90(6): 1151–1178.

Hann, R. G. 1973. *Decision Making in the Criminal Court System: A System Analysis.* Toronto: Centre of Criminology.

Hartnagel, T. 1978. "The Effect of Age and Sex Compositions of Provincial Populations on Provincial Crime Rates." *Canadian Journal of Criminology,* 20(1): 28–33.

Hartnagel, T., & J. Lee. 1990. "Urban Crime in Canada." *Canadian Journal of Criminology,* 32(4): 591–606.

Hastings, R. 1997. "Crime Prevention and Criminal Justice" in T. Fleming (Ed.), *Post-Critical Criminology.* Toronto: Prentice Hall, pp. 315–329.

Hills, S. 1971. *Crime, Power and Morality.* Scranton, PA: Chandler Publishing.

Hindelang, M., R. Hirschi, & J. Weis. 1981. *Measuring Delinquency.* Beverly Hills, CA: Sage.

Hirschi, T. 1969. *Causes of Delinquency*. Berkeley: University of California Press.

Hogg, P. 1992. *Constitutional Law of Canada* (3rd ed.). Scarborough, ON: Carswell.

Huizing. D., & D. S. Elliott. 1986. "Reassessing the Reliability and Validity of Self-Report Delinquency Measures." *Journal of Quantitative Criminology*, 2(4): 293–327.

Hylton, J. 1983. "The Growth of Punishment: Imprisonment and Community Correction in Canada" in T. Fleming & L. Visano (Eds.), *Deviant Designations: Crime, Law and Deviance in Canada*. Toronto: Butterworths, pp. 411–430.

Irwin, J. 1970. *The Felon*. Englewood Cliffs, NJ: Prentice-Hall.

Jackson, M. 1983. *Prisoners of Isolation*. Toronto: University of Toronto Press.

Jaffe, P. G., B. J. Kroeker, C. Hyatt, M. Miscevick, A. Telford, R. Chandler, C. Shanahan, & B. Sokoloff. 1985. "Diversion in the Canadian Juvenile Justice System: A Tale of Two Cities." *Juvenile and Family Court Journal*, 37: 59–66.

James, C. E. 1989. *Seeing Ourselves: Exploring Race, Ethnicity and Culture*. Oakville, ON: Instructional and Human Resource Development, Sheridan College.

Johnson, H. 1986. *Women and Crime in Canada*. Ottawa: Solicitor General of Canada.

Jones, A., & B. Krisberg. 1994. *Images and Reality: Juvenile Crime, Youth Violence and Public Policy*. Washington, DC: Office of Juvenile Justice.

Jurgens, R. 1996. *HIV/AIDS in Prison: Final Report*. Ottawa: Canadian HIV/AIDS Legal Network.

Katz, J. 1988. *The Seductions of Crime: Moral and Sensual Attractions in Doing Evil*. New York: Basic Books.

Kelling, G., T. Pate, D. Dieckman, & C. Brown. 1974. *The Kansas City Prevention Patrol Experiment: Final Report*. Washington: Police Foundation.

Kennedy, L., R. Silverman, & D. Forde. 1991. "Homicide in Urban Canada: Testing the Impact of Economic Inequality and Social Disorganization." *Canadian Journal of Criminology*, 16(4): 397–410.

Klein, J. F. 1976. *Let's Make a Deal: Negotiating Justice*. Lexington, MA: Lexington Books.

Kymlicka, W. 1989. *Liberation, Community and Culture*. Oxford: Clarendon Press.

LaPrairie, C. 1983. "Native Juveniles in Court: Some Preliminary Observations" in T. Fleming & L. A. Visano (Eds.), *Deviant Designations: Crime, Law and Deviance in Canada*. Toronto: Butterworths, pp. 337–350.

Larsen, N., & B. Burtch (Eds.). 1999. *Law in Society*. Toronto: Harcourt Brace.

LeBourdais, I. 1966. *The Trial of Steven Truscott*. Toronto: McClelland & Stewart.

Lemert, 1967. *Human Deviance, Social Problems and Social Control*. Englewood Cliffs, NJ: Prentice-Hall.

Lewis, D. O., J. H. Pincus, M. Feldman, L. Jackson, & B. Bard. 1986. "Psychiatric, Neurological, and Psychoeducational Characteristics of 15 Death Row Inmates in the United States." *American Journal of Psychiatry*, 14: 838–845.

Linden, R. 1996. *Criminology: A Canadian Perspective* (3rd ed.). Toronto: Harcourt Brace.

Lipton, D., R. Martinson, & J. Wilks. 1975. *The Effectiveness of Correctional Treatment*. New York: Praeger.

Luckenbill, D. F. 1977. "Criminal Homicide as a Situated Transaction." *Social Problems*, 25(2): 176–186.

MacNaughtan Smith, P. 1974. *What Is Crime and Why Do We Fight It?* Toronto: Centre of Criminology.

Manson. A. 1989, April. Lecture presented at *The Fifteen-Year Review of Life Sentences*. Sumposium conducted at the University of Windsor, Ontario.

Marron, K. 1996. *The Slammer: The Crisis in Canada's Prison System*. Toronto: Doubleday.

Martinson, R. 1974. "What Works? Questions and Answers about Prison Reform." *The Public Interest*, 35: 22–54.

Mathews, R., & J. Young. 1992. "Reflections on Realism" in J. Young & R. Matthews (Eds.), *Rethinking Criminology: The Realist Debate*. London: Sage Publications, pp. 1–24.

McDonald, L. 1969. "Crime and Punishment in Canada: A Statistical Test of the 'Conventional Wisdom.'" *Canadian Review of Sociology and Anthropology*, 6: 212–236.

Meithe, T. D., & R. F. Meier. 1990. "Opportunity, Choice, and Criminal Victimization: A Test of a Theoretical Model." *Journal of Research in Crime and Delinquency*, 27(3): 243–266.

Melnitzer, J. 1995. *Maximum, Minimum, Medium: A Journey Through Canadian Prisons*. Toronto: Key Porter.

Mendelsohn, B. 1976. "Victimology and Contemporary Society's Trends" in E. Viano (Ed.), *Victims and Society*. Washington, DC: Visage.

Merton, R. K. 1938. "Social Structure and Anomie." *American Sociological Review*, 3: 672–682.

Messner, S., & R. Rosenfeld. 1994. *Crime and the American Dream*. Belmont, CA: Wadsworth.

Miller, W. B. 1958. "Lower Class Culture as a Generating Milieu of Gang Delinquency." *Journal of Social Issues*, 14: 5–19.

Morris, N. 1982. *Madness and the Criminal Law*. Chicago: University of Chicago Press.

Morris, N., & D. Rothman (Eds.). 1995. *The Oxford History of the Prison*. New York: Oxford University Press.

Morris, P. 1965. *Prisoners and Their Families*. London: Allen and Unwin.

Morris, R. 1997. *Prison Abolition*. Toronto: Canadian Scholars' Press.

Morris, T., & L. Blom-Cooper. 1963. *A Calendar of Murder: Criminal Homicide in England since 1957*. London: M. Joseph.

Morris, T., & P. Morris. 1963. *Pentonville*. London: Routledge and Kegan Paul.

Morton, J., H. Addison, R. Addison, L. Hunt, & J. Sullivan. 1953. "A Clinical Study of Premenstrual Tension." *American Journal of Obstetrics and Gynecology*, 65: 1182–1191.

Muncie, J., E. McLaughlin, & M. Langen (Eds.). 1997. *Criminological Perspectives: A Reader*. London: Sage.

Murphy, P. J., & L. Johnson. 1997. *Life-25: Interviews with Prisoners Serving Life Sentences*. Vancouver: New Star Books.

Nagel, W. H. 1974. "The Notion of Victimology in Criminology" in I. Drapkin & E. Viano (Eds.), *Victimology*. Lexington, MA.: Lexington Books.

Nergard, T. B. 1993. "Solving Conflicts Outside the Court System: Experiences with the Conflict Resolution Boards in Norway." *British Journal of Criminology*, 33(1): 81–94.

Nettler, G. 1984. *Explaining Crime*. Cincinnati: Anderson.

Nye, F. I., & J. Short. 1957. "Scaling Delinquent Behaviour." *American Sociological Review*, 22: 326–331.

Olweus, E. 1987. "Testosterone and Adrenaline: Aggressive Antisocial Behavior in Normal Adolescent Males" in S. A. Mednick, T. E. Moffitt, & S. A. Stack (Eds.), *The Causes of Crime: New Biological Approaches*. Cambridge, UK: Cambridge University Press, pp. 263–282.

*Strategic Planning Committee on Police Training and Education: A Police Learning System for Ontario: Final Report and Recommendations* (D. Scott Campbell, Chairman). 1992. Toronto: The Committee.

Osgood, W., J. Wilson, P. O'Malley, J. Bachman, & L. Johnsston. 1996. "Routine Activities and Individual Deviant Behaviour." *American Sociological Review*, 61: 635–655.

Packer, H. 1964. "Two Models of Criminal Process." *University of Pennsylvania Law Review*, 113: 1–68.

Peak, K. 1997. *Policing America: Methods, Issues, Challenges*. Englewood Cliffs, NJ: Prentice-Hall.

Perkins, C. A. 1997. *Age Patterns of Victims of Serious Crimes* (NCJ 162031). Washington, DC: Bureau of Justice Studies.

Quinney, R. 1972. "Who Is the Victim?" *Criminology,* 10: 314–322.

Regoli, R., & J. Hewitt. 1996. *Criminal Justice.* Englewood Cliffs, NJ: Prentice-Hall.

Reiman, J. 1990. *The Rich Get Richer and the Poor Get Prison* (3rd ed.). Upper Saddle River, NJ: Prentice-Hall.

Riedel, R. 1989. *The Victim's Guide to the Canadian Criminal Justice System.* Scarborough, ON: Centennial College Press.

Rosenbaum, A., S. K. Hoge, S. A. Adelman, W. J. Warnken, K. E. Flecther, & R. L. Kane. 1994. "Head Injury in Partner-Abusive Men." *Journal of Consulting and Clinical Psychology,* 62(6): 1187–1193.

Ross, J. I. (Ed.). 1995. *Violence in Canada: Sociopolitical Perspectives.* Don Mills, ON: Oxford.

Ruby, C. 1996. *Sentencing* (3rd ed.). Toronto: Butterworths.

Rush, G. 1994. *The Dictionary of Criminal Justice* (4th ed.). Guildford, UK: Dushkin Publishing.

Sacco, V., & L. Kennedy. 1998. *Crime Victims in Context.* Los Angeles: Roxbury.

Schmalleger, F. 1997. *Criminal Justice Today: An Introductory Text for the Twenty-First Century* (4th ed.). Upper Saddle River, NJ: Prentice-Hall.

Schmalleger, F., D. MacAlister, P. F. McKenna, & J. Winterdyk. 2000. *Canadian Criminal Justice Today.* Toronto: Pearson Education.

Schneider, H. J. 1982. "The Present Situation in Victimology in the World" in H. J. Schneider (Ed.), *The Victim in International Perspective.* Berlin: Walter de Gruyter.

Scott, G. (with B. Trent). 1982. *Inmate.* Toronto: Optimum.

Scull, A. 1983. *Decarceration.* Englewood Cliffs, NJ: Prentice-Hall.

Sellin, T. 1958. *Culture, Conflict and Crime.* New York: Social Science Research Council.

Shaw, C. R., & H. D. McKay. 1969. *Juvenile Delinquency and Urban Areas* (rev. ed.). Chicago: University of Chicago Press.

Sheldon, W. H. 1949. *Varieties of Delinquent Youth: An Introduction to Constitutional Psychiatry.* New York: Harper.

Sherman, L., & D. Weisburd. 1995. "General Deterrent Effects of Police Patrol in Crime 'Hot Spots': A Randomized, Controlled Trial." *Justice Quarterly,* 12: 625–648.

Siegel, L. J., & C. McCormick. 1999. *Criminology in Canada: Theories, Patterns, and Typologies.* Scarborough, ON: Nelson Thomson Learning.

Silverman, R. A. 1980. "Measuring Crime: A Tale of Two Cities" in R. A. Silverman & J. J. Teevan (Eds.), *Crime in Canadian Society* (2nd ed.). Toronto: Butterworths.

Spierenburg, P. C. 1984. *The Spectacle of Suffering: Executions and the Evolution of Repression.* Cambridge, NY: Cambridge University Press.

Sprott, J. B., & A. Doob. 1998. "Understanding Provincial Variations in Incarceration Rates." *Canadian Journal of Criminology,* 40(3): 305–322.

Stansfield, R. 1996. *Issues in Policing: A Canadian Perspective.* Toronto: Thompson Educational Publishing.

Stebbins, R. 1996. *Deviance:Tolerable Differences.* Toronto: McGraw-Hill.

Stenning, P. C. 1983. *The Legal Status of the Police.* Ottawa: Land Reform Commission of Canada.

Sutherland, E. 1966. *Principles of Criminology* (7th ed.). Philadelphia: J. B. Lippincott.

Sutherland, E., & D. Cressey. 1970. *Principles of Criminology* (8th ed.). Philadelphia: Lippincott.

Sykes, C. 1992. *A Nation of Victims: The Decay of the American Character.* New York: St. Martin's Press.

Tappan, P. 1960. *Crime, Justice and Corrections.* New York: McGraw-Hill.

Tittle, C. 1995. *Control Balance: A General Theory of Deviance.* Boulder, CO: Westview.

Tittle, C., & A. Rowe. 1973. "Moral Appeal, Sanction Threat, and Deviance: An Experimental Test." *Social Problems,* 20: 488–498.

Toby, J. 1957. "Social Disorganization and Stake in Conformity: Complementary Factors in the Predatory Behaviour of Hoodlums." *Journal of Criminal Law and Police Science,* 48: 12–17.

*Toronto Star.* 2000, April 16. pp. A1, A6.

Travis, F. T. 1990. *Introduction to Criminal Justice*. Cincinnati: Anderson.

Trent, B. 1971. *The Steven Truscott Story*. Toronto: Pocket Books.

Udry, J. R. 1988. "Biological Predisposition and Social Control in Adolescent Sexual Behaviour." *American Sociological Review*, 53: 709–722.

Vago, S. 2000. *Law and Society* (6th ed.). Upper Saddle River, NJ: Prentice-Hall.

van den Bergie, P. 1974. *Race and Ethnicity* (2nd ed.). New York: Basic Books.

van Dijk, J., & P. Mayhew. 1997. *Criminal Victimisation in Eleven Industrialised Countries: Key Findings from the 1996 International Crime Victims Survey*. Amsterdam: Netherlands Ministry of Justice.

van Dijk, J., P. Mayhew, & M. Kilias. 1991. *Experiences of Crime Across the World: Key Findings of the 1989 International Crime Survey*. Boston: Kluwer Law and Taxation Publishers.

van Rijn, N. 1999, July 24. "Police Caseload Doubles in 36 Years." *Toronto Star*, p. A1.

Verdun-Jones, S. 1997. *Criminal Law in Canada: Cases, Questions and the Code* (2nd ed.). Toronto: Harcourt Brace.

Vincent, C. 1990. *Police Officer*. Ottawa: Carleton University Press.

Visano, L., & K. McCormick. 1992a. *Canadian Penology: Advanced Perspectives*. Toronto: Canadian Scholars' Press.

_____. 1992b. *Understanding Policing*. Toronto: Canadian Scholars' Press.

Volovka, J. 1987. "Electroencephalogram among Criminals" in S. Mednick, T. Moffit, & S. Stack (Eds.), *The Causes of Crime*. Cambridge, NY: Cambridge University Press.

Von Hentig, H. 1948. *The Criminal and His Victim*. New Haven, CT: Yale University Press.

Walford, B. 1987. *Lifers: The Stories of Eleven Women Serving Life Sentences for Murder*. Montreal: Eden Press.

Wallerstien, J. S., & C. Wyle. 1947. "Our Law-Abiding Lawbreakers." *Probation*, XXV(April): 107–112.

Weinberg, L. S., & J. W. Weinberg. 1980. *Law and Society: An Interdisciplinary Introduction*. Washington, DC: University Press of America.

Wilson, E. O. 1975. *Sociobiology: The New Synthesis*. Cambridge, MA: Belknap-Harvard University Press.

Wilson, J. Q. 1975. *Thinking about Crime*. New York: Basic Books.

Wilson, J. Q., & G. Kelling. 1982, March. "Broken Windows: The Police and Neighbourhood Safety." *Atlantic Monthly*, 127: 29–38.

Winterdyk, J. (Ed.). 2000. *Issues and Perspectives on Young Offenders in Canada* (2nd ed.). Toronto: Harcourt Brace.

Witkin, H. A. 1977. "XYY and XXY Men: Criminality and Aggression" in S. A. Mednick & K. O. Christensen (Eds.), *Biosocial Bases of Criminal Behaviour*. New York: Gardner, pp. 165–197.

*Wolfenden Committee on Prostitution, Pornography and Homosexuality*. 1966. London: Home Office.

Wolfgang, M. 1958. *Patterns in Criminal Homicide*. Philadelphia: University of Pennsylvania Press.

Wolfgang, M., & F. Ferracuti. 1967. *The Subculture of Violence*. Beverly Hills, CA: Sage.

Wolfgang, M., R. M. Figlio, & T. Sellin. 1972. *Delinquency in a Birth Cohort*. Chicago: University of Chicago Press.

Young-Rifai, M. 1982. "Victimology: A Theoretical Framework" in H. J. Schneider (Ed.), *The Victim in International Perspective*. Berlin: Walter de Gruyter.

Zamble, E. 2000. "Community Supervision : Current Practice and Future Directions." CSC Web site. Available: www.csc-scc.gc.ca.

# Index

and limited rationality, 81
pleasure/pain calculus, 73
principles of classical thought,
73–75
proportionality, 74
rational choice theory, 78–79
rationality, 74
routine activities theory, 79–80
and social structure, 80–81
transparency, 75
classism, 29–30
Cleaver, Eldridge, 190
closing arguments, 167–168
Cloward, Richard, 93
Cochrane, Johnny, 164, 165
Coffin, Wilfred, 176, 218
cognitive theory, 88
Cohen, Albert, 93–94
colour of right, 56
Columbine High School, 93
commission, 50
Commission of Inquiry into Certain
Events at the Prison for Women in
Kingston. See Arbour Commission
community-based alternatives to prisons, 207–208
community service orders, 223
elder panels, 224
electronic monitoring, 225
European context, 222
fine options, 225–226
mediation services, 223–224
nonviolent offenders, 223
restitution, 226
restorative justice, 226
sentencing circle, 224–225
tethering, 225
community corrections, 208
community interest groups, 102–103
community policing, 105, 121,
137–139, 259–262
and crime prevention, 259
critics of, 261
desirability of police presence,
261–262
foot patrols, 260–261
community service orders, 223
comparative trends, 32–33
compensation, 241–242
Compensation for Victims of Crime
Act, 244
composition of police, 133–134
concurrent sentences, 173
conflict criminology, 96–97
conflict model, 48–49
consecutive sentences, 173
conspiracy, 51
constables, 129
Constitution Act (1867), 143
Controlled Drugs and Substances Act,
244
corporate crime, 103
corporate deviance, 29
corporate interest groups, 103–104
*corpus delicti*, 51
correctional officers, 195
Correctional Service of Canada, 184,
186, 197, 223, 224–225, 226
corrections, 5–6

*see also* prisons
criticism of, 6
federal institution, 8
provincial institution, 8
systemic biases, 30
treatment needs, 8
Corrections and Conditional Release
Act, 243
court procedures, 2–3
court system, 4–5
appeals, 151
courts of appeal, 144
federal, 145
levels of, 5
provincial, 143–145
structure, 142–145
superior courts, 144
Supreme Court of Canada, 145
trials. *See* trials
youth, 152–155
courts
creation of law, 110
role of, 11
systemic biases, 30
victim services, 242–243
youth, 153–155
courts of appeal, 144
crime
by age, 37–39
causes of, 9–10, 16
*see also* theories of crime
commission, 50
corporate deviance, 29
*versus* criminality, 21
dark figure of, 20–21
defined, 21, 47
definition of, 10
expressive, 77
incidence of, 18
index (FBI), 22
instrumental, 76
measurement of, 16
media portrayal of, 15
omission, 50
patterns of. *See* crime patterns
prevalence of, 17
prevention of. *See* crime prevention
questions about, 248–249
by race, 41–43
rate, 18–20, 23
recording. *See* crime statistics
by region, 33–37
by sex, 39–41
and social ecology, 43–44
and social thinking, 10
street, 29
theories of. *See* theories of crime
violent, 39–40
crime etiology, 69
crime patterns
age, 37–39
comparative trends, 32–33
economic disparity, 37
and gender, 39–41
historical trends, 31–32
race, 41–43
regional, 33–37
social ecology, 43–44

statistics, 27
young offenders, 37–39
crime picture. *See* crime statistics
crime prevention, 80, 120–121
community policing and, 259
factors behind, 257–259
government funds, 258
neighbourhood watch, 257–258
schools, role of, 258–259
target hardening, 257–258
techniques, 256
crime statistics
crime rate, 18–20
dark figure of crime, 20–21
demographics, 14–15
errors in, 27–30
incidence of crime, 18
longitudinal research, 26–27
official statistics, 21, 22–23
patterns in Canada. *See* crime
patterns
and preconceptions, 15
prevalence of crime, 17
purpose of, 16–17
self-report survey, 23–24
and summary conviction offences,
22
systemic biases, 27–30
unofficial statistics, 21, 23–27
victimization surveys, 24–26
CrimeStoppers, 175
Criminal Code, 4
amendment of, 48, 50
Bill C-89 amendments, 243
conspiracy, 51
criminal negligence, 51
decriminalization. *See* decriminalization
duress, defence of, 57–58
espionage, 51
faint hope clause, 215, 219
felonies, 50
mental capacity, 55
misdemeanours, 51
necessity, defence of, 57–58
obscenity provisions, 59
statutory law, 49
treason, 51
Victim Fine Surcharge (VFS), 244
victim impact statements, 240
victimless crime, 53
and victims, 243
Criminal Injuries Compensation
Boards (CICBs), 240, 241–242
criminal insanity, 54–55, 87
criminal intent, 52
criminal justice system
challenge for, 105–107
components of, 2
corrections, 5–6
court system, 4–5
goal of, 8–9
history of, 71–72
police, 4
process under, 6–9
criminal law
conflict model, 48–49
criminal offences, elements of,
51–53

# Illustration Credits

p.   5:   RCMP/GRCP
p.   8:   The Canadian Press/Jonathan Hayward
p.  28:   The Canadian Press/*Winnipeg Free Press*/Ken Gigliotti
p.  37:   The Canadian Press/AP Photo/Susan Sterner
p.  52:   The Canadian Press/*Ottawa Sun*/Fred Sherwin
p.  58:   National Archives of Canada/PA141503
p.  72:   The Granger Collection, New York
p.  97:   The Canadian Press/*Winnipeg Free Press*/Joe Bryska
p. 106:   The Canadian Press/*Winnipeg Free Press*/Joe Bryska
p. 111:   The Canadian Press/*Maclean's*/Mike Pinder
p. 118:   Ontario Provincial Police
p. 123:   The Canadian Press/Chuck Stoody
p. 146:   The Canadian Press/Tom Hanson
p. 154:   Prentice Hall Archives
p. 164:   Paul McCusker
p. 168:   *The Toronto Star*/P. Edwards
p. 191:   Prentice Hall Archives
p. 199:   The Canadian Press/*Toronto Sun*/Alex Cairns
p. 213:   The Canadian Press/AP Photo/Mpozi Mshale Tolbert
p. 225:   The Canadian Press/Kevin Frayer
p. 234:   Courtesy of Amnesty International
p. 238:   Marko Shark
p. 257:   Dick Hemingway
p. 260:   Metro Toronto Police

Figure 2.2 adapted from *International Crime Statistics 1989-90*, Interpol; Figures 2.3–2.7 prepared using data from Statistics Canada, CANSIM, Matrix 2200 and Catalogue numbers 85-205XIB and 85-002; Figure 2.8 prepared using data from Table 4.6 of the *Final Report of the Commission on Systemic Racism in the Ontario Justice System*, Queen's Printer for Ontario, 1995; Figure 2.9 adapted from *Canadian Urban Victimization Survey*, Ministry of the Solicitor General, 1982.

Statistics Canada information is used with the permission of the Minister of Industry, as Minister responsible for Statistics Canada. Information on the availability of the wide range of data from Statistics Canada can be obtained from Statistics Canada's Regional Offices, its World Wide Web site at **www.statcan.ca**, and its toll-free access number 1-800-263-1136.